RESEARCH AND EVALUATION FOR BUSY STUDENTS AND PRACTITIONERS

A Survival Guide

(Third edition)

Helen Kara

First edition published in Great Britain in 2012
Second edition published in Great Britain in 2017
Third edition published in Great Britain in 2023 by

Policy Press, an imprint of
Bristol University Press
University of Bristol
1-9 Old Park Hill
Bristol
BS2 8BB
UK
+44 (0)117 374 6645
bup-info@bristol.ac.uk

Details of international sales and distribution partners are available at
policy.bristoluniversitypress.co.uk

British Library Cataloguing in Publication Data
A catalogue record for this book is available from the British Library

ISBN 978-1-4473-6627-0 hardcover
ISBN 978-1-4473-6624-9 paperback
ISBN 978-1-4473-6625-6 ePub
ISBN 978-1-4473-6626-3 ePDF

Cover design: Qube Design

Bristol University Press and Policy Press use environmentally responsible
print partners

Printed and bound in Great Britain by CMP, Poole

To my parents, Julie and Mark Miller, who taught me to read, write and think, gave me a love of learning, and encouraged me even when my choices were different from their own.

Contents

List of figures, tables and boxes

Figures

Tables

Boxes

About the author

Dr Helen Kara has been an independent social researcher and writer since 1999 and an independent scholar since 2011. Her background is in social care and the third sector, and she works with universities, non-profit organisations, the European Commission, and other organisations and partnerships around the world. Helen is a Director of We Research It Ltd, an Honorary Senior Research Fellow at the University of Manchester, and a Fellow of the Academy of Social Sciences. She teaches research methods to researchers of all kinds, and loves to demystify the processes of writing and research.

Acknowledgements

Some time after publication of this book's second edition, I realised I had made one of the worst mistakes an author can make. I had left someone out of the Acknowledgements whose contribution should have been recognised. In this third edition, let me begin by rectifying that mistake. Sharon Inglis of Staffordshire University inspired Chapter 3 in the second edition, which is Chapter 4 in this edition, and I am grateful to her for the idea.

My thanks go to the interviewees who provided all the quotes for this book. I am also grateful to six anonymous proposal reviewers and two anonymous manuscript reviewers. Thank you all for making helpful and constructive suggestions I was very happy to implement.

Thank you to everyone who has bought or borrowed, read, recommended and used the first or second editions. You have all helped this book to grow and develop; it would not have reached a third edition without you.

Policy Press is a great publisher to work with. Philippa Grand and Emma Cook oversaw the initial stages and Paul Stevens and Georgina Bolwell brought the book to fruition. I am grateful for their help and guidance.

My families – Millers, Rounds, Denyers, Holmeses, Mengells and Parrish-Joneses – are unfailingly supportive. My friends and colleagues are excellent (you know who you are). And the biggest thanks of all, for constant love and support, go to my beloved Nik.

1

Introduction

Chapter summary

This chapter includes:

- Information about being a researcher
- A discussion of some reasons for doing research
- A comparison of insider and outsider research
- An introduction to doing research or evaluation
- Some of the issues that can arise in managing or commissioning research or evaluation
- A discussion of terminology used in the field
- An outline of the book's structure
- An introduction to the case studies, Ana and Ali, that run through the book

Introduction

This book is for both students and practitioners in public services. By 'public services' I mean services run by society for society, such as health, social care, criminal justice and education, from pre-school to university. Some public services are paid for by the state from our taxes, and others are run as charities, businesses or social enterprises. 'Practitioners' are people who work in these services, whether paid or unpaid. We are all users of tax-funded public services such as health, education and waste disposal, and many of us use other public services at different times in our lives.

'Research' means systematic investigation designed to answer one or more questions. In the current climate, research is becoming an increasingly common requirement of public service jobs. This may be workplace research, such as evaluation of a service or intervention, a service user satisfaction survey, a skills audit or training needs analysis. Or it may be academic research such as a diploma or a Master's degree for the purpose of professional development or to support career progression. The differences between workplace and academic research are not as pronounced as you might think, because good quality research demands most of the same approaches and techniques, regardless of context.

There is also less difference than might at first appear between academics, practitioners, students and service user/carer researchers. People move much more freely between educational and practice roles these days. Any academic or practitioner may also be a service user and/or a carer, and/or be studying for a qualification. Work across disciplinary boundaries is also more common, whether by multidisciplinary teams or by a single researcher who has, and wants to, use knowledge from more than one discipline. I use the term 'practitioner' in this book as a general term for anyone doing research while working in a public service, whether that work is paid or voluntary, informal or formal, and whether their research is under the auspices of an organisation or an academic institution.

I have worked as an independent researcher in public services since the late 1990s. After a while, practitioners began to ask my advice about their own research projects. I decided to write this book because I have seen at first hand some of the difficulties practitioners encounter when they are faced with the need to do research. As part of my preparation for writing the first edition, I conducted 20 in-depth interviews with public service practitioners. These practitioners had a wide range of roles (see Appendix 1), and all had experience of doing research on top of a main job, whether for their employer or for a qualification. Some also had experience of doing research as service users, or of supporting service users or other practitioners through the research process. I asked them how they managed to do research on top of their main jobs, and what advice they would give others who found themselves in a similar position. The insights they gave me were invaluable. Quotes from their interviews can be found throughout this book, and a different font has been used to distinguish them, for example:

> I think, obviously naively, where's the book that will tell me what to do? It doesn't exist because it's more complex than that. There's no one book that will say, 'If you want to research this, do this'.

As this interviewee suggests, this book is not an instruction manual that will lead you step by step through your research project. That's because there is no such book. Writing a comprehensive instruction manual for research would be as impossible as writing an instruction manual for a city. You have to find your own way through your research, just as you would have to find your own way around an unfamiliar city, and this is your guidebook. Within these pages you will find much useful advice about places to go – and places to avoid. Then it's up to you whether you go to the recommended places, or the dangerous places; the risk is yours. Think about it, though. Careful use of a guidebook can help to increase enjoyment and reduce stress when you are in an unfamiliar place. Similarly, this book is designed to help maximise enjoyment and minimise stress as you navigate through your research project.

This third edition has four more chapters than the second. It includes a chapter on research ethics. There are two chapters on collecting primary data instead of one, with the first covering conventional methods and the second covering creative methods. There are two chapters on analysing data instead of one, with the first covering quantitative analysis and the second covering qualitative analysis. And there is a chapter on putting research into practice. Also, all references have been updated, and the entire text has been carefully revised. The draft manuscript was peer-reviewed by two anonymous reviewers, who made very helpful suggestions that were implemented in this final version.

The book is about research and evaluation because evaluation is a particular type of research that public service practitioners are often required to carry out. However, I'm not going to write 'research and evaluation' all the time, because that would become very tiresome to read. In this book, 'research' generally includes 'evaluation'.

Being a researcher

While you are conducting research or evaluation, you are a researcher (Davies, 2007: 6). It doesn't matter whether you are a novice or experienced, whether your project is one of many in your life or the only piece of research you ever carry out. While you are doing your project, you have the identity of 'researcher' to add to all your other identities: friend, colleague, sibling, parent, service user, and so on. You already know what those identities mean and how they interact. For example, you might be more likely to talk about your emotional problems to a family member than to a colleague. You will probably respond lovingly if a child wakes you in the night because they had a bad dream, but you might be less sympathetic if you were woken for the same reason by a noisy neighbour, for example.

Some common qualities of good researchers are:

Determined	Creative	Thoughtful
Intelligent	Tenacious	Organised
Reflective	Empathic	Meticulous
Conscientious	Thorough	Analytical
Self-aware	Assertive	Honest

Researchers also need to be skilled in reading, writing, thinking, generating ideas, making connections, dealing with people, negotiating, balancing competing needs and managing setbacks.

> From a personal point of view, I want to do it to the best of my ability.
> I have had comments like 'Just do enough to pass'. I think, 'Yes, I will',
> but I can't. It's not who I am.

This may look terribly daunting. I include it here because I think it's easier to find your way if you know where you're going. All identities are learned. You will have had experience of this during your life – perhaps you learned to be a university student, or a parent, or a sportsperson. So you can learn to be a researcher – and, like all identities, you learn it on the job.

All identities overlap and interact with each other. Nobody is 'just a shop assistant' or 'only a student'. We all manage multiple identities all the time. Nevertheless, adding a new identity to the portfolio can be a stressful process, even if it's one you would like to acquire. That process will be even more stressful if it's not an identity you want. You may feel resistant to the idea of taking on the 'researcher' identity, particularly if you loathe the idea of doing research and are having it forced upon you. Perhaps you have a Master's dissertation or thesis to complete, or your manager has delegated some evaluation research to you. But even if you hate the very idea and are determined only to ever do one piece of research in your life, it's worth doing it as well as you can. This is because you will inevitably use research in your work over the coming years and decades, and not all research is good research. The best way to learn to judge the quality of others' research is to do a good piece of research yourself.

One key research skill is communication. Even if you have good communication skills, embarking on research can leave you feeling like a bumbling amateur. I think this is because you're working from an unfamiliar identity – that of researcher – and you're putting other people into unfamiliar identities of their own, such as research participant, before you have acquired the skills to help this along:

> For people who haven't got a lot of experience in doing research, it gets very difficult when you're learning on the job, in front of your colleagues, in a whole new sphere of skills that you haven't actually got so you feel well outside of your comfort zone even though you're a very experienced practitioner. People feel very exposed and unsure, and that gets very difficult for a lot of practitioners who are very experienced to understand that they've got to go through that learning process.

Also, research inevitably includes a lot of 'first contacts', which are notoriously difficult for us humans who are predisposed to jump to conclusions (Kahneman, 2011: 83–4). This can be doubly difficult when a first contact is made electronically, perhaps by email or on social media, where there is more scope for misinterpretation due to lack of contextual cues. Whatever your first impression of someone you meet during the research process – whether favourable or unfavourable – try to keep an open mind about that person, and remember how little you actually know about them. Where possible, take the time to find out more. Kahneman points out that we often operate as if what we see is all there is (2011: 85), and so we are willing to reach a conclusion about someone's personality and potential on the basis of a very brief contact. In fact, people are astonishingly complex, and even a small investment of time and attention can often pay dividends.

Other key research skills, such as project management, negotiation and time management, will be covered later in the book. Although each of these is a skill that can be learned, and they are all essential for researchers, it is unusual to find these skills being covered in a book of this kind. Most research methods textbooks, while undoubtedly useful, are written as if research exists in a bubble, separate from everything else. My aim in this book is to acknowledge that research is part of life in all its messy complexity, and to demonstrate ways of managing the research process in its wider context without compromising research quality.

Why do practitioners do research?

> We do research all the time, don't we? If you want to buy a product for work, say we need some marketing materials produced, I'm not going to go with the first company, I'll go with the company that gives the best product at the best price. That's research.

Why are you doing research? Because you've been told to? To earn money? To please your manager? To improve your CV or help you get a qualification? To increase knowledge, improve practice or influence policy? For some other reason? Or for two or more of these reasons, combined?

One reason may be that the requirement for research to be conducted within public services appears to be increasing. I observed this in the 2000s, as an independent researcher working with practitioners in a range of public services, and 10 of the 20 interviewees for this book – from across the sectors – also said this was their experience.

From the 2010s, due to the worldwide economic downturn, there has been less money to outsource research. This means research has become part of the main job for more people. There are also positive reasons for this. One interviewee from the health sector spoke eloquently about this:

> Some reasons I can think of are:
>
> 1. Health professionals such as nurses access education at degree level and above now, which has changed in the last few years. This has increased the body of literature regarding nursing, midwifery and health visitors generated by those professionals.
>
> 2. Education at these levels creates more academically confident professionals who understand, can contribute to and can critique and apply research. They understand the benefit of research and how it can benefit patient care in a way that was not there previously.
>
> 3. Extended roles for nurses, midwives and health visitors have been developed over recent years, such as prescribing, which was traditionally the stronghold of the medical profession. The ability to manage complex issues and to make clear decisions requires higher-level skills.

4. The NHS is required to make best use of resources and deliver best possible outcomes for patients – evidence base is needed to inform this.

5. Patients are able to access information such as through the Web and health professionals need to be able to demonstrate that the treatments they offer are the best available in terms of safety and efficacy – this can be shown through research evidence.

Another interviewee, from the criminal justice system, said an increase in in-house research hadn't happened yet in the UK, but they could see it coming:

This whole research thing, it's something that is ripe for expansion. In America there's research and development departments in some police forces. There is in Australia; Australians in some respects are quite far ahead of the British in terms of establishing a police research culture. In Britain there's one or two research and development type departments but they're few and far between. I think if the police had the capacity to do their own research, the database that they have, if they had the ability to use academic analysis on their material, they would, I'm certain, be able to reduce crime quite significantly because they have the data that people would just love to get access to, but because it's confidential, you can't.

As these interview extracts indicate, practitioners in public services are ideally placed to conduct research that will improve those services. This applies whether research done by practitioners is conducted entirely in the workplace or is for an academic qualification. In some countries, and in some disciplines, research skills are a requirement for career progression at certain levels. For example, in New Zealand, social workers have to demonstrate that they can do a piece of evaluation or research before they can progress to senior clinician status. However, as the interviews for this book showed, public service workers are often required to do research with little or no training or support:

I know people who think research is just about going in and talking to people, and don't understand even that you shouldn't ask leading questions. There is something to having done your background research before you've done the research. It's not true that anyone can do it. I don't think you necessarily need formal qualifications, but to have read something about it, or done a training course, you would probably reap the rewards.

Formal training is seen as helpful but difficult to access for a number of reasons: budget restrictions, lack of local courses, lack of courses in the subject area and insufficient understanding of training needs:

> I don't think there's enough training courses available in this area. I
> don't think people understand, really, that things like training audits,
> skills audits, evaluation, all fall under research.

One interviewee had some advice for those starting a job involving research
when they had no experience of research:

> You need to set aside a day of your induction, sit with your line manager
> or ideally your head of department, and get them to show you what
> evaluations they've done, how they do it, and what they expect of you.
> So you're really seeing either a benchmark you're working towards, or
> the style of working practice.

This book will explain the fundamental principles and practices of research in
public services. It won't provide everything you need – no book can do that –
but it will give you a good grounding in the subject, as well as lots of practical
advice about how to manage the research process in tandem with the rest of
your life, and tips to save you time and stress. Here's an example:

 **TIP Develop a strategy for naming and storing document files on your
computer that will make them easy to find and retrieve.**

Some of the tips in the book, like this one, may at first sight seem to add extra
work to your load. Think, though: putting in a little time up front will save
you from having to sort out a tangled mess later on.

Backing up your work also benefits from a strategic approach. There are many
ways to back up. You can:

- transfer your work manually to a memory stick or an external hard drive
  (and, if you wish, from there to a different computer);
- set up a free email address via one of the many providers such as Gmail or
  Outlook and send your work to that address;
- use a free cloud-based service such as Dropbox, iCloud or Google Drive;
- use a paid back-up service such as SOS Online Backup or Carbonite.

Any of these processes will take only a few minutes to set up initially, and
just a few seconds to use each day. You should, of course, keep your back-up
somewhere away from your main data store; there's not much point backing up
onto a memory stick that you then put in the same bag as your laptop. Also, you
need to consider the wisdom of using cloud-based services for people's personal
data, which should be kept confidential. But between all the options, if you
take a little time to think it through, you should be able to set up an easy-to-
use system that will protect you against time-consuming and stressful data loss.

While you're working on a computer, get into the habit of pressing Ctrl+S (on a PC) or Cmd+Shift+S (on a Mac) every few minutes. This will save your latest work against computer crashes, power cuts or accidents.

Insider and outsider research

'Insider' and 'outsider' are opposites, but presenting them in this dichotomous way conceals the fact that they're actually two ends of a spectrum. If you're a practitioner conducting research within the service you help to run, or a service user researching the service you use, you're definitely an insider. However, it could be argued that anyone doing research in their own service is, in a sense, becoming an outsider, if they are taking on a researcher's identity in a setting where others are not researchers. But when are you definitely an outsider? When you've stopped working in, or using, a service? If so, do you become an outsider straight away, or only after a period of time? Or are you only, really, an outsider if you've never worked in, or used, that service? In which case, can anyone ever conduct outsider research on primary healthcare or school education? Conversely, how much research does an outsider have to do within a particular organisation before they become an insider?

There are pros and cons to both insider and outsider research (Robson and McCartan, 2016: 399–400). A comparison is set out in Table 1.1 (and I am indebted to Colin Robson and Kieran McCartan for many of the points made here).

As you can see, neither insider nor outsider research is 'best'. The answer to the question of which approach should be used depends on the nature of the research to be conducted.

There is more information about insider research in the 'Further reading' section at the end of this book.

Doing research or evaluation

For a long time, writers on research and evaluation have acknowledged that participating in such research – say, by completing a questionnaire, or taking part in an interview – may not be someone's top priority. Interviewees were also aware of this:

> It's okay doing research but if you can't get anyone to take part in it and you've got very low sample numbers it almost becomes pointless. It's never anyone's priority; it's only the priority of the person conducting it, never the recipient's.

I would go further. I think it's essential to acknowledge that there are times when conducting research or evaluation isn't even a *researcher's* top priority. There are times when looking after a sick child, a night out with friends, visiting a

Table 1.1: Comparing insider and outsider research

Insider research	Outsider research
Insider researchers have expert knowledge of their service that will help to inform the research	Outsider researchers have to spend time learning about the service
Insider researchers know where to go for help and information within their organisation	Outsider researchers have to spend time getting to know the people and politics of the organisation
Insider researchers may be attached to a particular view of their service	Outsider researchers bring a fresh, independent view to the research
Insider researchers may have more credibility with their colleagues and service users than an external stranger (although the reverse can also be true)	Outsider researchers have to build relationships and develop trust with service staff, volunteers and users
Insider researchers may have difficulty in challenging their colleagues' practice, or their own, even where research findings demonstrate that change is needed	Outsider researchers usually find it easier to challenge practice where necessary
Insider researchers are likely to have full access to confidential information	Outsider researchers may not have full access to confidential information
Organisations may be more willing to facilitate insider researchers' access to potential participants	Outsider researchers may find it more difficult to gain access to potential participants
Some participants will give fuller and more honest information to insider researchers who they already know and trust	Some participants will give fuller and more honest information to outsider researchers who they believe will maintain their anonymity
Insider researchers are well placed to oversee implementation of the research findings or recommendations	Outsider researchers have to let go of the research when it is finished, and leave the organisation to implement its findings or recommendations
Research done by an insider, with the full involvement of service users and colleagues, can greatly improve the working practices of the organisation	Research done by an outsider can become the focus of organisational discontent, at worst leading to the outsider researcher becoming a scapegoat

bereaved relative or going on holiday with your partner will come first. And quite right too.

There is an art in balancing research or evaluation with the rest of your life. Everyone will differ in the extent to which they prioritise research. I prioritise it highly because I love research and evaluation, and have made this my career since the late 1990s. For some people, research is a full-time job, or full-time study, and most people in either of these situations do not have difficulty finding time for their research. But for many people it is a part-time occupation, and for some, very part time. For example, someone who has been forced to do a service evaluation – by a manager they don't like, with no training or support, when they are sure they already know what the findings will be – is not likely to prioritise their research very highly at all.

Whether research is a high or low priority for you, and whatever your other commitments, this book will help you find ways to fit research or evaluation into your life. And it is important to balance research with the rest of your life, or there can be long-lasting consequences, as these interviewees found after neglecting friends and family in favour of research:

> I did not spend the time I should have with them and I know I lost lots of contact with relatives and friends that I miss now that I am semi-retired and have the time.

> I do feel that I probably lost a little bit of my social circle because I wasn't as accessible, I wasn't the party animal I had been. Now I'm trying to make up for it!

> Some friendships have been sacrificed, and relationships have been sacrificed. Some people need you to make that time and if you're not there to make that time, well, I'm okay with that. I think from an impact point of view, I've perhaps been more absent than other friends, but the people who have persevered, we've perhaps got a deeper relationship.

Although, as the last interviewee hinted, there can also be positive consequences for family and friends from spending time on your research:

> I think if it had an impact, it was a positive one. My son has a great intellect but really struggles with his dyslexia, he struggles with getting things on paper. He learned perseverance. I think some of my women friends would say it's a bit inspiring to see one of your friends doing that, and they've gone on and retrained and changed what they do.

Several interviewees suggested that you should think through your plans at the earliest possible opportunity, and talk them over with people you trust:

> People should seek others out who have done what they are proposing and sit down and talk to them about the ups and downs.

> Get some good sounding board people – they don't have to be researchers, but people you can talk to about the project, people you feel comfortable talking to about things.

Just as identities overlap and interact, so do the component parts of the research process. This book is written, like most books on research or evaluation, as if there are separate and discrete parts of the process: background reading, data collection, data analysis, writing up. Here is some of the reality:

- Reading in various forms is likely to occur throughout the process.
- Notes from your reading may be coded and analysed in the same way as primary data.
- Documents may be categorised as background reading, or secondary data, or both.
- Writing is an essential part of data analysis in particular, whether it be qualitative or quantitative, and of the whole research process in general (Rapley, 2011: 286).

These are just a few examples of the ways in which research processes interact and overlap. It is necessary to separate them for the purposes of discussion and teaching, but in reality, they are inextricable parts of a whole.

Nevertheless, there are transition points in research projects, and it is these that some researchers find hardest to handle:

> I finished gathering the raw data, and it sat there and looked at me for about three weeks before I actually did anything with it. Then I did a few graphs and tables....

Even after years of experience, I still procrastinate when faced with the blank page on which I need to start writing a research report. But these days I know that it is the constants of reading, writing and thinking that will carry me through the bumpier stages of the research process. So I read some of the notes I've written, and think about what I want to say, until I'm ready to start. Other people use different techniques, such as this interviewee:

> I've got a studying CD that involves quite a bit of Frank Zappa. It makes me laugh, it makes me relax, then I can get started. I need to find a way to relax. Music is my medicine.

Whatever works for you is fine. But if you don't yet know what works for you, I recommend experimenting with reading, writing and thinking.

Reading, writing and thinking permeate the research process (Hart, 2018: 6), and thinking is the most important of the three. Your thinking, like everyone else's, develops and moves on day by day. The fact that your brain is your most useful research tool is particularly helpful for busy practitioners, because you can think about your research or evaluation when you don't have time to do any of your other research work. You can make progress with your thinking in the shower, on the bus, at the supermarket – any time you have to be doing something that doesn't require much of your brainpower. As a researcher, your brain is your greatest asset, both for conducting the research itself, and for working out the best ways to manage the research process in the context of the rest of your life.

The other thing it's important to say at this early stage is that there is no such thing as perfect research or evaluation. Yes, the standards are high, and with good reason. Research should be rigorous, ethical and robust; researchers should be thorough and conscientious. If you don't yet have a good understanding of the reasons for this, you will by the time you've finished reading this book. But research and evaluation are never perfect, and can never be perfect, because they are conducted by, with and for people just like us, with all our conflicts and inadequacies. Planning and carrying out research or evaluation to a high standard, in the real world, is an enormous challenge – and can also be a source of great joy.

Managing and commissioning research or evaluation

It is difficult to manage or commission research or evaluation if you don't know how to do research yourself. In fact, it's not easy even when you do know how:

> I had to produce a commissioning document, interview all the organisations that applied, and make a decision based on their application and interview, which could really deliver what we were asking them to deliver? I don't think we appointed the best contractor, but we went on who scored the most points, and now, 18 months in and looking back, I'm not quite sure what I'd do differently but I know something needs to be different.

You will need at least a broad idea about research methods and the research process if you are to manage or commission research effectively. You also need a clear idea of what the research or evaluation is that you want to delegate or buy, and why you want that work to be done.

Useful questions to ask yourself include:

- What do you want the research or evaluation to achieve?
- What are the resources you can invest? (These may include funding, time, training, and so on.)
- How will you know whether you're getting good value for your investment?

- What steps will you need to take to maximise the likelihood of the research achieving your aims?

One key step is to figure out which methodology, approach and/or methods you think would be most appropriate to enable you to match your resources to the research you want to manage or commission. The information in this book should help you do that. I don't recommend being entirely prescriptive about the research design, as a researcher may come up with good ideas you haven't considered. This may be because they're more experienced in doing research or evaluation than you are, or simply because they're looking at the research question and design from a different angle. But it does make sense to be clear about what resources are available and why you are making those resources available, and to share that information with researchers at the earliest opportunity.

Another key step is to ensure that the person you charge with the responsibility for doing the research or evaluation actually has the necessary skills and abilities. Books like this may help, but nobody can truly learn to conduct research from a reference book.

Terminology

Some academic language is quite impenetrable. Here's an example:

> Unlike psychoanalysis, psychoanalytic competence (which confines every desire and statement to a genetic axis or overcoding structure, and makes infinite, monotonous tracings of the stages on that axis or the constituents of that structure), schizoanalysis rejects any idea of pretraced destiny, whatever name is given to it – divine, anagogic, historical, economic, structural, hereditary, or syntagmatic....

This is quite an extreme example, being taken out of context from a well-respected book by two French poststructuralists (see Deleuze and Guattari, 1987: 13). I do not include it here to criticise the book or its authors, who have made a unique and valuable contribution to social theory. However, many people do find their work, and that of other academics, quite difficult to read:

> Academic language, oh, ow, it made my eyes bleed, and that was really time-consuming. I still can't remember what 'hermeneutic' means.

> Sometimes, I'm sure some people would shoot me for saying this, when I've started to unpack some of it, some of it isn't complex in itself but it's the language that's used to make it complex. Like phenomenological analysis. You're analysing a phenomenon as experienced by someone else, that is fairly straightforward but the language has made it complex.

Luckily an increasing amount of academic work is written in more accessible language. However, each profession has its own jargon and other complex terminology, and this can also be a barrier, for example to educators or service user researchers. The profession of research, including evaluation, is no exception, and the language of research practice can be quite opaque:

> Some of the people I teach are expected to do small-scale research studies. Ninety per cent of them are practitioners within the service. They find the language quite difficult; it's a language they're not used to. Qualitative and quantitative research is not something that trips off the tongue.

> The language of research can put people off. I'm in practice and it's too academic for me.

In this book, I have tried to be clear about the meanings of the terms I use, and to use those terms consistently. But other writers will use some of the same terms with slightly different meanings, such as 'document analysis' where I have used 'document review'. And other writers will use different terms to mean the same thing, such as 'subject' or 'respondent' to mean a person who takes part in research, where I have used 'participant'. Also, I have not tried to include every possible research term in this book, just those that are necessary for understanding the points I want to make. I have prepared a Glossary of research terms that you will find at the end of the book (and also on https:// policy.bristoluniversitypress.co.uk/research-and-evaluation-for-busy-students-and-practitioners/companion-website). Where you see the companion website logo in the margin, this means that the material is also available online. As you read other people's work on research methods, you will inevitably come across new research terms and different definitions.

If you're doing research or evaluation you are likely to have to get to grips with some unfamiliar and challenging concepts. After all, you're doing it to learn. If you find complex abstract thought exciting and appealing, you'll find plenty to amuse you. If, on the other hand, you prefer simpler explanations, there is so much literature available that you should be able to find readable commentaries on the topics you need to understand.

 You don't have to read the unreadable.

As a researcher, it is as important to learn to identify and skip documents that won't help you as to learn to identify and read those that will (Langdridge and Hagger-Johnson, 2009: 19). There is information about how to do this in Chapter 7.

It has to be said that the language of public services can also be difficult and off-putting. There are some good glossaries and jargon-busters online if you are struggling with that terminology.

 Write definitions of new words on Post-it notes and stick them where you will see them frequently, such as on the inside of your front door, next to the kettle or on the bathroom mirror.

There is a useful resource for help with research vocabulary in the 'Further reading' section at the end of this book.

Structure of this book

Chapter 2 gives an overview of research. It introduces quantitative and qualitative research, and discusses the role of service users in research.

Chapter 3 explores research and evaluation ethics. It explains the current system of research ethics management, discusses researcher wellbeing, and outlines how and why it is important for researchers to think and act ethically throughout the research process.

Chapter 4 engages with some of the more complex concepts in the field: methodologies and some more specialised approaches to research (action research, evaluation research, arts-based research and digitally mediated research). The chapter discusses how these link with methods and the role of theory, and outlines the links between research, theory and practice.

Chapter 5 looks at how to choose a research topic and refine it into a research question. Research methods are introduced, and advice is given on how to write a research proposal or plan.

Chapter 6 discusses ways to manage the research process in the context of the rest of your life. Planning, organisation and time management are discussed in detail, and there is a lot of advice from practitioners who are experienced in research. The pros and cons of receiving support for research from employers are outlined. The need to reward yourself, and to look after yourself, as you do research, is emphasised. There is a summary of what works – and what doesn't work – in managing research.

Chapter 7 describes the similarities and differences between document reviews for workplace research and literature reviews for academic research. Information is given about how to conduct document reviews and literature reviews, together with advice on record-keeping, critical and strategic reading, finding open access materials, using libraries and making notes.

Chapter 8 explains the advantages and disadvantages of working with secondary data, and shows how to find secondary data on the internet. Chapter 9 covers the main conventional ways of collecting primary data, and Chapter 10 looks at creative methods of collecting primary data. Chapter 11 outlines some ways of preparing, coding, analysing and synthesising quantitative data, and Chapter 12 does the same for qualitative data.

Chapter 13 begins by identifying and dispelling some myths about the writing process. Then there is a full discussion of how to write research, with advice on how to structure, edit and polish your writing. The chapter explains how to avoid plagiarism and how to cite other people's work.

Chapter 14 looks at how to disseminate research, why dissemination is important, and the potential barriers to this process. The advantages and disadvantages of different methods of dissemination are outlined. The similarities and differences of workplace and academic research are discussed, as are the ethics of dissemination.

Chapter 15 discusses ways of putting research into practice. It covers research impact, ways of getting research evidence into policy, research implementation, knowledge exchange and the recent move to a more holistic approach.

Chapters 1–15 end with some suggested exercises, discussion questions and a debate topic – pick a side and argue for it against an opponent who takes the opposite view. It doesn't matter whether you agree with the side you are arguing for – the point is to gain skills in creating and developing arguments while learning about research methods.

Chapter 16 concludes the book with a summary of the key points made in the earlier chapters.

There are also recommendations for 'Further reading' at the end of the book.

CASE STUDIES

We will follow two case studies in each chapter. Their work will help to illustrate the points made in the book.

Ana is doing media studies. She is interested in the representation of non-heterosexual couples and families in the media. As a bisexual woman, Ana is an insider researcher. We will follow her progress as she works on her main research project for her degree.

Ali works in a big not-for-profit social care organisation with several departments. His department supports young families in need. The organisation's management has decided that someone from each department will evaluate the work of another department. Ali has been tasked with evaluating the department that supports unpaid family carers. We will follow his progress as he works on this evaluation.

EXERCISE

You are asked to advise a research commissioner who wants to fund three pieces of research:

    a. Evaluation of patient care in a hospice.

    b. Skills audit of civilian staff in a police force.

    c. Pilot study, in three local schools, of whether training teachers in oral storytelling techniques can improve educational outcomes for primary school children.

In each case, would you advise the commissioner to specify an insider or an outsider researcher? Why?

Discussion questions

1. How do you think research could benefit people's lives?
2. What would help someone to balance their new identity of 'researcher' with their existing identities?
3. If a friend told you they had to do some research and they felt daunted and scared, what would you say to them?

Debate topic

Insider research is more useful than outsider research.

2

Overview of research

Chapter summary

This chapter includes:

- An explanation of the differences between quantitative and qualitative research – and their similarities
- A discussion of the pros and cons of doing research alone or in collaboration with others
- An introduction to involving participants or service users in research and evaluation
- An outline of some highly time-consuming methods

Introduction

As a whole, research is complicated. There is no point pretending it is easy and straightforward. It is hard to do your own research well, and it can be difficult to understand other people's research.

The good news is that research and evaluation can be broken down into component parts that are much easier to understand. As you become familiar with each piece of the jigsaw, you will begin to see how they can fit together to create a whole picture. This will make it easier for you to plan and carry out research. It will also help you to assess research done by other people.

This chapter and the next will introduce you to some of these component parts. The terminology begins to become more demanding at this point, so you may wish to use the Glossary, which you will find at the end of the book.

Quantitative or qualitative?

In the simplest terms, quantitative research deals with *numerical data*, that is, things you can count or measure. Qualitative research deals with *textual data*, that is, words, and other forms of data, such as pictures, sound or multimedia.

Looked at another way, the two types of research can be held to express different philosophies or standpoints (Langdridge and Hagger-Johnson, 2009: 13). Classic quantitative research follows the more traditionally scientific or 'post–positivist' methodology where a hypothesis is formulated, with a defined 'independent variable' whose variation can affect a 'dependent variable' or outcome. The questions are 'What? How much? How many?' So a hypothesis might be that the amount of homework (independent variable) given to school pupils will affect their class test results (dependent variable). Numerical data about amounts of homework given, and test results achieved, would be collected and analysed using recognised statistical tests to produce numerical results.

Qualitative research, on the other hand, aims to provide an understanding of why things are as they are. Classic qualitative research follows a 'constructivist' methodology where it is held that understanding is constructed by researchers and research participants together, or an 'interpretivist' methodology in which multiple viewpoints are acknowledged. The questions are 'How? Why?' So a qualitative researcher who is interested in finding out about the factors affecting school pupils' class test results would be likely to ask pupils, teachers and parents or caregivers for their views, probably through interviews and/or group discussions. The resulting textual data would be coded and analysed using the researcher's own judgement.

These are very superficial descriptions of extremely complex fields. They make it look as if quantitative and qualitative approaches to research are very different from each other and completely incompatible. Researchers in one field may often trivialise or, at worst, demonise researchers in the other field:

> When I was doing my dissertation I went and saw someone who was a supervisor for quantitative research. I said I was using phenomenology, and he said, 'Well that's not really research is it?'

However, a closer look will show that quantitative and qualitative research are surprisingly similar in a variety of ways (Bryman, 2016: 402–3). For example, both are created by a researcher's judgement. Qualitative researchers often aim to record their judgements and present them alongside their findings, so as to allow readers to make their own assessment of the quality of the research. Quantitative research is often presented as though the researcher's judgements are irrelevant or even non–existent, with the quality of the research being defined by the method itself. However, quantitative researchers, like qualitative researchers, have to make judgements at every stage of the process, such as how to word a hypothesis, which variable(s) to choose, which sampling methods to use, which statistical tests to apply, what is of relevance in the statistical test results and how to present findings. There is no research of any kind without judgement, assumption and interpretation.

Whether you choose to use quantitative or qualitative methods should depend on your research topic and question(s). If you are interested in the extent to which reduced funding for non–profit health services increases demand on other health services, you would probably choose a quantitative method to help you answer your 'How much?' questions. If you are interested in the effects on a community of reduced funding for non–profit health services, you would probably choose a qualitative method to investigate your 'How and why?' questions. In either case, however, I would encourage you to consider whether there is scope for you to use both approaches together.

Quantitative and qualitative research methods are often complementary. For example, in the case of the school pupils and their test results mentioned earlier, the quantitative approach would give a useful overview of the topic, while the qualitative approach would fill in some detail. In visual terms, you could say that the quantitative approach provides the outline while the qualitative approach colours it in. The researcher may have chosen the quantitative method because of strong suggestions from elsewhere (for example, the literature, dissertation supervisors or research commissioners) that the amount of homework given to school pupils is the most likely predictor of class test results. They may have chosen the qualitative part of the research because of their own suspicions that other factors may also be relevant. Using both qualitative and quantitative methods in one research project is often known as 'mixed methods' research. The vast majority of evaluation research uses a mixed methods approach.

The philosophical underpinnings of research, and the different methodologies, are discussed in more detail in Chapter 4. Quantitative, qualitative and mixed methods research is discussed in more detail in later chapters. There are more resources on quantitative and qualitative research in the 'Further reading' section at the end of this book.

Solo or collaborative?

Some research and evaluation projects are led or carried out by a single researcher and others are done in partnership. Working in partnership can bring great benefits such as opportunities to learn from others and a shared workload. However, it also requires a high level of communication and management skills – perhaps even more than solo research – as these interviewees found:

> In the research I did most recently, one of the biggest problems we had was that the timetable was too tight and the brief was not clear enough. I think that was because people weren't working together, there were too many cooks in the pot. People were making decisions who had no research experience. A lot of it went belly up because of lack of communication between all the parties involved. The whole research project was delayed because some of the parameters weren't set out correctly at the beginning. It was all done in a rush really.

> If you're working in a group as well, don't trust that other people are going to do their job! You might want to make sure that whatever you've had your hands on, even if someone else is keeping the literature search file, keep your own to keep track of what you've done. If they don't do it at least you've got your bit. Then that means you don't need to get quite so angry with somebody else, because

> you've got something. If your qualification is dependent on lazy-ass getting their act together, or someone who's just had a baby … this is control freak speaking! But being a control freak is quite helpful in these circumstances.

Ideally, the choice about whether research is carried out by one person or several should be led by the research topic and questions. However, like these interviewees, there may be times where you have no choice about whether your research will be carried out by you alone or collaboratively. And 'collaboration' can mean working with other researchers, and/or other practitioners, and/or service users.

Involving participants or service users in research and evaluation

Involving participants in research is sometimes known as 'participatory research' or 'participatory action research'. Participatory research began in the 1970s and grew rapidly in the 1990s (Banks and Brydon-Miller, 2019: 3). The fundamental principle is that participants are involved from the outset and all the way through the research. This sounds straightforward but it can be difficult to manage in practice. It is very rare to involve participants in student research, due to the common expectation that students do their own research for an individual qualification. It is much more common to involve service users in evaluation.

'Service users' is a generic term for the users of public services, that is, all of us. Other names may be used for service users, such as patients, students, pupils, parents, caregivers, offenders or clients. Service users began to become involved in planning and delivering public services in the mid-1990s (Kemshall and Littlechild, 2000: 7). In the UK in the mid-2000s it became mandatory for service users to be involved in training social workers (Branfield, 2009: ix). Some other examples of service user involvement in the UK are:

- parents as school governors;
- pupils on school councils;
- health service users on primary care advisory groups;
- health service users in local involvement networks;
- health service users in hospital patient advice and liaison services;
- offenders on prison councils;
- offenders in probation service user groups.

There are similar systems of involvement in the USA, Canada, Australia and New Zealand, and presumably in other countries too.

The 21st century has seen a significant increase in service user involvement in research (Barber et al, 2011: 217). 'Involvement' denotes a higher level of inclusion than simply completing a questionnaire or taking part in an interview, although it may not be as comprehensive as in participatory research. That said, service users can be involved at all stages of research and evaluation, from planning and design to dissemination and the implementation of recommendations (Barber et al, 2011: 218). This has a range of positive effects, such as increasing access to participants, better-quality data and more relevant findings (Barber et al, 2011: 218–19). It also has some less positive effects. For example, as with participatory research, it takes more time to do research with the full involvement of inexperienced researchers, so it often costs more too (Barber et al, 2011: 219).

 If you're intending to involve service users in your research or evaluation, allow plenty of time to give them any support they may need to enable them to be fully involved.

One interviewee for this book had worked with service users throughout a project, which was a high priority for that researcher, but also created a range of problems to overcome:

> If you're going to use lay researchers, the training is most important. Also commitment. I did have a problem where people didn't turn up, I'd have to cancel or reschedule meetings with interview candidates because people didn't turn up that day. Sometimes people would be unwell, or not come in because of a conflict of priorities. I think the hardest part was the fluidity of participants. Those who started the project weren't those who ended it. Some people were more interested in setting up, some in the interviews, some in the data analysis. A very fluid group of people, and that was quite difficult. If I went back again, I'd probably try to have a different regime. My feeling is that having casual labour doesn't work. I'd rather take on four workers for a 10-hours-a-week contract that they could declare at the benefit agency over the whole duration of the project. That would be a lot more solid. With the casual workers, that was like juggling with jelly. There is also the issue that people were doing it mainly for the money, the £10 or £20 per interview. I don't blame them, when you're on benefits, but the primary driver for them wasn't the research itself. Some people would do more than they were paid for, some would get up and walk out of the room literally as soon as they'd earned their £15.

While service users can be involved in any stage of a research project, it may not always be appropriate for service users to be involved at every stage of research controlled by a practitioner. Equally, it may not always be appropriate for practitioners to be involved in research controlled by service users (Turner and Beresford, 2005: xii). A third option is for research or evaluation to be carried out in partnership between practitioners and service users (Fox et al, 2007: 133). As a practitioner, you can only define your research as 'user-controlled' if you are also a user of the service concerned. If you are not a user of that service, you may be able to work in partnership with service users when doing workplace research such as evaluation, although this kind of partnership is often unequal (Fox et al, 2007: 145). For academic research leading to a qualification, you will probably need to control the research (because it would be your qualification), with service users as participants or involved to a comparatively small extent.

In considering whether and/or how to involve participants or service users in your research or evaluation project, you need to think through a whole range of questions. It's not possible to provide an exhaustive list that will cover any project, but here are some examples to get you started:

1. How might participant or service user involvement benefit your research or evaluation?
2. How might your research or evaluation benefit any participants or service users who choose to become involved?
3. What are the characteristics of the participants or service users who might become involved? Are there particular needs for you to take into account? If so, what are these, and how might they affect participants' or service users' involvement in your research or evaluation?
4. To what extent would any participants or service users involved in your research or evaluation be representative of a wider group? What are the implications of this?
5. Might any of the participants or service users have some research or evaluation experience? If so, how might this help or hinder your research or evaluation?
6. Is there a way to reward participants or service users for their involvement in your research or evaluation?
7. What other ethical issues might you face in involving participants or service users?
8. Can you make contingency plans in case participants or service users change their minds about being involved?

For some people, involving participants or service users is good ethical research practice in itself, as long as the involvement is genuine and not tokenistic:

> Because I have certain principles about how to carry out research, I always enjoy working out how to value participants and make them feel as much an active part of the research as possible. I enjoy working with people. So you're not parachuting in and buggering off, they get something out of it. It's not always possible, but I like to get them involved in data analysis where I can.

The main ethical reason for involving participants in research and service users in evaluation is because their viewpoints can contribute to creating positive social change (Banks and Brydon–Miller, 2019: 1).

There are some resources on participant and service user involvement in the 'Further reading' section at the end of this book.

Highly time-consuming methods

There are several research methods that are usually too time-consuming for workplace, undergraduate or initial postgraduate research. Some examples are randomised controlled trials, systematic reviews and meta-analyses, ethnography and participant observation, and social return on investment. These methods may be used at doctoral level but, even then, I would encourage you to only use one of these methods if you're absolutely sure it's the best way to achieve your research aims.

Randomised controlled trials

Randomised controlled trials are experiments where participants are randomly allocated to an experimental group or a control group. These trials are often used in drug testing, where each person can be given pills, but only those in the experimental group are given pills that actually contain a drug. People in the control group are given pills that look identical but contain a harmless substance such as sugar. These trials may be conducted 'double-blind', which means that even the person administering the medication doesn't know which of the participants are getting the drugs and which are getting the fake pills. Some people regard this as the 'gold standard' of all social research methods (Robson and McCartan, 2016: 117). However, like all methods, it should not be used for its own sake, but only when it is likely to be the best way of answering the research question. Randomised controlled trials are difficult to set up and administer, and can have unique ethical problems. For example, sometimes drug trials have to be ended early if a drug proves to have unexpected and harmful side effects, or if interim results show that people in the control group are suffering because they are lacking a drug being given to those in the experimental group.

Systematic reviews and meta-analyses

A systematic review is, in theory, a review of all the research already conducted around a specific research question. The aim is to reduce bias (Petticrew and Roberts, 2005: 10) by establishing selection criteria for the inclusion of research in the review, such as methodological soundness (Petticrew and Roberts, 2005: 2). However, the selection criteria are defined by researchers and are therefore likely to carry biases of their own. For example, although a researcher may have the best intentions of including all methodologically sound research in their systematic review, different researchers will have different views of what constitutes 'methodologically sound'. One researcher might think sample size is an important criterion, so they decide to exclude any study with a sample size of less than 60 participants. This could mean they leave out several studies with fewer participants, which have relevant results. Another researcher might think sample size is just as important, but they decide to exclude any study with a sample size of less than 30 participants. This researcher might further decide that the findings of studies with 31–99 participants will be considered as indicative rather than conclusive. That may mean this researcher doesn't give enough weight to some studies with 31–99 participants.

A systematic review differs from a literature review because it is a review only of reported research, and doesn't include any other kinds of literature. (Literature reviews are discussed in more detail in Chapter 7.) The use of inclusion criteria is intended to make the review systematic, because the researcher systematically assesses research reports against defined inclusion criteria to decide whether or not to include those reports. A meta-analysis is similar to a systematic review, but also includes a statistical summary of quantitative findings.

So far this all sounds quite straightforward. In practice, however, conducting a systematic review or a meta-analysis can be a real challenge. Jesson et al (2011: 3) suggest that a systematic review shouldn't be attempted until a researcher has become a competent reviewer of literature using more conventional methods. They comment that conventional reviews 'often provide insights that can be neglected or passed over in the steps towards exclusion and quality control that are required in the systematic review model' (2011: 15).

In conducting a systematic review or meta-analysis, the researcher may be faced with a huge amount of data to analyse, and in some cases, many hundreds of research reports. Systematic reviews and meta-analyses are as subject to the constraints of time and budget as any other kind of research, and even generous allowances of both may not be enough. Then the application of the inclusion criteria may not be as easy as it looks. Not all research is clearly written, which can make it difficult to assess the quality of the method(s) used and the robustness of the conclusions drawn. Therefore, I would assert that systematic reviews and meta-analyses, however well intentioned, require as much use of judgement, assumption and interpretation as any other type of research.

This is not intended as a criticism of the systematic review or meta-analysis methods. These are worthwhile and useful exercises in some contexts, such as to assess the effectiveness of an intervention where a single study may not give the full picture, and so to increase the chances of knowledge gained from research being translated into practice (Jesson et al, 2011: 15; see also Chapter 15 for more about putting research into practice). However, it is important to remember that there is no such thing as a perfect piece of research, and systematic review and meta-analysis are no exception. My primary aim here is to emphasise that systematic reviews and meta-analyses should not be undertaken lightly.

Ethnography and participant observation

Ethnography and participant observation are two further techniques that should not be underestimated in terms of the time and effort needed to use them properly. Ethnography comes from the Greek words for 'people' and 'writing', and literally means 'writing about people'. Ethnographers often use the technique of participant observation, which involves living and/or working with people while observing their experiences. For example, Philippe Bourgois spent five years living with crack dealers in a deprived area of New York (Bourgois, 2002), and Nigel Rapport spent a year working as a hospital porter at a large hospital in Scotland (Rapport, 2008). Both men are, in fact, career academics, and spent their time observing the people they were living and working with, and writing about those people. The techniques they used come from the discipline of social anthropology, and are widely used by anthropology doctoral students, who do not find them easy. They are particularly difficult for novice researchers to undertake effectively (Davies, 2007: 168, 170).

Social return on investment

Social return on investment (SRoI) is a form of evaluation research. Specifically, it is a value-based mixed methods approach to all-round assessment of the social, economic and environmental return on investment. This encompasses a much broader conception of how change is created and what change is worth than a simple financial return on financial investment, or even a cost–benefit analysis.

SRoI was first conceived at the turn of the century, and the UK-based SRoI Network was founded in 2006. Use of the approach has developed rapidly worldwide to a point where it is now being promoted in legislation in some countries, such as in the Public Services (Social Value) Act 2012 in the UK. In other countries, such as Australia, recommendations have been made that the government should support the use and development of SRoI (SVA Consulting, 2012: 4).

Like the other methods in this section, SRoI can be time- and resource-intensive, particularly at the outset. But SRoI also has a lot to offer in providing a framework for how to think rigorously about the nature and quality of public services.

SRoI is based on seven principles:

1. Involve stakeholders.
2. Understand what changes.
3. Value the things that matter.
4. Only include what is material.
5. Do not over-claim.
6. Be transparent.
7. Verify the result.

I would argue that some of these principles should apply to any kind of evaluation, particularly numbers 1, 5, 6 and 7. It is perhaps within principles 2, 3 and 4 that the uniqueness of SRoI resides. These raise specific questions, which provide a useful framework for thought.

Central SRoI questions include:

- Who changes as a result of the service being provided? Does the service create change for its users? What about their families? Do the staff or volunteers of the service experience change? What about professionals referring people into the service, or accepting referrals from the service? Are there other people who change as a result of the service?
- In what ways do these people change? How do they know? How can they communicate the change to us?
- How can we measure the change? What is the evidence for the change?
- What is the change worth? Can the people experiencing the change express its value? Are there financial proxies we can use to express the value of the change?
- Is any of the change due to other factors apart from the provision of the service? Would any of the change have happened if the service didn't exist? Are there other ways the change could have been created even though the service does exist?
- Will the change persist beyond the point where someone stops using the service? If so, for how long?
- How much of the change is relevant? Can the service deliver outcomes which are required (or, conversely, blocked) by policy; needed by stakeholders; valued by stakeholders' peers who experience similar change from other sources; demanded by social norms; and/or have beneficial financial impacts?
- How much of the change is significant? Is the quantity of change too low for it to be significant? Is too much of the change caused by other factors for it to be significant? Would too much of the change have happened anyway, for it to be significant, even if the service did not exist?

Doing a full SRoI project is a sizeable undertaking, particularly if you have no previous experience. The approach always uses both qualitative and quantitative data, and requires a completely different approach to data analysis from any other type of research. And there are no short cuts. As a result, learning and using SRoI requires a lot of resources of time, energy and money (Javits, 2008: 2).

However, the SRoI principles and questions in themselves are a valuable free resource for social researchers. We can all benefit from considering these questions as part of any evaluation or other research project that focuses on the provision of public services. SRoI Network members have seen, in practice, that this process can improve the quality of service delivery, by its rigorous approach to identifying the actual change that really happens, rather than trying to find a level of change that doesn't actually exist. Sadly, the latter approach is still all too common:

> It's a one-week project and we still have to evaluate in terms of how much this has influenced their lives, when we know that's all about the long-term relationship rather than the quick wham-bam. It's 'Have

we changed your life?', which sometimes the organisation thinks is possible when it's not.

Given the speed with which SRoI developed, it is perhaps not surprising that some misconceptions about SRoI also arose. In particular, SRoI does not provide a basis for comparison between services or organisations, so it cannot be used as a short-cut to decisions about the allocation of resources. SRoI produces the 'SRoI ratio', which, at its briefest, says something like, 'For every £1 invested in the work of Super Service, £4 worth of social value is created.' It is tempting for people to focus on this at the expense of the associated narrative about change and value. If Mega Service creates £3 worth of social value for every £1 invested, that does *not* mean that Mega Service is less valuable, overall, than Super Service. Each SRoI will have been conducted in the context of each individual service, so the results are applicable only to that service. However, comparison between one SRoI and another of the *same* service, conducted after a suitable interval, can be useful (Nicholls et al, 2012: 11).

Conclusion

This chapter has provided an overview of some of the complexities in the research landscape. Methods can be quantitative, qualitative or mixed; research may be done alone or in collaboration with colleagues and/or service users; some methods are highly time-consuming. If this is all starting to seem a bit daunting, don't worry; we will go through the process one stage at a time. But first, in the next chapter, we will consider research ethics, which underpins every stage of the research process.

CASE STUDIES

Ana has to do her project alone because it is for her degree and must be all her own work. Although she cannot involve participants fully in her research, she intends to recruit some heterosexual and some non-heterosexual participants. She plans to find some stories about non-heterosexual couples and families in the mainstream print media, and interview people about their reactions to and views of those stories. This will be *qualitative research*.

Ali is also doing his project alone, but as part of his work and in an organisation with a strong evaluation culture. He would like to involve service users in his evaluation, but there is a problem: unpaid family carers are usually over-worked and under-resourced. Ali's evaluation will be mixed methods, with *some quantitative and some qualitative research*.

EXERCISES

1. Think of two research questions relevant to your own area of work or study:

    a. A question that would be best answered using quantitative research; and

    b. A question that would be best answered using qualitative research.

2. Imagine you want to involve service users or participants in your own research or evaluation project, or in one of the projects in the exercise at the end of Chapter 1. Use the questions from earlier in this chapter to help you think through the implications.

Discussion questions

1. Do you think quantitative research would be better conducted alone, or in collaboration with others? Why?
2. Do you think qualitative research would be better conducted alone, or in collaboration with others? Why?
3. Imagine you were collaborating to help with an evaluation of a university course. What ethical issues could you foresee?

Debate topic

It is always a good idea to involve participants in research and service users in evaluation.

3

Research and evaluation ethics

Chapter summary

This chapter includes:

- An explanation of research ethics management
- An outline of ethics through the research process
- A discussion of researcher wellbeing

Introduction

Ethics can be defined as the rules of conduct for a particular activity. This is not specific to research: there are medical ethics, legal ethics and sporting ethics, among many others. Many public services have their own code of ethics (or equivalent, for example, a code of conduct), but research ethics are different from service ethics (Fox et al, 2007: 104). Within research there are different ethical codes for different disciplines such as psychological research, social research and market research. These codes are broadly similar but with slightly different foci. Many can be found online.[1]

 Seek out the ethical code that is closest to your profession or discipline, and familiarise yourself with its contents at an early stage.

Research ethics have learned a lot from medical ethics. The basic principle of medical ethics, 'first, do no harm', can be useful for social researchers to keep in mind (Kumar, 2005: 214). Ethical dilemmas from medicine also provide useful illustrations of the fact that sometimes it is not possible to balance all competing interests and to 'do no harm'. For example, if someone is close to the end of life and too unwell to express their own wishes, their family may ask the doctor to do everything possible to prolong their loved one's life, which may not be medically advisable. If the doctor grants the family's wish, they may cause physical and emotional pain to the patient; if they refuse, they may cause emotional pain to the family – and risk repercussions such as a formal complaint being made about them. Researchers, too, can find themselves confronted by ethical dilemmas with no good solution, which need careful management.

Research ethics management

Every researcher will encounter ethical dilemmas. These can be minimised through careful planning and good research practice, but they can't be eradicated. Luckily, they're not usually matters of life and death. But social research does have the capacity to do great harm, to individuals, groups and society as a whole, if it is unethically managed.

Most central government departments, healthcare organisations and universities worldwide now have research ethics committees, known as 'institutional review boards' in the USA and by other names elsewhere. However, researchers will not always be required to seek formal approval from a research ethics committee. Evaluation researchers are rarely required to seek formal approval unless they are working in government-funded healthcare settings or universities. Many evaluation textbooks make little or no mention of ethics, in contrast to more general research textbooks. This does not mean that evaluation is unethical, or that evaluation researchers need not consider ethical issues. But it does mean that the culture around evaluation research is, overall, less concerned with ethics than for some other research approaches.

A number of interviewees found that a particularly stressful part of their research project was the process of obtaining ethical approval from research ethics committees. Not everyone has to do this, but it is becoming more widespread. The procedures of research ethics committees differ, but the application process is often long and complex. This does make you think through your research thoroughly at an early stage, which is a good thing as it will save you time later on, but it can also be quite onerous:

> We needed help to get through the local research ethics committee. Because we were working with NHS patients we needed their approval. It's designed for the boys, so if you're outside of that circle it's harder to get into. If you're part of the research community … the language they use is in-house language and it's alienating, it's very long-winded.

After application, there may be a wait of two or three months before the committee gives a response. Even then, it may not be approval. The application may have to be rewritten and resubmitted, with another lengthy wait for a response, or at worst, it may simply be refused. Although this might be for a good reason, it's frustrating and upsetting for the researcher. Luckily there are ways to mitigate this, as this interviewee found:

> It's such a steep learning curve, a lot of it, like ethics. Last week I went to an ethics committee for the research we're doing. That was really useful. It's the one I'll have to go to and I've been now, I've seen what

it's like. All the time it's been that ongoing appreciation of, while it's something you have to navigate through, it is important if your research is going to have value.

 Find someone else who has made a successful application to your research ethics committee, and ask for their help.

One interviewee's view was that the practices of some research ethics committees may themselves be unethical, such as in removing choice from potential participants:

> What I wanted to do was research asking people what they think about things. These people are quite capable of giving consent, so why does an ethics committee have to second-guess what people are going to say? This patronising attitude to asking people's opinions, it's still there. I haven't managed to make any inroads into ethics committees but other people have and they say people aren't allowed to have an informed choice. The second-guessing is there all the time.

It is worth considering that there are some circumstances in which even embarking on research could be regarded as unethical:

> There are so many consultations going on now that it's reached the ridiculous stage. One of the patients I spoke to had someone from a large professional consultancy firm come and ask questions about a month ago. Four years ago someone else from that company came and asked exactly the same questions and nothing changed since then so she said 'I'm not prepared to talk to you'.

At the start of the global COVID-19 pandemic in 2020, many researchers jettisoned plans for research or put existing projects on hold. This was because researchers realised everyone, themselves included, were involved in a potentially traumatic experience. As a result priorities changed rapidly, and until life settled down it would have been difficult at best, and probably unethical, to start most new research or continue most existing research.

Ethics through the research process

Generally speaking, it is during the primary data collection phase of research that people are most conscious of the need to be careful not to do harm to others. But ethical considerations should underpin every stage of the research or evaluation process (Robson and McCartan, 2016: 208; Kara, 2018: 2). To begin with, why are you doing the research or evaluation? Is it for your own benefit, for kudos in the workplace or to gain a qualification, or does it have a wider purpose? For many practitioners, their research, like their work in general, needs to achieve something worthwhile:

> I didn't want to do research just for the sake of doing research, because I think that's unethical. Whoever you speak to in the community needs to benefit from the research you're going to do.

As you plan your research or evaluation, you need to think through the ethical issues for each stage, and show that you have done this in your proposal (see Chapter 5 for more on this).

It might seem that working with literature or documents doesn't require any ethical considerations. However, as a researcher you have a responsibility to read carefully and give a faithful representation of others' work. If you don't take the time, and make the effort, to gain a full understanding of each text, you may misrepresent the author's views, which could harm their professional reputation – and yours. This does not mean reading uncritically; it is essential to form your own opinion on the merit of what you read. There is more about this in Chapter 7.

Use of secondary data also involves ethical considerations. Statistics and other numerical data are often presented as though they are neutral, but they are not value-free. Human beings have decided how to present the figures, what to include and what to leave out, and how to arrange the numbers they have included. Those human beings have their own agendas that may unconsciously – or consciously – influence their decisions. This is not an attempt to create some kind of grand conspiracy theory. However, I would suggest that you are as careful in reading numerical data as in reading literature and documents, to make sure you understand the arguments being put forward and can represent them correctly. I would also recommend a critical approach to numbers, as to text, to try to understand, as far as possible, the personal and political agendas that may have influenced their presentation. Secondary data is covered in more detail in Chapter 8.

Primary data collection is the stage where most people do consider ethical issues. Potential research participants must always be able to choose freely whether or not to take part in your research. This means they need full information about what you are doing, why you are doing it, what the extent of their involvement would be, how their data will be stored and the outcomes you expect. This is often provided as an information sheet given to potential participants to read before they decide whether or not to take part.

Research participants are usually volunteers, although some researchers think that, for ethical reasons, they should be given a tangible thank you – perhaps a nice pen to keep after using it to fill in a questionnaire, or a gift voucher at the end of an interview or focus group. In any case, in accordance with good volunteer management practice, research participants should not be out of pocket as a result of volunteering to take part, so any travel or other expenses they incur as a result of their participation should be reimbursed from the research budget. Also, where possible, you should usually conceal participants' identity and protect their anonymity, although there are some exceptions to this (Kara, 2018: 99–100). Information given to you by participants should remain confidential and should not be shared with other people. There is more about primary data collection in Chapters 9 and 10.

When working with secondary or primary data, you need to know about the data protection laws in force in the country or countries where that data originated. For example, at the time of writing, European Union (EU) member countries and the UK are bound by the General Data Protection Regulation (GDPR). The GDPR came into force in May 2018 and is designed to protect individuals' privacy. It sets out the ways in which researchers in the EU and the UK are permitted to collect and process data about individuals. I cannot explain data protection laws in detail (that would take a book of its own!), but it is ethically necessary for you to inform yourself about, and comply with, the data protection laws that affect your research.

Some research projects focus on vulnerable groups such as those with mental health problems, people with learning disabilities, bereaved people, children or homeless people. In these cases even more care needs to be taken to ensure that potential and actual participants are not harmed in the course of the research. Participants should be reassured that they can end their participation at any time if they wish, or withdraw their data at a later stage. You need to specify when they will no longer be able to do this, and I would suggest that this is the point at which you start analysing the data. Once the analysis is underway, it becomes more difficult to withdraw data fully because it will have contributed to your thinking.

Data analysis, too, should be done ethically. For a start, you need to use all the data you have collected, unless circumstances change and require an associated change in your project. Otherwise, if you collect data that you don't use, you have misled your research participants and wasted their time. (This is a good reason for keeping your research project to a manageable size.) Then you need to make sure that you are representing your participants fully and accurately. Your findings should be firmly and clearly rooted in your data. There is more about data analysis in Chapters 11 and 12.

Reporting on your research also has ethical aspects. Consider the needs of your readers and create your report to meet those needs. Make sure the structure is user-friendly, the narrative flows and the language is clear. Keep jargon and professional terminology to a minimum and, where these are absolutely necessary, give definitions. Be clear about how your conclusions spring from your findings and your findings spring from your data. As far as possible, ensure that your conclusions are dictated by the findings and the data you have collected, rather than by your own biases and preferences. And try to create the report in such a way that anyone reading, watching or listening to it will be able to judge this for themselves. Research reporting is covered in more detail in Chapter 13.

Dissemination also has its ethical aspects. It is difficult to summarise a research project on one side of A4, or a poster or leaflet while maintaining a true representation of all the literature, documents and data that have contributed to the research. There is also the question of to whom you disseminate the findings. Of course your manager, supervisor, commissioner or examiner will have to see your work. But what about the research participants? Do they have a right to see, and maybe even comment on, the results of your research? For some people, doing this is an ethical necessity:

> I think feeding back to the people you have involved in the research is something that should happen as standard every single time, and I think it should be built into a research plan. I don't think sending them a copy of whatever report you produce is good enough. I think it has to be something that definitely reflects what they've told you.

Dissemination methods are covered in more detail in Chapter 14.

Putting research into practice is an ethical act in itself, but it also comes with ethical considerations. It is only ethical to try to put research into practice if that research is high quality with robust findings. Also, using research evidence to create organisational or social change requires a lot of work, which can be exhausting for researchers. This will be discussed more fully in Chapter 15. There are more resources on research ethics in the 'Further reading' section at the end of this book.

Researcher wellbeing

Historically, research ethics committees have been focused on ensuring participants' welfare and reducing institutional risk, and researchers' welfare has largely been ignored. However, this is beginning to change, particularly in the UK, where some universities (such as Sheffield Hallam University) and practice associations (for example, the Social Research Association) are publishing guidelines on researcher safety.

Where there is little external recognition of the need to consider the safety and wellbeing of researchers, we have to take care of our own welfare. This is not always easy in the heat of a research project when you are trying to juggle competing agendas and manage everything else in life too. Keeping to your ethical principles can be a hugely stressful experience in itself, as this interviewee found:

> Our tutor decided, earlyish on, that she wanted us all to send abstracts off to a national research conference. That led directly into some of the biggest difficulties, ethically. For me, it was a nightmare, because we weren't doing a proper research project, we were doing a practice one, that was how it was presented to us, but that changed because of our tutor's ambitions, so then you've got this conflict. Then it gets very difficult to manage, because you're doing this because you want to get qualified, and your tutor holds a lot of power within that. My

own ethical position meant that at the end I didn't know whether I would fail because I'd stuck to my guns. That was a real personal journey for me.

The need to resist the power of others can also arise in workplace research, as this interviewee's experience shows:

We did have a moment before the stuff was collated where we were in the middle of a meeting. I hadn't done the coding yet but I had the coding categories. The other researcher and my boss sat down and started coming up with recommendations, and I was like, 'Hang on a minute, should we not be making recommendations after we've done all the collation and stuff?' Some of what they were saying did turn out to be relevant, but I felt very uncomfortable about that. I don't think there was any malice involved, it was enthusiasm, but we had to stop it.

This quote helpfully demonstrates that ethical problems can arise from people acting with the best of motives.

If you are conducting workplace research such as a service evaluation, you will need to make recommendations for putting the research into practice (Robson and McCartan, 2016: 499). This can be something of an ethical balancing act. On the one side, you have the need to accurately represent your findings, and on the other, you have limited resources. You may also be under pressure from managers or commissioners, like this interviewee:

They want me to find things other than what they've already found but there's nothing there. It's blindingly obvious where the problems are but they seem to want more and more detail. There's no point, it won't tell them anything different in the long run. Our biggest problem, I could have told them when they first did the survey, is that we haven't got enough staff to deal with the customers coming through the door, the footfall, it's just not possible. All the findings are people complaining about wait times. One day we had over 400 people through the door and four members of staff so what do people expect? I'm trying to turn it round to be positive, four members of staff, each saw 100 people that day, excellent bloomin' productivity. They're trying to get me to find something different, but in the long run it's all going to come out the same.

This kind of pressure is in itself unethical, and it is a researcher's job to resist such pressure and protect the views of research participants. This is not always easy. Some years ago, I did a service audit that involved gathering views from all the staff of a public service. The research commissioner told me not to include a question about salaries, as it was a contentious issue and the management didn't want it to be highlighted through the research. I agreed to this, thinking that as I was doing semi-structured interviews, it would come up anyway if there were strong feelings about the subject. Even so, I was surprised when every single person I interviewed said they were aggrieved by their low salary. Given this, I felt a duty to report it in the findings, so I did – and the commissioner was furious.

It can be very stressful to try to manage ethical difficulties where you have little or no control. Preparation is the key to foreseeing as many of these as possible and therefore minimising their impact. Many of the interviewees for this book emphasised the need to be well organised and to manage your time so that you can deal with ethical difficulties as they arise:

> The preparation work is the most challenging, most important and most difficult. Like the ethics process, getting ethics, getting a committee together. Once you get the research process going, it develops momentum and is quite fun and rewarding.

Doing research or evaluation in itself can be very stressful at times, particularly on top of a main job:

> It's the sort of thing that could bring on a panic attack if you think about it too hard.

> The pressure and stress on family life can be quite demanding, you've got to factor all that in. I have known marriages breaking up, I've got academic friends who've done so much work in academia that they've ended up divorced, you've got to be pretty careful.

It's essential that you plan ways to keep yourself physically, mentally and emotionally safe:

> Do what we all teach, that is, your research into what impact this work will have on your personal and professional life. Then plan accordingly and do not take too much on board as it could impact on your health etcetera.

It is not ethical to wear yourself out doing research or evaluation. This book will advise you on healthy working practices such as good time management that can help to reduce your stress levels.

Different people have different ways of reducing stress. Interestingly, some of the interviewees for this book advocated linking academic research as closely as possible with your main job to reduce stress, but this could evidently cause stress too. Other interviewees recommended keeping a clear separation between research and other work:

> You need be able to compartmentalise work: do the practice work, leave it alone, walk away from it, concentrate on the academic work. That's very, very important. What I've found is that crossover can have a significant impact. There's no point doing research while you're worrying about a particular case, or being with a challenging client and worrying about your questionnaires.

If you're doing workplace research, you may be able to enlist the help of colleagues, or work to recruit volunteers with suitable skills:

> One of the things that I want to do is get a student in who I can then delegate some of the work to, and I've been having a look at how I can go about doing that. Students do come with work attached but I think it would be worth it.

However, if you're doing academic research, it's all down to you.

Primary data collection is the phase that can be most obviously stressful for a researcher, particularly if you are working with a vulnerable group, as this interviewee did:

> I think my main worry was that I knew I was going to hear some very harrowing stories, and how could I prepare myself for that? There was nothing in the literature anywhere that discussed that. The only thing I found was on change management and how people deal with stress. That's one element of it but it didn't really answer my question. I took advice that a friend gave me about it's okay to be upset but don't be hysterical, and it's okay, you're not being cold, you're just deferring the emotion. But there was nothing written anywhere about that. In my uni class I actually brought this up, I was there with a couple of people who were social workers, they don't get any training on how to deal with things like that.

This interviewee prepared by thinking through the problems that were likely to occur. Searching the literature, asking friends' advice and bringing up the subject in class for discussion yielded nuggets of information and advice that they were able to use to prepare mentally and practically for the work ahead. This is excellent research practice.

Peer support can also be useful in reducing stress. I am part of a loose group of 'research buddies' who see each other through the long and difficult process, and are always available between get-togethers for support by phone, email or face-to-face. I find that invaluable. Social networking sites such as Facebook and Twitter are also very useful for this kind of peer support. Some people are happiest in groups, whether online or in real life, while others prefer chatting or meeting one-to-one:

We got together with people doing research once a month to talk about how it was going. That didn't work particularly well for me because I got anxious, I thought everyone else was doing better, but it did help for others in the group.

 Work out what kind of support will be most effective in reducing your stress levels, and make sure it's in place.

There is more advice on how to look after yourself in Chapter 6, and on researcher wellbeing in the 'Further reading' section at the end of this book.

Conclusion

The key take-away point from this chapter is that researchers need to think and act ethically throughout the research process. This includes paying attention to our own wellbeing; we cannot expect others to do that for us. It is ethically necessary for us to identify our own needs and, as far as possible, find ways to meet them. We cannot rely on the research ethics management systems to help us think and act ethically in research. All researchers need to hone their ethical awareness and practice throughout their research careers.

Some research is set within frameworks that are specifically designed to be ethical, and these will be discussed in more detail in the next chapter.

CASE STUDIES

Ana is keen to find stories showing a broad representation of the LGBTQIA+ community, and also concerned to find stories that would not be upsetting to read. These are both ethical considerations. It takes her a long time to find three stories in the press that she is happy to use with participants. These are: a story about a Member of Parliament coming out as lesbian and marrying another woman; a story about a poly family, including trans and bisexual members, with three people sharing an equal relationship over 20 years; and a story about a gay couple who adopted one-year-old brother and sister twins.

Ali knows it would not be ethical to ask over-worked and under-resourced service users to become involved in his evaluation project. However, in discussing this with the head of the carers' support department, he discovers that the department is in touch with former carers, and they have a small budget for this kind of involvement. Ali meets with two former carers, both of whom agree to become involved. Their first task is to think through the ethical issues and methods for the evaluation.

EXERCISES

1. Choose one of the following research projects and consider the ethical implications. How would you address these in practice?

    a. A local authority is concerned about the cost of providing 'safe house' refuges for women and children escaping domestic violence. They want to investigate ways in which they could reduce the cost of this service without decreasing client safety.

    b. A health authority wants to assess the satisfaction levels associated with end-of-life care in a large hospital.

    c. A criminal justice service runs a secure unit for under-18s who have been convicted of violent crimes. The senior management team want to review the education programme to ensure it prepares inmates as well as possible for their post-custodial lives.

2. Think about your own research and write down what you think you will need for your own wellbeing throughout the process. Then write down any steps you can take to ensure those needs are met.

Discussion questions

1. Do you think the system of research management through committees is ethical? Why?
2. Why is researcher wellbeing important?
3. Are there some parts of research where we need to pay more attention to ethics than others? If not, why not? If there are, which parts, and why?

Debate topic

Ethics is for philosophers in their 'ivory towers', not for life in the real world.

4

Methodologies, approaches and theories

Chapter summary

This chapter includes:

- Overview of methodologies, methods and approaches
- Explanation of positivist, realist, constructionist, interpretivist and transformative methodologies
- Definitions of ontology and epistemology
- Outline of action, evaluation, mixed methods, arts-based and digitally mediated research
- The role of theory in research and evaluation
- Links between theory, research and practice

Introduction

It's easy to get confused about the difference between 'methods' and 'methodologies', particularly as 'methodology' sounds like a posh word for 'method'. Even some textbooks get these terms mixed up, so it's not surprising that students and practitioners can find them bewildering:

> Methodologies, epistemology, quite complex ideas really, going back to the philosophical underpinnings of knowledge. I do find that quite challenging. I find it interesting, but sometimes you can get really bogged down in it.

In fact, methods and methodologies are not the same. They have a relationship with each other, and with research approaches and questions, which is both important and useful. This chapter will help you to understand the difference between methodologies, approaches and methods; the important concepts of epistemology and ontology, and how they relate to methodologies, approaches and methods; and the role of theory in research. This may sound complicated, and it can be made so, but that is unnecessary; we will go through it one step at a time. Definitions of all the key concepts can be found in the Glossary at the end of the book. These concepts can be explored in much greater depth than is possible in a single chapter, but the information here should provide you with enough understanding to create a successful research or evaluation project.

Methodologies, methods and approaches

A methodology is a coherent and logical framework for research based on views, beliefs and values. This framework guides the choices made by researchers. For example, a researcher might work within a participatory methodology, where researchers work with participants throughout the research process. This researcher would choose to involve their participants in the research process as much as possible. Conversely, a researcher could use a conventional ethnographic methodology to investigate social phenomena in their natural context. This researcher would involve themselves in their participants' lives as they collected their data, but would be unlikely to involve participants more fully in helping them to conduct their research.

Methods are the tools that researchers use to collect and analyse data, write and present their findings. Researchers may use the same tools with very different methodologies. For example, a participatory researcher and a conventional ethnographer might both use interviews. However, their choices about *how* they used the method of interviewing would be guided by their methodology. So the participatory researcher might train some participants in interviewing techniques and support them to interview other participants, while the ethnographic researcher would be more likely to carry out their own interviews.

There are also some ways to approach research that are not methodologies, because they are not coherent and logical frameworks, but they are widely used and understood. Evaluation is one example. The main point of evaluation research is to assess the worth or the effect of something such as a service, or an intervention (which may be medical, social, educational, and so on), or a policy. There are several types of evaluation, such as formative, summative and impact evaluation. There are also different philosophies of evaluation, such as realist (Pawson and Tilley, 1997) and utilisation-focused evaluation (Patton, 2008). These different types and philosophies of evaluation are based on different views, beliefs and values, so evaluation is not itself a coherent and logical framework. Therefore it is an approach rather than a methodology. Evaluation can be used within a methodological framework: for example, it is possible to do participatory evaluation. And many methods can be used to collect data for evaluation research: questionnaires, interviews, focus groups and creative methods, among others. Evaluation is often seen as purely workplace research, but academics also conduct and write about evaluation:

> If you've got a group of researchers doing evaluation, you can do really nice academic work and be published.

The methodology you use will depend partly on your research question and partly on your own views, beliefs and values. Methodology, method, approach and research questions are inextricably linked together (Mason, 2018: 32–4). Some people have strong views, beliefs and values, such that they will only ever use certain methodologies. For others, the research question comes first, and they aim to choose the methodology and/or approach most likely to help them answer that question.

Either way, methods come after research questions, methodology and approach in the research planning process. This is because you need to choose the method or methods that are most likely to help you answer the research questions and most in tune with your chosen methodology or approach. Using a method that is unlikely to answer your research questions is a complete waste of time. The more you know about research methods, the more skilful you will be in making suitable choices.

People who don't know much about research often misunderstand this sequence. Many times my clients have said things like, 'We need to evaluate the impact of this service so we thought we'd do a questionnaire', or 'We want to find out residents' views about their healthcare so we'd like you to do some focus groups'. These kinds of approaches to research miss out some vital steps in the process, which should go as follows:

1. What is your research question or questions?
2. Which methodology or approach will be most useful in addressing the research question(s)?
3. Which research methods will be most likely to help you find an answer to your research question(s)?

There are many methodologies and approaches to research – far too many to cover in detail here. This chapter will give a brief overview of five of the most common types of methodology and five of the most common approaches to research. The aim is to give you enough information to help you decide which kinds of methodologies and approaches you want to pursue. There is a 'Further reading' section at the end of the book to help you find more information on your areas of interest.

 Use the Glossary at the end of the book any time you need to refresh your memory about the meaning of a term used in research.

Positivist methodology

Positivist methodology comes from the natural sciences. Positivists believe in objectivity and see no role in research for intangibles such as emotion or personal values. Markers of quality in positivist methodology include reliability and validity. Positivist research is said to be reliable if it can be replicated and produce the same results. Validity refers to whether the research actually measures what the researchers intended to measure.

Positivists use observation and measurement to establish facts. They often use logic rather than theory, and believe they can control any variables that are not directly connected to the matter under investigation. Positivist research or evaluation will test a carefully formulated hypothesis. A two-tailed or non-directional hypothesis predicts a relationship or an interaction – for example, 'either men or women give more money to environmental charities'. A one-tailed or directional hypothesis predicts a phenomenon or effect – for example, 'men give more money to environmental charities than women'. Such hypotheses are commonly tested by collecting numerical data, which is analysed using statistical calculations.

Positivism can be criticised on a number of grounds, such as for rejecting values while itself being value-based, or for maintaining that people can observe something objectively – a stance that has been comprehensively discredited (Robson and McCartan, 2016: 22). Also, some people criticise its application to social science, arguing that it should be left with the natural sciences where it originated. Yet positivist methodology has a lot to offer in the right context and, perhaps because it is so highly regarded within the natural sciences, it is still very influential.

If you are going to use positivist methodology, you need to have (or be willing to acquire) a good knowledge of experimental methods and statistics. The kinds of research investigations that might suggest the use of positivist methodology include:

- Will low-income neighbourhoods benefit from credit unions?
- Is participation in arts activities beneficial for young people with learning disabilities?
- Is there a difference in access to legal services for people of different ethnic origins?

Realist methodologies

Realist methodologies use theory, recognise complexity and acknowledge context. They look for the 'How?' and 'Why?' in research or evaluation findings as well as the 'What?'

When realist methodology is used in academic research, the theory used is often 'grand' or overarching (Wright Mills, 1959), such as Marx's theory of social class, Foucault's theory of power or Butler's theory that gender is performed. In practice-based research or evaluation, people using realist methodology tend to draw more on 'middle-range' theory (Merton, 2012 [1949]), that is, the theories of people involved in the matter under investigation that can be tested and refined through research.

Following the work of Pawson and Tilley (1997) realist methodologies are often used for evaluation research. Pawson and Tilley's view is that every service, intervention and policy exists in a context (place, time, political and economic environment, and so on), and this must be taken into account in any evaluation.

For Pawson and Tilley, asking 'What works?' is too simplistic. The question in realist evaluation is more like 'What works, when, why, how and for whom?' So evaluators using realist methodology are unlikely, for example, to use a simple pre-/post-test design, which applies a test to people both before and after they take part in an activity or receive a treatment, and considers the results sufficient to evaluate that activity or treatment. Realist evaluators are more likely to test and develop people's theories about what is causing an outcome, identify and include other variables that might affect the outcome, and aim to explain and infer rather than judge.

Realist methodologies can be criticised for trying to do too much at once and for needing more resources of time and money than some other methodologies. However, they have proved useful in addressing complex research and evaluation questions.

If you are going to use realist methodology, you need to be comfortable with complexity and creative thinking. The kinds of research investigations that might suggest the use of realist methodology include:

- How does the work of a local mental health charity affect government-funded services in the area?
- Is there a difference in benefit between natural and artificial water features as part of public green spaces?
- Does performance-related pay improve teachers' performance?

Constructionist methodologies

Constructionists believe that social phenomena do not exist independently of people, and nor do they happen by chance, but they are constructed by social actors. Constructionists believe there is no independent reality for us to observe and measure, but multiple realities (Robson and McCartan, 2016: 24–5), potentially one for each person on the planet. Constructionism is explicitly value-based and subjective, and is therefore the opposite of positivist methodology (Robson and McCartan, 2016: 24–5):

> In the first interview, the person I interviewed I knew quite well. At one point she said to me, 'Of course in the world you and I inhabit…' and I thought hang on a minute, is it the same world or isn't it?

For constructionists, research often involves gathering and analysing different people's perspectives on the matter under investigation. People using a constructionist methodology would regard themselves as constructing research with participants rather than using participants for their research. Constructionism is linked with postmodernism, although the latter focuses on deconstruction as well as construction.

Constructionist methodologies can be criticised for being too specific and lacking in rigour. However, these methodologies have proved very useful for some kinds of research where the views of diverse groups of people need to be considered, such as public consultations.

If you are going to use constructionist methodology, you need to be comfortable with the idea of multiple realities. The kinds of research investigations that might suggest the use of constructionist methodology include:

- What kinds of amenities would local residents like in a new community centre?
- How could art exhibitions be made accessible for more people?
- What would help people feel safer while using an urban transport system?

Interpretivist methodologies

Interpretivist methodologies suggest that reality is interpreted by people as we work to make sense of the world we experience and of our place in that world (Robson and McCartan, 2016: 24). This has some similarities to constructionist methodologies in also being value-based and subjective, but it is not the same. Put simply, constructionists view meaning as constructed, while interpretivists view meaning as interpreted.

Interpretivist researchers believe they cannot understand why social phenomena occur if they don't first understand how the people involved in those phenomena interpret, or make sense of, what they experience. Like realist methodologies, interpretivist methodologies take context into account. However, interpretivists regard each context as distinct, and so do not expect research to be replicable.

Interpretivist methodologies can be criticised for being biased. Interpretivists might counter such an accusation by saying that bias is simply one form of interpretation, which can be identified, explained and integrated into research findings. Another criticism is that interpretivist research cannot be replicated.

If you are going to use an interpretivist methodology, you need to be able and willing to understand other people's perspectives. The kinds of research investigations that might suggest the use of interpretivist methodologies include:

- How do refugees and economic migrants experience living in a specific country?
- What is the quality of neighbour relations in cities, towns and villages?
- Can listening to music reduce pain?

Transformative methodologies

Transformative methodologies, as the name implies, suggest that research and evaluation will not only investigate but also create change. This type of methodology has a strong ethical focus that goes beyond the principle of 'do no harm' that is central to ethics in biomedical research. Transformative methodologies aim to reduce power imbalances (Kara, 2020: 45) – certainly among people involved in conducting research, and ideally also as a result of the findings.

Transformative methodologies were, and are, being developed primarily by people who have experienced discrimination, such as women, people of colour and disabled people. People within such groups – at first independently, later collectively – became angry about researchers studying them for personal gain with no resulting benefit, and sometimes actual detriment, to the groups being studied. They decided that if research was to be done about their lives, they would find a way to do it themselves:

> I ran a user-focused project, evaluation with mental health service users central to the research methodology – that was user-led research.

Any transformative methodology can be criticised for being too subjective and ambitious, setting itself up to reduce power imbalances but failing to make any real difference. However, some projects using transformative methodologies have demonstrated real impact. Rose et al (2002) conducted user-led research to study the effect of electro-convulsive therapy (ECT) on patients with mental illness, and their findings changed the way ECT was administered by clinicians in the UK (SCIE, 2007: 9–11). Similarly, European researchers used a participatory approach to investigate the exclusion of Europe's nomadic Roma people from many employment opportunities. The researchers, including Romani team members, presented their findings at the European Parliament, which led to changes in EU legislation designed to reduce Roma exclusion (Munté et al, 2011: 263). (There is more about research impact in Chapter 15.)

If you are going to use a transformative methodology, you need to be prepared to give more time and effort to your research than in using other methodologies. The kinds of research investigations that might suggest the use of a transformative methodology include:

- What is the best way to tackle substance misuse within a specific ethnic group?
- How can archival data support present-day activism?
- What are the support needs of new mothers with physical disabilities?

Ontology and epistemology

All methodologies are allied with positions of ontology and epistemology. These annoyingly long and complicated words conceal fairly straightforward concepts. Ontology (literally 'the study of being') refers to how the world is known, while epistemology (literally 'the study of knowledge') refers to how that knowledge of the world is learned (Ormston et al, 2014: 6). Everyone has ontological and epistemological positions, although these can change over time. For example, part of your ontological position might be a firmly held belief that each person should take full responsibility for their own welfare – or an equally firm belief that everyone should share responsibility for the welfare of everyone else. These positions would be likely to align you with, respectively, the right or left of the political spectrum.

An example of an epistemological position is someone's view of illness. For example, illness could be seen as:

- caused by independent entities such as viruses and bacteria (positivist);
- due to a complex range of factors in a specific context (realist);
- created through people's actions and decisions (constructionist);
- different for different people (interpretivist);
- a combination of the above, and also affected by wider social structures such as poverty and ethnicity (transformative).

It is worth identifying your own ontological and epistemological positions, because your view of the world, and the way you think things are known, will inevitably influence the way you do research or evaluation (Bryman, 2016: 28–30). This is, in part, because your ontological and epistemological positions are likely to make some methodologies and approaches more attractive to you than others.

Table 4.1 summarises the ontological and epistemological positions of the methodologies outlined above. While it is not exhaustive, and there is some disagreement about terminology and categories, it provides a useful 'rule of

Table 4.1: Methodologies, ontologies, epistemologies and methods

Methodology type	Positivist	Realist	Constructionist	Interpretivist	Transformative
Subdivisions include:	Post-positivist	Critical realist	Postmodernist Grounded theory	Phenomenologist Symbolic interactionist Hermeneutic	Participatory Feminist Emancipatory/ activist User-led Decolonising
Ontology (how the world is known)	Facts and phenomena exist independently of people	Facts and phenomena are entwined in complex contexts	People construct facts and phenomena	People interpret facts and phenomena	People, facts and phenomena can combine to create change
Epistemology (how that knowledge of the world is learned)	Through observation and measurement	Through assessment of complexity in context	By creating meaning from experience	By identifying and interpreting multiple realities	Through relationships with people and the environment
Methods likely to be used	Randomised controlled trials, surveys, technology-based methods	Mixed methods	Interviews, arts-based methods, discourse analysis	Interviews, focus groups, participant observation	Arts-based methods, interviews, community-based research

thumb' guide to the concepts discussed so far in this chapter, and also points to the links between methodologies and methods.

Action research

The term 'action research' was coined in the 1940s by the German–American social psychologist Kurt Lewin (1890–1947). Action research is an approach that enables groups of people to investigate their own situation or practices, either on their own or with help from professional researchers, to find out how they can make positive changes.

Action research was initially used within organisational research, and has expanded into other fields such as education (Robson and McCartan, 2016: 200). Collaboration is at its heart, and it is characterised by a repeating cycle of 'plan, act, observe, reflect', as shown in Figure 4.1. This has clear parallels with the evaluation cycle shown in Figure 4.2, and indeed, action research can be used for evaluation purposes.

Figure 4.1: The action research cycle

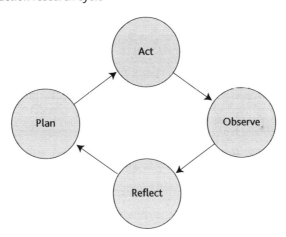

Action research resists a clear definition (Whitelaw et al, 2003: 8–9) but, in essence, it is an iterative process of reflection and problem-solving in groups or communities. Problems addressed through action research are those that affect members of the group or community carrying out the research. The process of action research involves identifying a problem, collecting information about the problem, deciding how to solve the problem, trying out the solution, seeing if the solution works, and so on. Ongoing action research can be thought of as a spiral, rather than a cycle, because each iteration builds on the last.

Participatory action research (PAR) arguably takes this a step further, as it 'aims to produce knowledge in an active partnership with those affected by that knowledge, for the express purpose of improving their social, educational, and material conditions' (Bhana, 2006: 430). PAR and its close relative, participatory appraisal, grew from work done by activists in South America and Africa. The differences between action research and PAR stem from their differing histories, but their use in practice has highlighted the many similarities they share (Bhana, 2006: 431).

Lewin was one of the first people to recognise the potential for linking research with social justice (Robson and McCartan, 2016: 200). Although action research is an approach rather than a methodology, Lewin's work has informed the development of several transformative methodologies such as activist and decolonising methodologies. It is not surprising, therefore, that action research and PAR are often used with transformative methodologies, and have a similar ethical focus. Action research can also be used with constructionist, interpretivist and realist methodologies.

Evaluation research

Evaluation is an approach to assessing the value of a service, intervention or policy:

> People want to know what's important about what they're doing.
> They're very evaluation-focused, they want to know what works and
> why and what doesn't and why.

There are a number of types of evaluation, chief among them being process, outcome and impact evaluation. Each of these will ask similar questions, for example, 'What is working well?' and 'Where and how could we make improvements?' However, the focus of each is different.

Process evaluation focuses on *how* a service, intervention or policy helps its beneficiaries. For example, a process evaluation of a health service might collect data about the number, length and frequency of appointments, and the nature of treatment provided, as well as changes in symptoms, to try to identify the optimum system for healing.

Outcome evaluation focuses on *what changes* for beneficiaries. For example, an outcome evaluation of a health service might collect data about changes in symptoms, and about other factors that could affect patients' health, to try to identify the difference made by the service to patients.

Impact evaluation focuses on the *effect* of a service, intervention or policy. For example, an impact evaluation of a health service might collect data about what has (or hasn't) changed in patients' lives as a result of the service. Those changes could be positive or negative, intended or unintended: from unwelcome drug side effects to improvements in health such that a patient can return to work or once again care for beloved grandchildren:

> I did the basic audience research, finding out about how people found
> out about us and demographic data so we'd know our audiences better.

Evaluation of our activities, and one-off pieces of research, finding out how people responded to our brand.

These three types of evaluation are not mutually exclusive. Any two, or all three, may be combined in a single evaluation project. Figure 4.2 shows the evaluation cycle.

Figure 4.2: The evaluation cycle

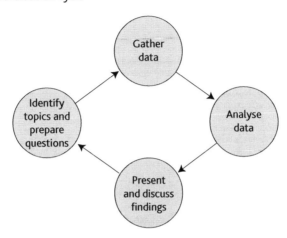

Conventionally, research has been carried out to answer questions and increase knowledge. Evaluation research has an added purpose of making recommendations for future action:

> That's a big thing between uni and work: at uni you don't have to make recommendations, you just have to present your findings, but at work you have to make recommendations.

As we have seen, evaluation research works well with realist methodologies, and can also be used with transformative methodologies, particularly participatory frameworks.

Mixed methods research

Formal research began as a quantitative, positivist discipline, with qualitative research developing much later (Ormston et al, 2014: 11). The initial idea of mixing methods involved combining quantitative and qualitative methods of collecting data:

> I interviewed four policymakers – two national, two local – and I did a questionnaire around leadership with my peers in different local authorities.

These days, mixed methods research can be entirely qualitative (Ritchie and Ormston, 2014: 44), or entirely quantitative, or a combination of the two. Also, methods can be mixed at any or all stages of the research process. For example, you might:

- collect data using one method;
- analyse that data in two different ways to check whether the findings are the same or not;
- disseminate your findings through a newspaper article, a website and an exhibition.

One of the problems with mixing methods is that, as shown in Table 4.1, different methods are associated with different approaches and methodologies. Of course some methods can be used with more than one approach or methodology, but there is no method that can be used with every approach or methodology. Table 4.1 also shows that each type of methodology is associated with a different ontological and epistemological position, that is, a different view of reality. This can cause difficulties for researchers who want to combine methods that look at things in different ways. Difficulties mainly occur at the data analysis stage, and suggestions for how to manage this are given in Chapter 12.

> With quantitative data that's a very easy skill for someone who's got a very analytical methodical mind. And I think that's why research and evaluation takes a combination of skills, because I'm not very good at analysing the open questions, the qualitative, summing up what exactly is the thing they're trying to say?

Partly as a result of these potential problems, mixing methods needs careful thought and planning at the research design stage. Some people think adding new methods can be a useful way of rescuing a research or evaluation project that isn't going to plan, but this is rarely a good idea (except, perhaps, at the dissemination stage). As always, the methods you use should be selected to ensure that they give you the best chance of answering the research question. This applies as much to mixed as to unmixed methods.

Mixed methods research can be used with any methodology. Evaluation researchers almost always use a mixed methods approach. And mixed methods designs may include arts-based or digitally mediated research methods, to which we now turn.

Arts-based research

The arts and research have a closer relationship than many people realise. They have some facets in common, such as paying close attention to a phenomenon and representing it for an audience. Artists of all kinds use research in their work, and for some their artistic practice is a form of research (Barone and Eisner, 2012: 24).

Research has made use of all kinds of art forms: visual arts, performing arts, music, creative writing, and so on. Increasingly, researchers are seeing the potential for the arts to make a contribution to research practice. Arts-based research may be particularly useful when working with sensitive topics or people with whom communication is difficult for linguistic or cognitive reasons. Also, arts-based methods can be used at any stage of the research process, from design to dissemination (Leavy, 2015: 18–19):

> It's about looking at the whole project. I'm quite a visual person so to map it out, time for interviews, time for ethics, so to get that timeline.

The current debate in arts-based research is around what level of artistic skill a researcher should have (Kara, 2020: 29–30). Some people think a researcher should have an equivalent level of ability in any branch of the arts they wish to use as they have in research. Others think the arts should be accessible to all, and that if using an arts technique – however badly – enables learning, then it is worthwhile. A third option, which I would endorse, sits between the two and considers the content and context of the research before deciding whether or not the researcher can manage on their own. For example, if you are investigating the social priorities of six-year-old schoolchildren by asking them to draw pictures of what they like doing best after school, you don't need a high level of artistic skill to collect and analyse that data. However, if you are working with community-based researchers who want to present their findings as a drama production, you need to consider bringing a professional drama worker on to the research team, unless you have good drama skills yourself.

Arts-based research is quite a new field so the terminology is still shifting and changing, but here are some examples of arts-based research that are quite well established:

- Photo-elicitation: photos are used to prompt discussion in interviews – the photos may be taken specifically for the purpose, or already in existence (for example, family photos or pictures in magazines).
- Poetic inquiry: poetry is written for research purposes, as data or to help with analysis.
- Mapping: maps are created, or used as prompts, for data collection.
- Storytelling: for data collection or reporting research findings.
- Drama: for presenting and disseminating findings.
- Art exhibition or installation: for disseminating findings.

Arts-based research works well with interpretivist, constructionist and transformative methodologies, and can also be used with realist methodology. Arts-based methods can also be used within action and evaluation research.

Digitally mediated research

Researchers of the 21st century are embracing the possibilities offered by smartphones, apps, social media, dedicated analysis software and other such technological options. Technology can be useful at all stages of the research process (Kara, 2020: 39). Among other options are:

- Skype, WhatsApp, Zoom, email etc can help researchers to work collaboratively, even if they're based in different countries.
- Gantt charts or project management software can help with planning and designing research.
- Online search tools such as Google Scholar and the Directory of Open Access Journals can help with context-setting or literature reviews.
- GPS can help researchers to find places for meetings with participants, gatekeepers or colleagues.
- Apps can be written to enable data collection online or via smartphones.
- Audio and video recorders can be used for data collection.
- Smartphones can record audio, video or written notes.
- Public QR codes can be used to collect data for place-based research.
- GoPro helmet cameras or drones, and software, can be used for outdoor research.
- Primary data can be collected online, either proactively (for example, through an online survey) or reactively (for example, by collecting posts from social media).
- The 'open data' movement means a great deal of 'big data' is freely available online.
- Skype interviews and online focus groups can enable data collection with geographically scattered groups of people.
- Computer software can be used to help analyse quantitative and/or qualitative data.
- Word processing software can be used to prepare research reports.
- Microsoft PowerPoint or Prezi software can be used to present findings.
- Video and/or social media can be used for dissemination.

In recent years it has become quite fashionable to use social media for research, particularly for participant recruitment, data collection and dissemination. Social media offers a huge amount of detailed information about people's lives and interactions, which makes it an appealing prospect for researchers. However, research using social media presents new ethical difficulties. Not everyone is online, and not everyone who is online uses social media. Also, people who are on social media may not reveal their true identities, so it can be difficult to be sure who your participants are or which group(s) they represent. This can also make it difficult to be sure you're obtaining fully informed consent – or even any consent at all. Yet it's important to take care to obtain informed consent, even with material that is in the public domain (such as on open blogs or Twitter), because the person who generated the content wouldn't necessarily be happy for it to be used as data for research.

Here is a cautionary tale. In mid–2014 researchers from Facebook published details of an experiment in which Facebook users' exposure to emotional content was manipulated (Kramer et al, 2014: 8788). This research was in accordance with Facebook's data use policy to which users had consented by ticking a box when they joined Facebook. However, many Facebook users felt that they had not given informed consent to participating in such research. When the research was published, there was such an outcry on social media that the researchers had to apologise. As a result, the editor of the journal that had published the research printed an 'expression of concern' about its ethical status.

Digital mediation can also create barriers for researchers. Information overload is a perennial problem. Content published online is of variable quality and reliability. Those outside university systems won't have the necessary passwords for access to all peer-reviewed electronic literature (although there is an increasing amount of open access literature – see Chapter 7 for more on this):

> If you want practitioners that are evidence-based you've got to have time to do it, to read, to keep up to date. Is it easier because of the internet? Possibly, but you can become overloaded, there can be too much information. There need to be tools to enable practitioners to research.

Digitally mediated research or evaluation also requires some level of skill on the part of both researchers and participants. It works well with positivist and realist methodologies, and can also be used with constructionist, interpretivist and transformative methodologies. Digitally mediated methods can also be used within action and evaluation research.

The role of theory in research and evaluation

Theory is a way of making sense of some aspect, or aspects, of the world around us. For the purposes of research, theory can usefully be divided into three types:

1. Formal theory, based primarily on thought, such as Marxist theory, postmodern theory or attachment theory.
2. Informal theory, based primarily on experience, such as a police constable's theory of how best to manage an unruly crowd.
3. Generated theory, built as part of the research process.

There are also some specific theoretical underpinnings to evaluation research. Research can be seen as a way to link formal, informal and (where appropriate) generated theories with a view to increasing knowledge and improving practice.

Formal theory plays a more explicit role in academic than in workplace research. If you are doing academic research, you will need to engage with formal theory, particularly when you are defining your research question and discussing your findings. If you are doing workplace research, you probably won't have to engage with formal theory, but doing so is likely to improve your research. This is because each research method is rooted in a theoretical perspective, that is, a particular way of making sense of some aspect of the world. The better you understand the rationale behind that way of making sense, the more effectively you will be able to use the method (Rose, 2012: 45) and disseminate the findings:

> Research sits in a void if it's not theoretically connected.

Yet, engaging with formal theory can be difficult for a number of reasons – it can be hard to read, hard to understand and even difficult to find:

> It's a bit of a challenge to apply theory when there isn't a lot of theory, you have to pull it from other schools of research.

Informal theory is often undervalued, perhaps because it is drawn from lived experience rather than being written down by academics. But, as a way of understanding the world, informal theory can be every bit as valid as formal theory (Glasby, 2011: 89):

> When I first came to academia, I shied away from my practice experience because I thought it's not academic, but now I realise that was stupid. I teach some subjects that are a real quagmire, and I can tell them what it means in practice, like when I worked with this person and the challenges we faced. Part of the reason you're here isn't just your academic skills, it's because you've been in practice. It's all part of the thing we're all banging on about all the time about theory into practice.

> Research is almost a hidden extra but it's such an important part of the work that we do. From my perspective as a nurse, in nursing we don't do enough research. As nurses, we're hands-on, we're coalface with patients, relatives, care providers, we see the impact of that care, and yet we don't utilise that information.

Writing down your own informal theories can be a useful process, which may help you define your research questions and hypotheses. Qualitative data collection often involves collecting the informal theories of practitioners, service users and others. Informal theories are like close-ups, while formal theories can take a wider view in a broader context. The most insightful research often, explicitly, uses both.

Generated theory is theory that is built from the research you conduct. The most common formulation is 'grounded theory', to signify that the theory is grounded in data. Grounded theory takes a unique approach to unifying theory with method and methodology (Strauss and Corbin, 1998: 14):

> I learned that you can generate your own theory, and I think that is something you have to learn, because – particularly in my bit of the world – you are presented with THE theories about child development, how children learn, staff training and development, and you think ooh, all these famous people have done all this, and actually you can generate your own and it is valid if you've got the data to back it up and you can talk about the way you've analysed it and why you've done it like you have.

Researchers who work to generate theory collect some data and analyse it using emergent coding – that is, focusing on whatever they can perceive in the data (see Chapter 12 for more on qualitative data coding). They identify analytic categories or themes, and the relationships between them. Then they collect some more data and analyse that too. They continue moving back and forth between data collection and analysis until they reach 'saturation', that is, they are no longer able to identify any new categories or themes or relationships. This enables the development of 'an integrated framework that can be used to explain or predict phenomena' (Strauss and Corbin, 1998: 15), that is, a theory.

There is a wide range of evaluation theories and they change over time (Alkin, 2013: 6). Some types of evaluation are 'theory-driven', that is, a detailed theory is devised for the service being evaluated (this is sometimes known as a 'logic model'), and is used to guide the evaluation (Christie and Alkin, 2013: 25). Others are based on wider theories, such as justice theories or decision-oriented theories (Christie and Alkin, 2013: 37, 40) or, as we have already seen, realist theories:

> I've done plenty of evaluation myself, commissioned work, and the assumption seems to be that to do an evaluation is to get very direct and clear answers to questions that are set and important to the funders which is fine, that's all good, but I think sometimes what escapes that process is the other knowledge researchers can bring to that, particularly with respect to theoretical development. Situations where evaluators say it's brilliant but we're just doing evaluation, it's a lost opportunity to do that theoretical development, we need to know more than whether a service is working for a group of people, the data can lend itself very well to theoretical development.

So it is clear that there is, or can be, a strong link between evaluation and theory. In fact there is (or should be) a strong link between theory, all types of research, and practice.

Theory, research, practice

Again, these are not separate entities – at least, they shouldn't be. In an ideal world, there would be a cyclical relationship between them, as shown in Figure 4.3.

Figure 4.3: Theory, research and practice, a cyclical relationship

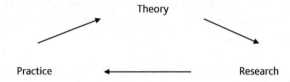

In the real world, there are a number of barriers to this relationship, such as organisational and sector cultures, lack of time and insufficient understanding. Then there is the human instinct to sort ourselves into groups on the basis of identity. Some academics see practitioners as so immersed in their day-to-day work that they can't stand back and take a wider view, while some practitioners see academics as out of touch with real life. Also, poor research practice by some academics and practitioners causes disillusionment among service users, which really doesn't help. Another barrier is the lack of resources and/or willingness to disseminate the findings of research and evaluation (discussed in more detail in Chapter 14).

These barriers can be particularly frustrating for practitioners, who can see how theory and research could be used in practice to benefit their service users:

> There are a lot of jobs within the police where research as a function could revolutionise the way policing is done. The growth in analysts, that's very interesting. What the analysts do is look at crime intelligence and look at patterns. It's a type of profiling, but it can go deeper than that. If they could learn to be sophisticated enough to use different sociological theories, based on a sample of live data that they have, they would be able to come up with explanations and action plans for how to address crime in that particular area.

One of the best ways to break down these barriers is to do research and evaluation well and make good use of its findings. This book shows you how.

Conclusion

This chapter has clarified the difference between research methodologies, research methods and research approaches, and discussed some of the major methodologies and approaches. We have defined and explained the concepts of ontology and epistemology, and looked at the role of theory in research and evaluation. It is really important that you have a good understanding of these topics before you begin designing your research project. If it is too late for that, you and your research will still benefit from gaining that understanding now.

CASE STUDIES

Ana plans to use interpretivist methodology with feminist theory because these fit with her epistemological and ontological positions. She wants to collect interview data, using the media stories to enhance the interviews and so – she hopes – elicit richer data. Because the stories are from the mainstream media, Ana knows some of her interviewees may already have seen one or more of them. However, she carefully chose one from a newspaper, one from a women's magazine and one from a men's magazine, so she thinks her interviewees are unlikely to have seen them all.

Ali wants to use realist methodology and theory because he finds them useful for evaluation. He explains this to the service users who are working with him and they are in agreement. They also all agree on the need to use more than one method of collecting data, because evaluations in their organisation focus on processes, outcomes and impact.

EXERCISES

1. Which methodologies and/or approaches, which methods and what type of theoretical approach would you choose for each of the following research questions?

   a. Does the use of 'health diaries' (for recording food, drink and exercise) help obese diabetics to lose weight?

   b. What is the value of a home handyperson service for people aged 80 or over living in the small town of Burrenford?

   c. What would attract more people to use a mobile library?

   d. What are the main difficulties faced by professionals moving from one public service career to another, for example, social workers becoming probation officers, or teachers joining the police?

   e. What is the best way to reduce crime in Delbright, an inner-city neighbourhood?

   Bear in mind that 'research methods' is not an exact science, so there may be a range of possible answers to these questions, particularly in the types of research where context is important. The aim is to come up with an answer that is 'good enough' and fit for purpose. If possible, discuss your choices with your peers.

2. Work out your own ontological and epistemological perspectives. Which kinds of theories and methods are aligned with your perspectives? How do you feel about that?

Discussion questions

1. Do you think you could use more than one methodology within a single research project? If not, why not? If you think you could, why and how would you approach that project?
2. What could be the role, or roles, of theory in evaluation research?
3. To what extent is research necessary in linking theory and practice?

Debate topic

Theory is impractical.

5

Topics and proposals

Chapter summary

This chapter includes:

- Advice on choosing a research or evaluation topic
- Information about how to refine your topic into a question
- A discussion of how to use your research question to guide your data collection
- Consideration of how much data you need, and whether it should be quantitative or qualitative
- An outline of sampling techniques, including probability and non-probability samples
- An overview of what constitutes evidence for research
- An introduction to writing a proposal
- Some information about research funders

Introduction

It can be tempting to rush through the early stages of the research or evaluation process and plunge straight into data collection. This is a bad idea. The more careful thought and exploration you put in at the start, the more time you will save yourself later on. This chapter will guide you through the process of choosing and refining a research topic and writing a research proposal. These are the first building blocks for the construction of your research, and it is always easier to build on solid rather than flimsy foundations.

Choosing a research or evaluation topic

Choosing a topic can be a challenge, particularly if the choice is wide, such as research for a Master's dissertation or evaluation within a whole organisation. Where possible, the best approach is to focus on whatever interests you most (Robson and McCartan, 2016: 49):

If you're going to do a postgrad and you have the opportunity to design your own question, make sure it's something that *really* interests you because you won't like it halfway through anyway.

Research can be a hard and lonely journey, and a passion for your topic will help you to keep going through the difficult times.

 Choose the research topic that you find the most interesting.

Some people have topics chosen for them, whether they are doing workplace or academic research. This may feel like a blessing in the short term, but people who are not enthusiastic about their research topic may have difficulties later on:

> I was talking to a colleague, someone else has chosen her topic for her, she's not committed to it. We've got some great topics she was really interested in doing but they were saying 'no'. She's got something she's not that interested in, you can see her commitment wavering, she's already off her timeline.

> One of the other problems that can occur is that services will decide what the research or the evaluation topic needs to be, and the person who's undertaking the research may well not actually be that interested in that area but because it's a topic that's defined by the service they've got to do it, and that gets very taxing in terms of their personal motivation to continue.

People in positions of power, such as funders, supervisors and managers, may attempt to influence – or even decide – your choice of research topic. If you are lucky, their interests and yours will coincide, but this seems to be quite rare. Where possible, I would advise you to resist such influence and focus on your own interests.

If you have to do a piece of research or evaluation on a topic you don't find particularly interesting, the best way to get through it is to identify likely positive outcomes. For example, you will learn from the process; the qualification would look good on your CV; it should earn you brownie points with your manager. Stay focused on those outcomes as you carry out the research.

 Write the positive outcomes that are likely to come from your research on Post-it notes, and stick them in places where you will see them every day.

In some cases, doing a project on someone else's topic may give you leverage to ask for extra support, whether in terms of study time, help with administration or other resources to make your life easier. This can also apply if you choose your own topic and it is closely related to your work. This will be discussed more fully in Chapter 6.

If you are intending to do academic research, you may be able to draw on existing workplace data, which can save a lot of time and effort. But it is still essential to make sure the topic interests you:

> One of the areas of advice I give is if possible do what I did. I was involved with some of the research officially within the police at the time, I got permission to use that as a base for my academic research. If people haven't decided on a specific subject, I say, 'Look at what the force is doing. If there are any areas that fit, see if you can get permission to latch on and use some of that data.' It can give a tremendous boost at the beginning.

Refining your topic

Whether you choose for yourself or the choice is decided for you, your topic is likely to start by being huge and vague. Two examples are:

- How does education help people to succeed?
- What does our organisation do effectively, and where could it be improved?

These are important questions but they are much too big to research as they stand. So you need to narrow your focus.

Photography offers a useful parallel. If you take a camera and point it at a landscape without focusing on something specific, the result will be unsatisfying: half sky, half land, altogether nothing much. However, if you focus on a gnarly tree in the foreground, and include enough scenery to give it some context, you could have an interesting and appealing picture. In a landscape, there are many different things you could choose to focus on: cattle on a hillside, dew-pearled cobwebs, a hovering hawk. The same applies to research.

Whether you are doing academic or workplace research, the tools you use to refine your topic into useful questions are the same: reading, writing and thinking. The way to formulate research questions is to read, and think, and write, and think some more. Reading other people's work in your topic area will help you to clarify your own thoughts, provide useful definitions to consider and offer ideas for how to conduct your own research. Thinking about what you've read will help you to develop your ideas. Writing down your thoughts will help you to clarify those ideas. Thinking about them again will help you to develop them further.

The huge vague topics mentioned earlier could be refined in many different ways, but in all cases you need to move from concepts (which are not measurable) to variables (which are) (Kumar, 2005: 56). 'Success' and 'effectiveness' are both concepts that are not, of themselves, measurable, but can be measured by identified variables such as individual income or service take-up rates. Let's consider the topic of how education helps people succeed. To refine this, you would need to consider questions like: What level of education are you interested in: pre-school, child, teenage, college/university or adult? Do you want to take into account factors such as gender, ethnicity or socioeconomic status? How do you define 'success'? It might take a lot of reading and thinking and writing before you come up with your research question: What is the relationship between exam results and income for Asian men 10 years after finishing compulsory education?

You could go through a similar process with the topic of what an organisation does effectively and where it could be improved. Researching the effectiveness of a whole organisation, even a small one, is an enormous task, so to begin with you would need to define 'effectiveness'. Then you would need to consider questions like: Using your definition of 'effectiveness', which parts of the organisation do you think are effective now? Which do you think could be more effective? Can you evaluate one effective and one less effective part of the organisation, for the purposes of comparison, with the aim of learning lessons that could be applied more widely across the organisation? Write down your questions, write down your answers, and develop your thoughts:

> I think the most important thing is to know what question you're going to ask.

Taking the time to define your research question or questions is the only way to give a clear focus to your research project (Booth et al, 2016: 38–9). This may seem time-consuming and onerous, particularly when other things are clamouring for your attention, but having clearly defined research questions to refer back to will save you much time and effort later in the process.

From question to data

In the same way that your research question is derived from your topic, your methods of collecting data should be derived from your research question. Again, you can work out how to do this by reading, thinking and writing. You may already have read an existing study and want to use the same method yourself, which is fine as long as you say where you got the idea. Alternatively, Chapters 8, 9 and 10 of this book introduce a variety of data collection methods, and the research methods literature explains these and other methods in more detail. The important thing is to make sure that the methods you use are those most likely to help you find accurate and useful answers to your research question:

> Once you've narrowed down your question, I enjoy designing research to fit the question because it's a bit of a puzzle, isn't it, and you know

there's not a right or wrong answer, you've just got to justify. And there may be limitations of time or money, so they've got to be built in.

So, for example, let's say a local authority has had a lot of complaints about long waits at bus stops. It wants you to do some research to find out whether the bus company it subsidises with taxpayers' money is providing the correct level of service. At first you think about talking to people as they get off the bus, to ask how long they had to wait for the bus to arrive at the start of their journey. However, common sense tells you people's perception of time varies depending on all sorts of factors, so the data you produce from such questioning probably wouldn't be very accurate. It might still be useful to collect, because complaints are likely to be based on people's perceptions, but you will need additional data for comparison. You realise you could find out about the intended and actual frequency of bus services, which would be useful. Reading some other research into bus passenger experiences leads to the idea of spending some time at bus stops, observing how long people wait and how frequently buses come along. You decide that combining those three methods – asking people about their perceptions, checking the frequency of bus services, and observing people and buses at bus stops – should give you enough information to answer your research question.

Of course there are many other decisions to make. How will you ask people about their perceptions? Will you conduct a brief interview on the street or hand them a questionnaire? How will you find out about the intended and actual frequency of bus services? Is this information available online, or do you need to contact the bus company, or go and look at timetables at the bus stops? How will you manage the direct observation? Which bus stops will you go to, on what days and at what times, and for how long? How will you record the data you collect?

For some people this is a very enjoyable part of the process, while others find it more difficult:

> I find formulating the questions to be the most difficult part. I know what I want to find out, I have no problem identifying where I want to be and what the outcomes of that information are, but I actually think choosing the right questions is a skill and I'm not quite sure, always. I still haven't mastered that although I'm learning from what I see people change my questions into.

> I like writing questions and thinking about what to ask people, wording things so that they understand. I like writing questionnaires and discussion guides and thinking what we need and how to get what I want from the research process.

The information in Chapters 9 and 10 will help you to start thinking about these subjects, and research methods books such as those listed in the 'Further reading' section at the end of this book will give you more detailed information.

How much data?

When doing research for the first time, it is common for people to think that the more data they collect, the better their research will be. This is not necessarily true (Davies, 2007: 53), as this interviewee found out when they were planning their Master's dissertation:

> The initial design was overly ambitious, completely over the top. My initial thing was about interviewing policymakers, national and local; a questionnaire to peers in the region; two focus groups; and using secondary data as well. And I then reflected with a friend who said, 'This is ridiculous, that's more than I'm doing for my PhD.'

Consider this. Ipsos MORI, which conducts opinion surveys, regularly carries out research on the whole of the adult UK population – around 53 million people – using a representative sample of only around 1,000 people.[1] However, almost everyone has an opinion, while not everyone is a victim of crime. The Crime Survey for England and Wales aims to reach almost 50,000 people each year, from a total population of around 48 million aged 16 and over (Home Office, 2011). This is one of the largest social research surveys in the UK, but even so, at around 0.001% of the population, it is a much smaller sample than most people would guess to be adequate.

The surveys conducted by Ipsos MORI and the Home Office (which carries out the Crime Survey) are based on decades of experience. The difficult question for most practitioners is: How much data will be enough? It's often less than you think:

> I found out later that for my dissertation I only needed to speak to 20 people for it to be a valid qualitative study, and I spoke to 129. That's the difference between doing it for work and doing it for uni. You're not told at any point how many people you should do.

Ideally, you need to collect enough evidence to be able to answer your research question in full. In practice this isn't always possible, so sometimes you have to settle for a partial answer. However, this is rarely due to lack of data. It's more often due to unforeseen circumstances, such as the research or evaluation uncovering new factors that need to be taken into account but can't be addressed within the current research due to limitations of budget and timescale. That's not a problem as such, and it certainly doesn't mean the research has been badly done. It just needs to be clearly explained so that the next steps can be taken in a follow-up piece of research, whether that is done by you or by someone else.

Qualitative or quantitative methods?

As we saw in Chapter 2, the distinction between qualitative and quantitative research is not as clear as it seems. At its simplest level, there are always numerical aspects of qualitative research – the number of people interviewed, the age of respondents, the size of the geographical area covered – while quantitative research is reported in words that may have different meanings for their readers than they do for their writers (discussed in more detail in Chapter 7). Also, as we saw in Chapter 4, there is a growing movement towards 'mixed methods' research, which draws on the best that each approach has to offer, as appropriate to the research question(s) under consideration.

There are many ways to describe quantitative and qualitative research, but essentially, quantitative research is based on numbers while qualitative research is based on data in the form of words, pictures, audio, video, and so on.

Quantitative research terms include:

- Independent variable: a measurable characteristic that changes in the course of the research.
- Dependent variable: a measurable characteristic that stays constant in the course of the research.
- Nominal data: data in categories with labels, such as categories of ethnicity.
- Ordinal data: data in ranks without a defined numerical distance between them, such as the first, second and third places in a competition.
- Interval data: data in ranks with a defined numerical distance between them, such as age in years.
- Questionnaires: data collection instruments that don't require the presence of the researcher.
- Statistics: analytic calculations for describing data and using samples to make inferences about populations.

Qualitative research terms include:

- Interview: a data collection method that usually involves one researcher and one or two participants.
- Focus group: a data collection method that usually involves one or two researchers and several participants.
- Observation: a data collection method that usually involves one researcher and many participants.
- Ethnography: a data collection method that usually involves one researcher and many participants over a sustained period of time.

- Action research or participatory action research: a data collection method that involves participants in helping to construct the research alongside the researcher (see Chapter 3 for more on this).
- Content analysis: a technique for analysing the content of data.
- Thematic analysis: a technique for identifying and analysing the themes in data.

There is a Glossary at the end of the book that contains definitions of these and other research terms.

You can use quantitative or qualitative methods, or both, to test a hypothesis. A hypothesis is a hunch, guess or suspicion about something unknown. For example, you might hypothesise that your service would function better if managers had a fuller understanding of service users' priorities. You could test this by evaluating the service, training managers in service user awareness, then evaluating the service again after a period of time to find out whether or not it had improved. You don't have to have a hypothesis to do research (Kumar, 2005: 73), but in practice, many researchers do have one or more hypotheses, whether or not they define them as such. Hypotheses can help you to keep a clear focus on the core of your enquiry, but on the other hand, they may prevent you from seeing other factors that might be of interest (Bryman and Cramer, 2009: 5).

Some people find quantitative research more appealing; others prefer qualitative research. It is rare to find a researcher who is equally comfortable in both modalities. Whichever is your preference, I would urge you not to ignore the other approach. There are two main reasons for this. As a researcher, it is important to let your research question(s) dictate your methods rather than the other way around. And as a research user, you need to be able to read, understand and evaluate all kinds of research.

Sampling techniques

In most research projects it is impossible to involve everyone who might be relevant to the research question or questions. There are exceptions to this. For example, in workplace research, it would be necessary to involve everyone in a company or department if you were conducting a skills audit or training needs analysis. Also, if you were doing research in a prison, you could perhaps include all the prisoners and/or staff. In an evaluation of a small specialist service, you might be able to include all the staff and service users.

In most kinds of research and evaluation you need to sample the population – that is, involve some of the people (the sample) from all the people you could involve (the population). Effective sampling makes it possible to draw conclusions about the population. On the other hand, sampling leaves room for error, because you have to use the findings from the sample to make calculations or inferences about the whole population that may not be correct. It is important to be aware of this while you're deciding on your sampling strategy.

The guidance on sampling is more precise for quantitative research than for qualitative research. However, in any research project, whether quantitative or qualitative, sampling may be constrained by time or budget limits. Also, no matter how well you plan your sampling technique, your plans may be overturned if potential participants don't turn up or refuse to participate, or if actual participants drop out part-way through your data collection or decide to withdraw their data at a later stage. It is worth thinking this through as thoroughly as possible at an early stage to prevent problems later.

Samples don't only consist of people (Robson and McCartan, 2016: 276). For example, in the transport survey described earlier, the researcher would also be thinking about suitable samples of place (How many bus stops, and which ones?) and time (Do people experience longer waits at certain times, say, at weekends, or when people are commuting to work?).

It might be undesirable to make firm decisions about your sampling strategy at the outset. You may wish to build in room for manoeuvre in case of unexpected findings early in the research or evaluation process. For example, the researcher for the transport survey may use local knowledge to hypothesise that people would experience the longest waits on Sunday evenings, and so decide to visit bus stops then. During the first session of data collection, three separate passengers mention that buses are often late on weekday mornings. The researcher is glad of the flexibility to add in some observations at those times.

If you are using qualitative methods such as interviews or focus groups, you may wish to continue until you are no longer hearing much new information. This is known as reaching 'saturation', a term drawn from grounded theory (see Chapter 4 for more on this), and it is often held to be good practice. The difficulty is that you won't know at the outset whether you will reach saturation in 10 interviews or 100, so you may have to set an upper limit that is suitable for your timescale and budget.

Your sampling strategy should be shaped by your research questions and how you are planning to approach those questions. Constraints of time and money will also play a part. For example, it might be fascinating and useful to compare whatever you're studying with a similar situation on another continent, but few practitioners can afford to do international research (although archival research can sometimes help here – see Chapter 8 for more details).

Probability samples

In probability samples, every member of the population has the same chance of being selected as part of the sample. This means you need two things: a 'sampling frame', which is a list of all the members of the population with their contact details, and a way of generating random numbers. Tables of random numbers[2] are available online.

With probability sampling, the larger the sample, the more robust your findings will be. But as you can't go on and on collecting data, you will need to decide how large is large enough. In statistical terminology, you need a sample with the 'power' (that is, size) to allow you to make inferences about the population. There are a number of web pages that offer calculators of statistical power[3] to determine the answer to this question.

The most straightforward type of probability sample is **simple random sampling**, where you use random numbers with your sampling frame to randomly select the required number of research participants.

If you don't have access to random numbers, or if you want a quicker way to sample, you can use **systematic sampling**. Here, you do need one number generated at random to select the first research participant, but then you choose the other participants from the sampling frame at regular intervals, for example, every third or every tenth person.

You can also do **stratified random sampling**. This is useful if you want to make sure, for example, that you include equal numbers of men and women, or equal numbers of people from different age groups. For this to be possible, the relevant information needs to be included in your sampling frame. Then you can divide the sampling frame into two or more parts, for example, one for men and one for women, or one for each of your defined age groups. After that you pick the same number of participants at random from each subset of the sampling frame.

One benefit of probability samples is that you can use inferential statistical techniques to calculate how likely it is that your findings could have occurred by chance. This helps to reduce the impact of any sampling errors, and makes your findings more generalisable (Bryman and Cramer, 2009: 6). If you're not comfortable with numbers, don't be put off, because there is a range of computer applications that can do the calculations for you. There is more information about this in Chapter 11.

Non-probability sampling

It may not be possible to create or gain access to a sampling frame. For example, if you're interested in the effect of custodial sentences on prisoners' extended families, or the impact of a health service on its users' carers, you probably won't be able to find or build a list of those families or carers. In research like this you have to use one or more types of non-probability sampling. Also, qualitative researchers, who are not interested in using inferential statistics, are likely to choose non-probability sampling techniques.

With non-probability sampling, a larger sample doesn't necessarily mean more robust findings. In fact, some reputable research uses a sample of one, such as for a case study. In these research projects, the participant is studied in great detail, and the richness of the investigation is held to compensate for the lack of sample size. (There is more information about case studies in Chapter 10.) However, in most research projects using non-probability sampling, you will have to make a judgement about how many participants to seek.

Convenience sampling effectively means choosing the first participants you can find who are willing to help. This is useful for some tasks, such as piloting questionnaires or interview questions, or in conjunction with other sampling techniques. However, I wouldn't recommend its use alone, as it is too vulnerable to researcher and other biases.

Quota sampling is akin to stratified sampling in that the population is divided into groups. The aim then is to find participants within those groups in proportion to the total number of people in each group. So, if you wanted to research a community care service, with 40 users, an estimated 100 carers and 16 care workers, you might decide to talk to 10 users, 10 carers (one per user) and 4 care workers. The perceptive reader will have noticed that this focuses on the numbers, and there is still a decision to be made about how to select the individual participants. Convenience sampling is often used here, although other non–probability sampling techniques may be used.

Purposive sampling is where the researcher uses their own judgement about which participants will have most to contribute to the research. Again, this is best used alongside other types of sampling, to reduce bias.

Snowball sampling is where you use one participant to lead you to others. This is particularly helpful when you're trying to research groups that are difficult to contact, such as gang members or freegans.[4]

There are other types of sampling (see, for example, Robson and McCartan, 2016: 277–81), but these are the main ones used in practice-based research. More resources on sampling are given in the 'Further reading' section at the end of the book.

What is evidence?

In some quarters there is a lot of argument about what constitutes evidence. Anecdote is often considered to be the lowest of the low when it comes to evidence. However, if you collect a large number of anecdotes, perhaps through a series of research interviews, they may then become data, which, once analysed and reported, yields useful evidence. Furthermore, you can use a single story from one interview as a quote to illustrate a point in your research report or thesis, and that is seen as perfectly proper. Yet the quote is indistinguishable from an anecdote.

So why isn't an anecdote generally held to constitute evidence? Especially when it often does in everyday life? People listen to the anecdotes of trusted friends or family members, about which plumber to use or which restaurant to avoid, and use those as evidence on which to base their own decisions. But I'm sure most people have followed someone else's anecdotal recommendation and had a completely different experience from the one they were led to expect. This is why, in research terms, a single anecdote does not count as evidence – a single view is not likely to be representative of a wider population.

Researchers, whether qualitative, quantitative or mixed methods, are seeking evidence that is representative of a wider population. Anecdotes may contribute to this – even in quantitative research, anecdotes told to the researcher may influence the planning or conducting of research. We love anecdotes because they are stories, and a single story is much more likely to change our view of the world than even the most robust statistical finding (Kahneman, 2011: 174). Nevertheless, anecdotes alone, even lots of anecdotes, are unlikely to constitute strong enough data for a competent research project. Even if your research project was designed to study anecdotes, you would need to use academic literature, documents and probably some secondary data, as well as collecting anecdotes of your own.

So, anecdotes collected for a research project may become data, as may diary entries, meeting minutes, photographs, collages, video recordings and any number of other constructions and artefacts. This data becomes evidence through the process of analysing it and reporting findings. However, you still need to consider what kind of evidence you are producing.

Some research commentators talk about a 'hierarchy of evidence', with randomised double-blind controlled trials seen as the 'gold standard' and personal experience having the lowest value. This seems to me far too simplistic. For sure, if I'm going to take a new drug, I'll be reassured to know it's been through a randomised double-blind controlled trial or six. However, if I'm considering trying a new brand of chocolate, I'm happy to base my decision on a friend's personal experience. These could be described as two ends of the research spectrum: both are based on evidence, and certainly the way the evidence is collected and assessed is much more rigorous in the former than the latter. But which type of evidence is appropriate depends on the context of your enquiry. For much research using constructionist, interpretivist or transformative methodologies, personal experiences are perfectly acceptable as evidence.

For you, as a researcher, the important thing is to aim to produce the type of evidence that fits your research question. If you're interested in the impact of a new piece of legislation on certain organisations, a randomised double-blind controlled trial will get you nowhere, but a well-conducted piece of mixed methods research might well produce evidence to show how many organisations are affected and in what ways. The advice in this book will help you to conduct good quality research that will produce robust evidence.

Writing a proposal

Most would-be researchers or evaluators need to persuade a tutor or manager that they have a good idea and a sensible plan, and some need to bid for funding or tender for a contract. Any of these involve writing a proposal. A proposal is a short document explaining what you intend to investigate and why, and how you intend to carry out the research or evaluation. A proposal is essential for most academic research, research funding applications and commissioned workplace research. Even if a proposal is not essential for the research or evaluation you are doing, it is good practice to write one. The process of writing the proposal will help you to clarify your thoughts and decisions. Also, the proposal can be used to help you plan your research process, and for reference during that process to make sure your work stays on track. And, as one interviewee pointed out, it can give credibility to your research in your workplace:

> Every researcher should put together a formal proposal. I think if you make it a formal thing, people are more likely to pay attention and make the time for it, rather than something ad hoc. It's about formalising it and showing the importance of it. I think once you've done that, got something in writing and a formal procedure that you're going to follow, people see it as part of your job rather than an additional thing you have to squeeze in.

As we saw earlier in respect of data, one major mistake that new researchers make is to think that more equals better. People who are not experienced in research may also think they need to read as much literature or as many documents as possible. This is not true – although it can be difficult to work out what to include and what to leave out (Barker, 2014: 63). There is more information about this in Chapter 7.

The people assessing your proposal will be more impressed with one that is SMART – specific, measurable, achievable, realistic and time-based – than with one that promises a great deal but is, by definition, highly unlikely to deliver. It is important to estimate how much time your research will take, taking into account the time you need for other aspects of your life (Jesson et al, 2011: 4), and there is more advice on how to manage your time in Chapter 6 of this book.

Your proposal should include information about:

1. Your topic area.
2. Your research or evaluation question or questions.
3. The background information you are drawing on.
4. Why your research is important or worth doing.
5. Whether or not you are involving service users, and why.
6. Ethical considerations.
7. A timetable for your work.
8. Data collection:
   - What you intend to collect.
   - How you will collect it.
   - How much you plan to collect.
   - Why you think this will enable you to answer your research or evaluation question(s).
9. How you will prepare and analyse your data.
10. How you intend to disseminate your findings.
11. Who could benefit from your conclusions and how they might benefit.
12. References.

For your proposal to be truly convincing, it should be readable and understandable by someone who has no prior knowledge of your plans. It was allegedly

Albert Einstein who said, 'If you can't explain it simply, you don't understand it well enough.'

 Test your proposal on a family member or friend, to make sure it is completely clear, before submitting it to a tutor, commissioner or funder.

It's not just the explanation that needs to be simple; it is the research or evaluation itself (Silverman and Marvasti, 2008: 434). Complicated research does not equal better research, and writing a proposal is a good way to assess whether or not your plans are sufficiently straightforward.

The process of writing a proposal may seem like a tedious chore, especially if you're longing to get on with collecting your data. However, time spent thinking through your plans well enough to write a convincing proposal will undoubtedly save you from time-consuming problems later on, so it is definitely worth doing.

Research funders

Funding for social research may be obtained from local and national government departments, charitable trusts and research bodies, and research councils or their equivalent, which are usually mostly or entirely government-funded. These include:

- UK Research and Innovation (UK)
- Jisc (Joint Information Systems Committee) (UK)
- National Endowment for the Humanities (USA)
- National Science Foundation (USA)
- Social Sciences and Humanities Research Council (Canada)
- Australian Research Council
- Research Australia
- Health Research Council (New Zealand)
- New Zealand Council for Educational Research.

It is difficult to get funding from any of these bodies unless you are a professional academic. Even then, it's not easy. Each department, trust, body or council will have its own application system, most of which are quite onerous. Also, some of these processes will have deadlines that don't suit your project. However, I don't mean to put you off, because if you think you have a chance of securing funding, it's well worth having a go. This is especially true when you can include an element of funding to free up your time, for example, to pay for someone to do your main job for a while so that you can concentrate on your research or evaluation.

If you decide to apply for funding, you need to write a killer proposal, using all the advice outlined in this chapter and the rest of the book, and make sure you work through the application process with meticulous accuracy and thoroughness.

All the points in this section apply equally to those tendering for a research or evaluation contract.

Sometimes small pots of money are made available to fund research or evaluation conducted by practitioners in public services. These are not usually widely advertised (at least, not in the UK), so if you want to find out what's available, you will need to do some judicious searching online. The application systems for these pots are not usually as onerous as for research councils, government departments, and so on. Nevertheless, you still need to write a really good proposal, and to be scrupulously careful to provide whatever the funders require.

Conclusion

This chapter demonstrates that you need a specific research topic with answerable research questions; a plan for collecting data that will not yield more data than you can analyse; and the ability to explain your proposed research clearly and understandably. It also shows you how to complete these tasks. Following the advice and guidance in this chapter will produce a firm foundation on which to build your research.

> **CASE STUDIES**
>
> Ana's research question is: How are non-heterosexual couples and families represented in the media? She is also interested in how the representations she has found will affect their readers, and wonders whether heterosexual and non-heterosexual people will be affected differently. She decides to try to do 20 interviews, 10 with heterosexual people and 10 with non-heterosexual people. She will use a combination of purposive and snowball sampling, starting with people in her networks and asking them for introductions to others in their networks.
>
> Ali's question, for his evaluation of the department that supports unpaid family carers, is three-fold: What works well? What could be improved? How could those improvements be made? He discusses sampling and amounts of data with the service users who are working with him. Together they decide to use a questionnaire with all the carers they support, and then some interviews to follow up on responses where more detail would be useful. They will use quota sampling for the interviews to ensure they reach carers from different genders, age groups and ethnicities. Ali's co-researchers offer to conduct the interviews, and he is pleased to accept.

EXERCISES

1. Here are some research topics. Pick two and construct a suitably focused research question for each.

    a. How can levels of bullying be reduced among junior school children?

    b. What would reduce the isolation of older people living alone?

    c. What does the fire service do well, and where could it be improved?

    d. How could convicted thieves be persuaded not to re-offend?

    e. What could help a maternity ward to operate more effectively?

    f. What measures could be taken to increase the use of a public park?

    g. How can run-down holiday resorts be regenerated?

2. For one of your research questions, think through what kind of sample you would choose to use. Also consider the ethical implications of the research.

Discussion questions

1. What do you think are the most important decisions in planning a research project, and why?
2. In your profession, field or discipline, what is regarded as good evidence? To what extent do you agree with this, and why?
3. What advice would you give to a friend or colleague who needed to write their first research proposal?

Debate topic

The only good data is numerical data.

6

Managing your research or evaluation project

Chapter summary

This chapter includes:

- Information about planning
- Advice on organisation
- An overview of time management principles
- An outline of support some people may get from employers, and its limits
- A discussion of creative time management
- The importance of rewarding yourself to help with motivation
- The need to look after yourself
- A summary of what works, and what doesn't work, in research or evaluation project management

Introduction

Research isn't a sprint, it's a marathon. Successful completion of a marathon takes planning, organisation and time management. This chapter will help you to learn techniques for these essential parts of the research and evaluation process. It contains a great deal of advice from practitioners who are experienced in conducting research, in the hope that their hindsight can be your foresight.

Research by Richard Wiseman from the University of Hertfordshire in 2009 (reported in *The Guardian* newspaper on 28 December 2009; see Sample, 2009) showed that people were more likely to stick to their New Year's resolutions if they followed six easy steps:

1. Made a plan for their project.
2. Broke down their overall goal into smaller goals, for each week or fortnight, which were SMART (specific, measurable, achievable, realistic, time-based).
3. Told their friends and family about their goals.
4. Rewarded themselves whenever they achieved one of the smaller goals.
5. Kept a diary of their progress.
6. Regularly focused on the benefits of success.

These steps are also ideal for helping researchers to complete their projects successfully.

Planning

The people I interviewed for this book were unanimous about the need to plan research carefully. You may feel inclined to skip this section. Perhaps you don't think there's any point in reading about planning, either because you're not a natural planner, or because you're already good at planning. Either way, I would advise you to read on. If you're not a natural planner, don't worry; project management is a skill that can be learned. If you are already good at planning, this chapter covers specific ways of planning research that will help you to complete your project and meet deadlines more easily:

> I used to have to plan my year at the beginning of the year, my family life, my work, my academic studies, planning is essential, good planning and time management.

The process of planning isn't always easy, but putting work in at this stage will save time later:

> The first major hurdle is going to be the planning.

Not everyone finds preparation and planning to be difficult. In fact, for some people, it's the easiest part:

> I love sitting down and doing concepts, and making action plans of where this could lead and where I need to go to find it out. I love fleshing out beginnings of projects, I really enjoy that part … if it's going to be a project that's collaborative you really have to start from that blank page. I like looking for resources, sources of information, people I might have to talk to.

First, you need an outline plan for your whole research or evaluation project. If you've written a proposal, as suggested in Chapter 5, this can form the basis of your plan. If not, you'll need to start from scratch. Either way, you should be able to break down your overall plan into a few chunks such as: background research, writing your proposal (or plan), collecting data, analysing data, writing up your research, dissemination. Then you can break down each chunk into monthly goals, bearing in mind that you are likely to be working on two or more chunks at the same time in most months. The next step is to break down your monthly goals into weekly to-do lists. Then each day you can refer to your list to make sure you're on track.

It's best to make weekly to-do lists just a week or two ahead of the present day rather than for the whole project at once. Life is full of surprises, as is research, so sometimes plans have to be changed. It is essential to build in time to deal with unexpected occurrences at all levels, from running out of milk to serious illness. It is equally essential not to use unexpected occurrences as an excuse for procrastination.

Visual learners may prefer charts to lists. Perhaps the best-known type of project management chart is the Gantt chart. Figure 6.1 shows a Gantt chart for the outline plan of a simple research project lasting just a few months.

Figure 6.1: Gantt chart for a research project

Task	Sep	Oct	Nov	Dec	Jan	Feb	Mar
Reading	XXX	XXX	XXX	XXX	XXX	XXX	
Working on proposal		XXX					
Collecting data			XXX	XXX			
Analysing data				XXX	XXX		
Writing	XXX	XXX	XXX	XXX	XXX	XXX	
Writing report				XXX		XXX	
Dissemination					XXX		XXX

You can see from the chart that this researcher plans to read throughout the project, do the research proposal at the start, then data collection that overlaps with data analysis. Two chunks of formal writing are planned, the first in December – perhaps for an interim report, if one is required, or just to get ahead – and the second in February, when most of the other work has been done. Dissemination is also planned in two chunks, one in January – perhaps to report interim findings at a meeting or seminar – and one in March, when the rest of the research work is finished.

As with all the other skills you'll be using during your research, you will get better at planning as you go along:

> I think the planning is the key for people, and just believing that actually you can manage this, people do it all the time, there's a massive community of people just ferreting away at this kind of work.

Organisation

Once you've got the planning sorted, you need to be organised in how you use that planning:

> Be extremely organised with your time and block off time in your diary each day or week to do research.

> I used to highlight things and have charts and graphs all over the place telling me what was coming up and what I needed to do by then. I have it all in my head these days but it's important to plot and plan things.
>
> Good administrative set-up right at the start is not time wasted. I wish I'd known that. It's about trying to manage the process and feeds into how you manage when you've got work and family and domestic and all that other stuff going on. You need a level of organisation that can help to manage the research.

If research forms part or all of your job, that will help. Conversely, doing research as part of a non-research main job can be particularly challenging. Research adds pressure to already pressured non-research jobs and, in these contexts, is often a low priority compared to other aspects of people's work. People interviewed for this book spoke of how they experienced this:

> Evaluation, the stuff that's statutorily required, it's easier I think to structure in time to do it. It's the more non-statutory stuff that is going to be very difficult to figure in. Getting a skills audit done is going to be difficult, it all keeps being crowded out by other needs. Getting some research done around marketing and publicity is going to be very difficult. But those are things that have to happen.
>
> The way things work out in academia now is that because you have teaching, if you want to be research active you basically have to use whatever time you can. During term times you can have such a high teaching load that you would effectively have to stop researching if you were to work to rule.
>
> Quite often it's easy for that kind of thing to fall to the back of your priority list. It's not meeting the bottom line at the end of the day. Everything is always deadline-driven. You have to continuously remind other people that evaluation is also important.

Planning, organisation and time management are the three keys to successfully fitting research obligations in with the rest of your work. Even then, as these quotes show, you can end up putting in extra hours. Yet professional practice and service delivery can benefit enormously from research and evaluation and, as we saw in Chapter 1, this is being recognised more widely.

Time management

Time management is more of an art than a science, but there are some basic principles that can help you to manage your time more effectively without compromising the quality of your work or your life. First of all, make sure everyone close to you knows you have research to do, and that it's a priority for you:

> If you want to do research you've got to be upfront about that with yourself and other people and you have to prioritise it and make it happen because nobody else will.

If people know you're doing something that matters to you, they're more likely to accept that you need to spend time on it:

> Because it was for my dissertation, and had an end point, it wasn't going to go on for ever, my mum said, 'Don't worry, we'll see you once you've reached the other end.' Most people were like that.

> You need your family behind you, or your support networks behind you, they need to be aware of the commitment involved.

> There is something about it won't go on for ever, and I think, certainly with the social life, if friends and family know what's going on then hopefully they can understand that you're just not so available and they'll still be there at the end and won't have buggered off entirely!

Second, and counter-intuitively, it is not always the case that more time equals more productivity. In fact, people are often more productive when they work in short bursts in between other activities:

> When you've got family, it's pulling aside a sensible chunk of time. If you had a whole day and went and sat in the library, you'd probably file your nails, you wouldn't use the time properly.

> Because I'm reporting to the chief exec, I'm trying to make time because it is fairly important, so I take time out of my normal job. It's the only way to do it.

> I've tried to set aside certain times when I focus on *my* work – usually part of Saturday and Sunday – or later in the evenings after dinner.

> I'm an anal calendar lady! I allocate time. It sounds so ... [giggling] I allocate slots of time, now I use an Outlook calendar, I'm not technically savvy but I think it's the absolute best thing since sliced bread.

It's a common misconception that you need a whole free day, or even a whole week, to be able to work on your research. Small chunks of time, well used, can be very productive. A colleague told me recently that twice a day, while she cleans her teeth with her electric toothbrush in one hand, she holds her eReader in the other hand and reads for two minutes until the toothbrush's timer sounds:

> I'm not one for sitting in libraries, I like to read while I'm waiting for the bath to fill up or something like that.

It takes only five minutes to read one page of a book, enter data from a questionnaire into a spreadsheet or think about a problem you are facing. In a quarter of an hour you can make notes from a chapter you have read, search online for journal articles on a particular subject or make a few phone calls to set up interviews. In half an hour you can transcribe part of an interview, read a journal article or write 250 words of your research report or thesis. Small chunks of time are very valuable for researchers; the art lies in learning to use them well:

> I do think if you don't do something fairly regularly, it becomes like an enormous mountain and you just don't want to do it even though you do.

It's also useful to identify thinking time, perhaps when you're doing repetitive tasks that don't need much thought, standing in a queue or walking to the bus stop:

> I was doing research for my course that wasn't directly work-related, and because I was a police constable at the time, I had lots of time where I was walking the beat or other duties that weren't taxing where I could think about things.

A third useful principle is to remember that you can say 'no'. If you are in the habit of saying 'yes' to every invitation and request for help, or even to most of them, try being more selective. One way to do this is, instead of giving an immediate response to an invitation or request, take time to think about whether you really want to accept. Another option is to ration yourself. For example, in the last three months of writing the first edition of this book I restricted myself to two social activities per week. In the final month, I reduced this to one social activity per week. I explained my plans to my family and friends, and they were very understanding.

One very helpful piece of advice is to look at your to-do list, and do the job you least want to do first of all.[1] There are two reasons for this. First, if you leave that job till last, it may well not get done at all, because motivating yourself to do an unpleasant job is harder when your energy is low. Second, if you do it first, the other tasks feel easier to tackle.

Another useful piece of advice is to identify your time eaters. Everyone has these and they're all different. Using social media, pottering in the garden, playing computer games, talking on the phone, watching TV – normal, everyday activities, in which you can lose anything from a few minutes to several hours. When you have identified your time eaters, work out a way to allow yourself enough time to do the things you love without either feeling deprived or encroaching on the work you need to do to achieve the goals you have set yourself. Social media is one of my great time eaters because I love to communicate, so I restrict the amount of time I allow myself on social media sites, and where possible, hide or ignore the associated time eaters like online games.

Time management isn't easy, as this interviewee discovered:

> That's something that you do need to work in, a bit of time management and a bit of time out, I wasn't particularly good at that. I am a bit of a Last Minute Lulu. I think timelines and working to deadlines, there needs to be training and support around that, I didn't get that right.

Many people think every waking hour is filled, but there is almost always scope for better time management. If you're unsure how you could manage your time better, I suggest you do a time audit. Write out a blank schedule on a sheet of paper, or use a spreadsheet, with days of the week across the top and half-hour slots down the side. Then fill in your actual activities. Be honest! The first few entries might look as shown in Figure 6.2:

Figure 6.2: Time audit example

	Mon	Tue	Wed	Thur	Fri	Sat	Sun
6.30 am	Tea; shower						
7 am	Breakfast						
7.30 am	Walk dog						
8 am	Read magazine						
8.30 am	Housework						
9 am	Data entry						

Completing the audit over an entire week enables you to see exactly how you're using your time. This then makes it possible for you to decide where adjustments could be made. For example, on looking at her audit, this person realises that she gets up at 6.30 am, but doesn't start work on her research project until 9 am. This leads her to wonder whether she really needs two-and-a-half hours for her morning tasks. After some reflection, she decides that she does need to dawdle through the first half-hour, to ease herself into the day. She also needs to walk the dog for half an hour, as this is useful exercise for her as well as for her dog. However, she thinks she could compress the other one-and-a-half hours into 45 minutes, by leaving out the magazine reading, taking 20 minutes over breakfast rather than half an hour, and doing 25 rather than 30 minutes of housework. Now she can start work on her research project at 8.15 am, having freed up another 45 minutes in her day.

Where possible, play to your strengths. So if you're a morning person, don't try to do creative research work late in the evening, and vice versa.

Support from employers

Some employers of people interviewed for this book were supportive in a few ways, such as by paying for academic courses or providing study leave or administrative support, and a few were very supportive. However, none were entirely supportive without requiring anything in return, and some sought to benefit from their employees' research without having provided any support at all:

> I was working for a local authority and they paid for me to do my course at uni. I had time, I think it was one day a week in term time to come to uni, they were full days teaching. Then I had some days of study leave as well, not loads, but it was good, it was there.

> Work agreed to pay for it.... I had to do all the rest myself.... My manager agreed that I could leave early once a month to go and attend what was referred to as a learning circle, so you could talk about your research and hear other people's research, so I did get time for tutorials.

> It benefited the organisation. When I was promoted they put me into special departments at headquarters to use the knowledge. The organisation never paid for any of it but they certainly got a return from it at the end of the day.

Most people conducting workplace research, or work-related academic research, said they had to fit it in as and when they could among all their other tasks:

> I am expected to do research as part of both jobs. The time is part of my working hours, I must factor it into my working day.

> We had to squeeze it in where we could. We were all aware that was not the best way of doing it, but it was a case of needs must.

> 'Normal' work has to take priority as it's my job – and sometimes this is really frustrating, especially when you feel you're at a crucial point with something and have to put it to one side.

Surprisingly, this was even the case for academics:

> Officially – and this is important – officially, in my faculty we get a number of days out of our full year's work which can go towards scholarly activity. So at the most basic you should be able to block out days to either write bids, but also then if they're successful to carry out the research. So the university I think would say it's contributing those days. But in practice it's very hard to take those days. I've just booked five of them out in my electronic diary, so that anybody in my team can see when I am on a research day, and people don't respect them, they ask you to come in for a meeting so it is a bit frustrating.

> My post is 70% teaching and admin and 30% research. It works as long as I can keep the teaching within the 70%, that's really the trick! And that's the hard bit, so it's recognising that the 70% for the teaching takes up entire chunks of time when there isn't any research time, but then scheduling in research time to make sure you've got adequate time to do things you need to do.

Interviewees who did receive support from their employer, however little, evidently found it helpful:

> I think what helped was my manager valued my studies. We discussed it and I felt that he valued academic research and doing it, and his supervision in that area was really good. He valued what I was doing, in supervision he'd say, 'I found this article from the *British Journal of Social Work*', and that was really helpful.

And some employers were notably more supportive, particularly those that could see their organisation stood to benefit from the research:

> My employers were very supportive. Even though it was extensively my own time, they allowed me to talk to the trainees across several districts and use the work support networks, and allowed me to write that research up. The only precursor was that once I'd finished the paper I sent a copy to them.

> They contributed admin support, they contributed help and advice.... Work were brilliant, actually. Because they were going to get the benefit of it.

But this can also come with a cost, as the employer then has an investment in, and so may claim partial ownership of or control over, your research. This can create situations that are difficult for employees to handle, because employers have more power than employees, and can apply pressure in all sorts of ways:

I think there was an element towards the end of apprehension because they weren't sure what they were going to get because they hadn't seen any of the writing. From my point of view that was additional stress. I ended up writing two different sections, one for my dissertation and one for my employer. That probably wasn't the best use of my time but I was worried about it so they got the big results before they got the dissertation.

It's compulsory, it's part of my contract of employment, which gives it a slightly different tone. I do it within the university. It's been more challenging in terms of having the time to do it. After I started it I had to intermit, to take time out from doing it. It clashed with a lot of my teaching, and when I raised it, and said, 'How can I manage it?' – hoping they would review my teaching – they said I would have to intermit which was quite frustrating. I felt blocked, they were telling me I had to do it, but I've had to manage and navigate my workload to do it rather than being supported to do it.

Most interviewees ended up doing at least some of their research work in their own time, even if it was workplace research:

This report's basically been pretty much handed over to me. There are pages and pages of stats and things. I'm trying to make something out of it. I get it done by bringing it home, to be honest.

There were a lot of late evenings and a lot of takeaways in the office.

If you do academic study as part of your continuing professional development, even with some study leave from your employer, it will eat up a lot of your 'leisure' and other time:

One of the things I found to do with research is that any academic course is very difficult to fit in and you have to learn to make use of time. You have to be very focused and dedicated.

As a researcher, sometimes the line between personal and professional becomes very blurred, it's because you get involved in projects and have commitments and deadlines and things that you drive yourself that bit harder.

People spoke about how they managed this:

My studies took place in the evenings once the children went to bed and at some weekends when I was against deadlines.

I didn't get out much!

I sleep less. True fact. It was sleep less or give up on family time. No contest really.

Also, it can be hard to switch off:

It's always there, so even if you do decide you're having a weekend off, it's still there. I can remember having weekends off and I couldn't concentrate on what people were saying to me because I should have been working on that chapter or that bit of data analysis.

It's like a little rucksack you take with you everywhere. You wake up and think about it, you go to bed and think about it, you don't get any peace, it's constantly there.

Even with effective time management, it can be a heavy load:

I worked stupid hours. I worked pretty much seven days a week. I got very knackered and pushed myself a lot. I couldn't really see any other way of doing it, though, there was no other way. It was a lifestyle, maintaining that family–work–study balance, but I wanted to study. I really needed to study to keep my brain going, I needed to be around for my family, and I needed to work because I couldn't afford anything. I didn't want to give any of those things up. It was 'work hard now, it'll pay off later' type of thing.

And effective time management is essential:

The thing I've tended to do always in my research time is to consider that there need to be specific hours that are given to it. During my time as a research fellow, they gave me one day a week … so I gave it one day as well … half the weekend. It's recognising that whatever you choose to do is fine, but you've got to have the hours to do it.

I also try to link, kill two birds with one stone, so the research we're doing is around a particular aspect of adult social care but I also teach in that area so by looking into it for the research, that can feed into my teaching. I do that where I can.

 Negotiate for support from your employer, wherever possible, while retaining as much autonomy as you can.

Creative time management

Conducting research or evaluation requires flexibility of thought. This applies to the research work itself, and to managing the research process. You need to be able to take an open-minded and creative approach, both to conducting your research and to managing your research. Inflexible thought will hamper your progress at every stage.

The kinds of inflexible thoughts that create problems for time management include:

> I can't start working on my research until all the housework is done.

> There's no time for my research in the working day, because I am either in meetings or people are in my office asking me about stuff.

> My children's needs must come first.

Words and phrases like 'have to', 'must', 'can't,' 'no time', 'always' and 'never' often signal inflexible thoughts.

 Use these words and phrases to identify your own inflexible thoughts. Then create a more flexible version that will help you with your research.

Of course housework is necessary, but it is rarely 'all done'; there is almost always something else that can be tidied or cleaned or de-cluttered, so the key here is to do only what is necessary and leave the rest for another time. For workplace research, techniques such as putting a 'Do not disturb' sign on the office door for an hour or two or, for those in shared offices, booking a meeting room to work alone for a while, can work wonders:

> It might be about taking yourself out of the environment, so you can focus, because when you're there, particularly if you're in the social sector, people are so needy and greedy, you might need to make yourself unavailable at particular times. Be clear about that. If you can't respect the value of what it is that you're doing then nobody else is going to.

Children's needs are indeed paramount, but don't have to be met by just one person, even if s/he is a single parent – relatives, friends and other parents can help to share the load. These interviewees offer real-life examples:

> Sometimes you just have to live in a bit of domestic chaos. It's disruption to the routine, and I do resent that a bit. I don't want to have

> to be stumbling over piles of laundry and books, but I also recognise that there's a deadline. The laundry is never going to end but at least the research project will.

> If I have half an hour at work before a meeting, I'll do half an hour of searching for the text that I need. I can build it into my day.

> My experience as a single parent, that really is difficult. My boyfriend was brilliant. Once a week he would take my daughter from school, feed her, be with her for the evening, and I would have that evening to work like a crazy lady.

The point here is that you almost always have a choice. You don't *have* to watch the next episode of your favourite TV programme; you are choosing to do so. It is not *essential* that you complete the crossword and Sudoku puzzles in the daily newspaper; it may be an enjoyable part of your usual routine, but it's still a choice you make, every time. Nobody is *making* you go out with your friends every week: for sure, they like your company, and you like theirs. They may encourage you to join them, but in the end it is your decision.

Of course, for people with heavy workloads, this can apply in reverse. It may feel as if you *must* spend evening after evening at your desk – but it's still a choice:

> I think in terms of having a life, it won't happen unless you make it happen. You've got to say, 'Right, enough is enough.' A concrete example: a friend, we sometimes go out for curry, he was saying, 'Can you do this week?' And I was saying, 'I can't, I've got this and this and this to do', and then I thought, 'What's important here?' I said 'yes' to the curry. You've got to make a conscious decision.

The key factor in managing decisions like these is self-discipline. Self-discipline is a term that makes many people recoil, because to them it means all the hard tasks and none of the enjoyable activities. The stereotype of a self-disciplined person is someone who rises at dawn, exercises vigorously for an hour, takes a quick shower, eats muesli, works hard all day, and so on. But that is more about self-control than self-discipline, and although self-discipline requires some self-control, they are not one and the same (Dienstmann, 2021: 9).

Self-discipline has two key components: habits and responses. Most people have one or two bad habits, such as eating too much junk food, smoking, drinking too much alcohol or too many diet drinks, watching too much TV, procrastinating, not exercising enough (or at all). If we want to change our bad habits into good habits, we need self-discipline. We also need self-discipline in our responses to others. Toddlers haven't developed this yet and throw massive tantrums during which they may kick, punch or bite anyone who tries to calm them. As adults, it is self-discipline that helps us remain calm in the face of provocation.

If you don't practise self-discipline – and this is the real kicker – *you are actually practising indiscipline* (Dienstmann, 2021: 29). There is no middle ground. Every time you collapse on the sofa for a full evening of TV viewing, or yell at a driver for not paying attention, or give in and buy the cake you had earlier decided to forgo, *you are practising indiscipline*. Self-discipline or indiscipline is a choice, and you make that choice, every single time.

If you practise self-discipline it can become your superpower. This doesn't mean avoiding pleasure (Dienstmann, 2021: 50). It means deciding what you really want to achieve, and figuring out how to achieve those things while also taking good care of yourself. That requires a sensible balance between work and leisure, obligations and treats.

 If you would like to improve your own self-discipline, keep a self-discipline journal to record your goals and plans and reflect on your progress.

Self-discipline is an essential skill for researchers, whether their research is workplace or academic or both.

Another essential skill is negotiating:

> There were two of us. We convinced the person in HR [Human Resources] to give us our CPD [continuing professional development] hours for actual study time. So we'd have a Friday working from home on CPD leave where other people were going on courses. We did some negotiating like that, it helped at the crucial moments where you've got something to submit.

The classic stereotype of a good negotiator is someone who is hard-nosed and out for everything they can get. Negotiating skills were developed by business people who were competitive, aggressive and comfortable with using unethical methods such as deception and manipulation to get what they wanted. This does not sit easily alongside ethical research. Luckily ethical negotiating skills have developed, such as through the work of Professor Robert B. Cialdini, a very experienced academic and psychologist from the USA who published the second edition of a useful book, *Influence: The psychology of persuasion*, in 2021.

Cialdini has identified seven 'levers of influence' that can help us to negotiate ethically. These are:

1. Reciprocation: offering something you can give in exchange for something you want.
2. Liking: people will be easier to negotiate with if they like you and you like them.
3. Social proof: negotiation is more likely to be successful if the desired outcome fits with social (or institutional, professional etc) norms.

4. Authority: people in authority, if they are also trustworthy, are more likely to be successful in negotiations.
5. Scarcity: people assign more value to things that are rare or exclusive.
6. Consistency and commitment: people like to see themselves as consistent, so gaining one commitment from someone is likely to make it easier to gain other similar commitments from that person.
7. Unity: people are more likely to say 'yes' to someone with whom they share an association.

Of course these levers can be used in unethical, exploitative ways, principally by manufacturing or engineering them (Cialdini, 2021: 446). To use them ethically, they need to be in existence already. Take this interviewee's report of a negotiation:

> I have had to have quite strong words with the assistant director, go through his timetable and get him to see he is not giving us the time he is committed to giving us. I've got a commitment from him that he will book in the time he is going to spend each week. That will help.

This interviewee used the lever of consistency and commitment. The assistant director was already committed to giving his subordinates a certain amount of time, but wasn't meeting that commitment.

Here is another example:

> I bribed my son to do the techie work for me. He made all the tables and charts for my Master's. He must have been about 12. And he's so savvy, and I think it helped him feel involved.

This interviewee used the lever of reciprocity, giving her son things he wanted in return for his help, plus increased self-esteem. And you can see that, in both of these examples, the levers already existed in the situations; they were not fabricated but available for use.

Cialdini's negotiators are self-aware, aware of others, honest, assertive and creative. Researchers also need these skills to manage the research process. Here's a great example of this in practice, from an interviewee who completed a part-time Master's degree while supporting herself financially and helping to care for her little brother, who is over 20 years younger than her:

> Explain to your tutors from the off, not apologising for it, but explain that you have a lot of responsibilities and you're juggling very many balls and you strive to keep on top of it but there is always a risk that something may take precedence, like family. Not like in a way that you're being a martyr, but just say, 'This is what I have going on in my life, research is important to me but these things might come into play.' I ended up bringing my brother to a field trip, I didn't want to miss the

field trip so I took him on the trip, and it actually showed people that, yes, there's a real child involved. In a way it made it a bit better when people actually saw that I had a child to look after as well.

 If you would like to improve your own negotiating skills, think about Cialdini's levers of influence and how you can use them ethically in your own life.

Reward yourself

Rewarding yourself for completing tasks will help your motivation. You can give yourself small rewards several times a day. Everyone has different ideas about what constitutes a reward. That doesn't matter; what matters is that you can identify rewards that work for you: 10 minutes on a social media site, a drink and a snack, or a walk around the block. On a daily level, I might promise myself that when I have reached my daily word count, I can call a friend for a chat; or when I have finished today's data entry task, I can have a break and do the crossword with a cup of tea.

Completing bigger tasks deserves bigger rewards. So, after the first draft of the first edition of this book went to the publisher, I spent a week catching up with friends. After the final draft was done, I took a holiday with my partner. Again, you need to identify rewards that work for you, whatever those might be: tickets to a show or a sporting event, time with family or friends, a new book or a new item of clothing.

Also, if you fail to complete a task as planned, don't beat yourself up. Life gets in the way, and people make mistakes. The last thing you need is to spiral into a vortex of feeling like a failure, deciding there's no point in trying, and giving up on your research. Regroup, replan and keep going.

Look after yourself

It is essential that you take care of yourself because nobody else is going to do that for you. Other people may help – someone might make you a meal, or listen to your woes. But it is your responsibility to keep track of, and maintain, your physical and mental health. For optimum research/life management you need to:

- Eat a healthy, balanced diet, with a few treats.
- Take regular exercise.
- Make sure you get enough sleep.
- Have regular breaks in your daily, weekly, monthly and annual routines.
- Find time each day and week to do some things purely for enjoyment.
- Network with other researchers for peer support.
- Ask for help when you need help.

- Learn from your mistakes, but don't dwell on them.
- Celebrate your achievements.

Highlighting the need to eat and sleep may seem obvious, trivial or irrelevant. Some people claim to do their best work in caffeine-fuelled all-nighters. They are likely to be deluding themselves. Research has demonstrated that food is necessary for the exercise of willpower, and sleep for good decision-making (Baumeister and Tierney, 2012: 49, 59–60). Willpower and good decision-making are key ingredients of successful research.

Keeping a research diary or journal can help you to manage your research and your life. Some people advocate the use of research journals for reflective learning, or learning from the process. A journal can certainly be useful for this, but it also has other potential benefits: as a way to express uncomfortable feelings or concerns; as a place for anything from the unspeakable to thoughts you really don't want to forget; or simply as somewhere to offload:

> I did keep a journal, and the journal was really useful, and that was from the research qualification because you had to do it for that. Initially I thought, 'This is a pain', but actually having the journal was really useful. The journal I used more about my experiences of the subject I was studying, the wake up screaming at 4 o'clock in the morning type stuff, and to reflect on things I'd had to do in my work life that I hadn't felt comfortable about.

Journaling expert Nicole Brown defines journaling for research as 'a way of thinking through making, doing, creating and recording for the purpose of discovery, grounding, professional development and creativity' (Brown, 2021: 8).

> At the moment I'm doing a diary of each time I have a project about who's come, how they're interacting with each other, how I've felt about it. That was encouraged by the last person in my job and my line manager, that's been quite useful doing a learning journal.

Some professions, such as nursing, regularly make use of learning journals (Alaszewski, 2006: 10–11), so you may be comfortable with this technique. Even if you have no experience of diary writing and feel appalled at the very idea, I would encourage you to give it a try. There is no right way to keep a research diary (Silverman and Marvasti, 2008: 304), which, comfortingly, means there isn't a wrong way to do it either. I am an ad hoc journal writer at best, but I do find it useful to write down odd thoughts and feelings and bits and bobs as I work through the process of conducting research or evaluation. In the day-to-day business of research work, such a huge amount of information passes through your thoughts and senses that it's easy to forget even very relevant pieces of information or ideas (Jesson et al, 2011: 58). It is surprising how often my ad hoc records of oddities prove useful when I'm writing my research reports.

You also need to take care of yourself within the process of conducting research. Potentially, research can endanger you physically, emotionally and politically, and it is your responsibility to keep yourself safe. Most of the physical dangers consist of spending too long sitting at a desk staring at a screen. However, the data collection phase may at times lead to physical danger for researchers. Some researchers will be sharply aware of this possibility, such as Simon Winlow in his investigations of cultures of violence and organised crime (Westmarland, 2011: 133–7). For others, it may come as a surprise.

Here's an example from my own experience. Soon after I became an independent researcher, I was asked to evaluate a partnership-based mental health service. To do this, I needed to interview users of the service, some of whom were in secure psychiatric wards. I'd had previous experience of locked wards, so the prospect didn't faze me. Arrangements were made for the ward staff to identify willing and able interviewees. When I arrived at one hospital, the nurse in charge pointed to a man sitting in a side room with a glass panel in the door, and said, 'There's your first interviewee. He said he's happy to do it, but he's a bit unpredictable with strangers, especially women.' My jaw must have dropped, because the nurse grinned and added, 'Don't worry, we'll keep an eye on you.' My pulse was racing but I tried to appear calm as I went into the side room to begin the interview. Luckily, the interviewee was even-tempered and helpful, but the interview felt very long and I was relieved to reach the end. I still don't know what 'a bit unpredictable' meant, but I certainly didn't feel safe, and the regular appearance of a concerned face in the glass door panel did more to prolong my feeling of alarm than to reassure me about my safety.

People generally are 'a bit unpredictable'. Some people don't like researchers, or intellectuals, or clever dicks. Someone may be sexist, or racist, or uncomfortable around people who dress in certain ways. A participant may have been angered by something unconnected with your research, and choose to take it out on you. Or someone may just be in a bad mood. Whatever the reason, you can't assume that everyone will be well mannered and helpful, and that you will always be safe. So take appropriate precautions. If you are going out alone into an unfamiliar environment, you should make sure someone knows where you are going and when you expect to be back, so they can take action if you don't return on time. Don't research topics that could take you into dangerous encounters unless you are confident that you can manage such situations. Be aware of the possibility of danger, and be prepared to abandon a piece of data collection if necessary.

Finding yourself in physical danger takes an emotional toll, but researchers can also be in emotional danger without any physical risk. Interviewees for this book talked of distressing experiences in researching subjects such as chronic illness or bereavement. As with physical danger, when it is obvious that a topic may lead to emotional danger, steps can be taken to manage this, although there seems to be little advice available on how to do so. One interviewee really grappled with this situation, and their experience also shows the importance of planning:

If anything in actually doing the research that was the bit that worried me, there were some people I knew were having end-of-life care, and I knew some bits were going to be harrowing. It's not just about how I deal with it, but how to deal with someone who is getting upset. Maybe because of the research I was doing, I knew about that but I didn't read it anywhere. I prepared an exit strategy, I had ready prepared statements I could use that were comforting but would call an end to the research interview and enable me to calm them down, make sure they were safe and happy and okay and remove myself from the situation. I had to use them once when a woman got very distressed, and they worked, but I have to tell you, thank God I had them, because if I hadn't had that at my fingertips I don't know what I would have done. I'm pretty intuitive, and I probably would have handled it okay, but you can't guarantee, and knowing what I'd planned to do meant the planning kicked in. Having the steps written down and in the back of my head helped me manage that situation. I like people, that's why I do social research, but having ideas about how to deal with it meant that I wasn't flustered and panicked, because what she needed was somebody calm. And bless her, she rang me the next day to thank me, and to apologise for being upset. I think I'd have been more upset if she hadn't been. It's not just how you're going to handle your own emotions, but how you're going to handle someone else's.

Sometimes you can't see it coming. For example, I have conducted research and evaluation for services working with mental ill health and drug misuse. Both are areas where I have enough experience and knowledge to be reasonably inured to the misery involved. However, on several occasions, I encountered parents who had been forcibly separated from their children because of their situation, and their grief was intense. I found this very upsetting, because I couldn't do anything but listen and sympathise, and that wasn't enough; it felt like trying to treat an amputation with a sticking plaster.

Again, with emotional danger, you need to take appropriate precautions. If you have a distressing encounter, take some time for yourself as soon as you can after the event. Find someone supportive to talk it over with, ideally someone who will help you sort through your feelings and find a sensible perspective. Write about it in your journal – or, if you don't keep a journal, write about it anyway: the act of writing will help you to process the experience, and the write-up may prove useful as data. (This might seem a horribly callous thing to say, but everything is potential grist to the researcher's mill.)

Political danger is another difficulty you may come across in your research work. What I mean by 'political danger' is that everyone has their own agenda and some people may try to hi-jack part or all of your research for their own ends. You may experience this from managers, commissioners, supervisors, tutors, participants, colleagues and others, at any stage of the process, from plans to dissemination and beyond. Yet this kind of hi-jacking isn't always malicious, or even intentional. The interviewee quoted in Chapter 2, who had to stand firm against another researcher and their boss when they were getting over-enthusiastic and trying to make recommendations before the data had been analysed, reflected on this:

> The danger from my point of view was, some people come up with an idea they don't want to let go of, and the idea works from one angle and won't work from another, and I was worried that we could go far too far down that road. Then the research might say something else but the idea wouldn't be let go of. So I nipped that in the bud, and said, 'Hang on, all this information's in my head but the coding may turn up something I haven't seen, and that's the point of coding.'

At times, however, hi-jacking can be absolutely intentional. For example, I was once asked to evaluate a residential service. The commissioner was completely open about the fact that they wanted to close the service down, and asked me to find evidence that would support their plans. I was equally open with them, saying that I was not prepared to work to their agenda, but I was prepared to conduct a professional independent evaluation and present my findings. The commissioner accepted this and gave me a contract for the work. My findings did not support their plans to close the service, as its users, its staff and staff of partner agencies who referred users to the service were all unanimous in their opinion of its high value, and this was supported by monitoring and other data. So the commissioner couldn't use my evaluation report as evidence to support their plans, but they were very nice about it, paid my invoice, and, sadly, found another way to close down the service.

In both of these examples, the researcher's job was to remain fully aware of what they were doing, why they were doing it, and how they were doing it, and to hold those boundaries in place when others tried to bend them. This is the best way to maintain your political safety as a researcher. It won't protect you against every political danger, because research is in itself a political act, and you can find yourself treading on unexpected toes. But boundary management is a great safeguard, as well as being a sound ethical way to conduct research. Also, in these situations, you need to have and use good negotiating skills and effective ways of managing your research relationships.

Conclusion

Table 6.1 summarises what works, and what doesn't, in managing the research process on top of your main job.

But, as I said in Chapter 1, I can only write the guidebook. Now you know where the safe places are, and which paths might lead to danger. What route will you take?

Table 6.1: What works, and what doesn't work

What works	What doesn't work
Being clear and realistic about your workload from the start	Putting off thinking about the work you need to do – and then putting it off some more
Establishing a routine for studying so that you work at the same times each day or week	Waiting until you're in the right mood to start studying
Finding or creating a quiet, uncluttered space in which to study so that you are free of distractions	Trying to study with the TV or talk radio playing, social media flashing up messages on your computer screen, children running in and out
Turning off your phone and letting your voicemail take messages	Trying to concentrate while your phone is beeping and ringing
Working in blocks of 30–90 minutes, with short exercise or snack breaks in between of 5–10 minutes	Working for long periods without breaks – you can't maintain concentration
Using time when your mind is under-occupied – for example, while exercising, waiting for a bus, walking to the shops – to think about your research	Putting your research out of your mind except when you're at your desk
Taking proper breaks: at least one day off a week and one holiday a year	Studying for days, weeks, months on end without a break
Setting milestones and rewarding yourself for each one you reach	Beating yourself up for failing to meet deadlines
Sharing experiences and support with other people doing similar work	Trying to do the work and cope with the pressure all on your own
Eating nutritious food	Living on junk food and coffee or fizzy drinks
Taking regular exercise	Sitting hunched over your desk all day

CASE STUDIES

Ana knows time management is not her strong point and that poses a risk to her research. She carries out a time audit for a week and is surprised to find out she spends around 20 hours each week watching TV. As she prefers to work in the evenings, she decides to make time for her research by working for at least an hour a day, Monday to Thursday, after her evening meal and before watching TV. She will also allocate a few hours each weekend to her research, at a time to fit in with her social commitments.

Ali's employer expects him to do his evaluation during his working hours, but this is not as straightforward as it sounds because he also has a busy full-time job helping to support young families in need. He has to be highly organised to make the evaluation happen while keeping on top of his own job. Ali finds technology helpful. He and his service user co-evaluators agree to use a project management app on their phones to help them manage tasks and deadlines, and to keep everything in one place, including their messages.

EXERCISES

1. What are your time eaters? How could you spend less time on them without feeling deprived? If you find these questions difficult to answer, do a time audit, as shown in Figure 6.2.

2. Keep a diary of your research work for one week. Write down what you have done, and what you have thought about, each day. At the end of the week, read over the entries, and consider (a) what they teach you about your research work and (b) whether this is an exercise worth repeating.

Discussion questions

1. Why is it important to be organised when you are doing research?
2. When and why should research be a high priority to (a) individuals; (b) organisations; (c) society as a whole?
3. How could a researcher benefit from keeping a reflective learning journal?

Debate topic

Holidays are for wimps.

7

Background research

Chapter summary

This chapter includes:

- An overview of the difference between document and literature reviews
- Why and how to keep good records
- When and how to read critically or strategically
- Ways of finding useful academic journal articles
- How to do a document review
- How to do a literature review
- Advice on using libraries, making notes and knowing when to stop

Introduction

Whatever kind of research or evaluation you're doing, some background research is always helpful. This can range from just a few project documents and perhaps one or two pieces of national policy for a small evaluation, to several hundred items of published and 'grey' literature for a full-scale literature review:

> When you're dealing with material that you can engage with and understand, the bit where it's exciting, firing off all sorts, the thrill of it, it's the bit that's pleasurable.

The main point of background research is to provide the context for your own research or evaluation. As a result, much of the work on this is best done early in the research process – although it may also be necessary to include any legislation, policy and/or key articles or books that are published as you do your research. Also, you may decide to do more background research at a later stage, such as if your data analysis reveals something unexpected and you want to put that finding into context for your readers.

Document review or literature review?

If you're doing research for postgraduate academic study, you will be required to do a formal literature review. This is covered later in the chapter. If you're doing research in and for your workplace, you will need to do a document review.[1] So what is the difference?

In conducting a literature review for academic research, you start from the literature and work towards your research topic, using the literature to help you develop your research questions. This is partly because many topics in the field of social studies can be addressed from a variety of angles. So, if your topic is the impact of custodial sentences on the families of offenders, you could look at, for example, the emotional impact, the economic impact or the health impact. Each of these would require you to read a different body of literature. Let's say you are most interested in the health angle. That could lead to another decision: physical or mental health, or both? Again, there will be different bodies of literature depending on what you choose.

In conducting a document review as the background for workplace research, you start from your research question or questions and work out which documents you need to include. So, if you were evaluating a project to improve the health of families of people in custody, you might need to include the project's original funding bid, minutes of steering group meetings, job descriptions of staff and volunteers, and relevant policy from the government's health and criminal justice departments. That kind of document review is quite easy to manage, but in other research projects it can be a much larger and more complex undertaking.

For example, let's say you work in a service that is set up to give debt and benefit advice. You notice that an increasing number of your service users have mental health problems – perhaps because of the closure of a neighbouring service, or the reduction of social stigma around mental health, which means more people are open about their condition, or a wider change in policy, or for some other reason. Your manager develops an informal theory that your service is not entirely meeting the needs of people with mental health problems, and asks you to do a piece of research to find some evidence, one way or the other. The research questions are: Are we meeting all the needs of our service users who have mental health problems? If not, what do we need to change to ensure that we do meet all their needs? Your manager wants you to collect primary data from interviews with service users, and also to carry out a document review to research best practice in service provision for people with mental health problems. This will involve you spending time on the internet tracking down documents from sources, including:

- specialist mental health organisations, such as Mind and SANE in the UK, Mental Health America in the USA or Mental Health Australia;
- other service providers in a variety of fields that have produced guidance about working with people who have mental health problems;

- research organisations and think-tanks, such as the Joseph Rowntree Foundation, Demos and The King's Fund in the UK, or the American Institutes for Research in the USA, which have published relevant research;
- national government departments.

This sounds very complicated, but actually, all you have to do is put your search terms into a web-based search engine, and it will find documents for you.

What your search terms will be is another question. Whether you see your background research as a literature review or a document review or something between the two, your work will be richer if you don't limit your reading to your own subject or discipline. Of course you have to limit your reading in some ways, or you'd never do anything but read. Nevertheless, a bit of lateral thinking can greatly enhance your research or evaluation. So, for example, in the project mentioned in the previous paragraph, as well as looking for information about best practice in service provision for people with mental health problems, you might also look at best practice in occupational health for the purposes of comparison. If you were researching the impact of custodial sentences on the families of offenders, you might do some reading around other ways in which a family member can be temporarily separated from the family home, such as through being in the forces or being kidnapped, to see whether these experiences have parallels or contrasts that might throw light on the experiences of offenders' families.

 Rather than reading only from your own subject or discipline, think laterally about which bodies of literature might help to throw light on your research question(s).

Whether you are conducting a document review or a literature review, you may wish to draw on 'grey' literature and ephemera. 'Grey' literature refers to research reports and other documents that are not formally published but may be available in hard copy and/or electronic formats from individuals, organisations or governments. Examples include research that has not been peer reviewed (including most evaluation reports), policy documents and technical reports. Ephemera are also written in hard copy and electronic formats, and are not intended to be kept or stored. These include zines, leaflets and social media updates such as tweets.

While I am suggesting you read as widely as you can, there is a danger for avid readers. When you are searching through documents or literature, it's easy to get side-tracked and go off on an interesting tangent:

> If you're reading a lot, you can go through bibliographies and keep on going and going and going. You can find yourself getting distracted by insignificant things which are interesting but have no relevance to you or anyone else.

While this may be enjoyable, if it is not potentially or actually relevant to your research questions, it is a poor use of your research time. Of course, if you have all the time in the world, go right ahead. But most of us need to exercise some self-discipline in this situation:

> Go back to what your research objectives were. If what you're doing isn't helping you get there, then stop.

In this chapter, I have drawn a distinction between a document review and a literature review, because the former is usually referred to in workplace research and the latter in academic research. But this is not a hard-and-fast distinction, and there are many areas of overlap between the two. Depending on the approach taken and the literature available, one person's document review may look much more like someone else's literature review, or vice versa. As I have already said, they are both forms of background research that can provide the wider context for your work, which is useful for you and for the readers and users of your research. They also both offer:

- a chance to clarify parts of your thinking about aspects of your research questions;
- an opportunity to hone your research questions against the work of others;
- support for the importance, necessity or relevance of your research;
- a way to find and develop your own standpoint.

And they both require:

- careful and critical reading;
- considerable thought;
- the making of connections between theories, ideas and perspectives;
- the development of a new view of the subject.

The requirement to develop your own standpoint, and a new view of the subject, can be quite daunting. It is more onerous for academic researchers, who *must* produce original work, than for workplace researchers, who *should* produce original work. But any research that ignores this requirement is likely to be poor research. The good news is, it's not as hard as you might think, and the way to do it is simply to keep reading, thinking and writing. Your standpoint already exists; the reading and thinking you do will help you identify and express it through your writing. Your new view of the subject, which you will convey in the completed research, does not exist at the start. In fact, it may not exist until close to the end. Nevertheless, it is essential, because whether you are doing a document review or a literature review, the final result should not simply be a list of 'person 1 says this, person 2 says that'. Of course you need to include some explanation of the thoughts, ideas and concepts put forward by the key writers in your field. But your view will influence the synthesising of those thoughts, ideas and concepts, from your own standpoint, such that the result is unique (Silverman and Marvasti, 2008: 98).

The words 'unique' and 'original' are quite scary for some people. It can help to step back and take a wider perspective. A commonly used phrase is 'the whole body of human knowledge', so let's compare that to a human body. Nobody knows how many cells a human body contains, but estimates suggest there may be approximately 10 trillion, or 10 to the power of 14, or 100,000,000,000,000 – which is a very big number. Every time you touch another person's skin, several of your cells rub off on them, and several of their cells rub off on you. Similarly, as you read and learn, cells of knowledge will rub off on you – but your research only needs to add one tiny cell to the whole body of human knowledge.

Record-keeping

Whether you're doing a document review or an academic literature review, you need to keep an accurate record of what you read, where you found it, and how it might fit in to your research (Hart, 2018: 216). This is because, at a later stage, you will need to explain what documents and/or literature you have drawn on in your research, and how you assessed and analysed them. The best way to keep these records is to make a grid for yourself and fill it in as you go along:

> We had a learning circle and one of the other people was talking about how he organised his reading and his notes, and I suddenly thought, 'I could have been doing that, it sounds like a really good idea.' And it was dead simple, it was a grid: author, title, publisher, date, very brief précis of what it was about and whether you liked it or not, another section that had quotes related to what you were interested in. I added another column later on that said, 'This would work in chapter so-and-so.' I'd got about six different reading lists at the time and could I find anything? Could I heck. It was about how I organised it, and that was the turning point.

This interviewee kindly gave me permission to use an example of their grid in this book, which you will find in Appendix 2.

You can make a grid on the computer in a spreadsheet or a text document, or on paper if you prefer. There is no set format for a grid; the important thing is to work out what you need to include for your own research project. Figure 7.1 shows another example. There is a third example on page 30 of Jesson et al (2011).

Figure 7.1: Example of a literature grid

Reference	Where found	Where stored	Key message	Fits where?
Bunting, M. (2004) *Willing slaves: How the overwork culture is ruling our lives*, London: HarperCollins.	Library	Notes in folder	Work is too stressful	Links emotion and work – discussion section

If you use spreadsheet software, you can use a similar grid system in much more detail. For example, you might have columns headed:

1. Number
2. Date
3. Author
4. Title
5. Publisher
6. Edition number
7. Where found
8. Where stored
9. Quote/page
10. Main subject(s)
11. Key message
12. Why is this important?
13. Who agrees with this?
14. Who disagrees with this?
15. Where might it fit into my research?

The sorting function of spreadsheets is a very useful tool in helping you manage and process your reading material, especially if you've read a lot of literature. For example, you could sort on 'main subject' to see whether you've read enough across each of the different subject areas; you could sort on 'edition number' to check whether there are any books that might have a more up-to-date edition than the one you've read; and you could sort on 'author' to help you construct your bibliography.

This may seem complicated and time-consuming, but it will save time later on (Jesson et al, 2011: 28), as this interviewee acknowledged:

> The literature search, if you are very clear at the beginning about the different elements of this, set that up right at the beginning and keep it up to date, that means you don't actually have to go back and try and dig that information out later. It's about trying to reduce the amount of work. Good administrative set-up right at the start is not time wasted. I wish I'd known that.

You are, of course, free to copy any of the grids in this book for your own use if you wish. However, I would urge you to spend a little time thinking through what you need to record for your own purposes. It is likely that an adaptation of a grid will work better for you than simply copying one as it stands.

Some people don't like grids and spreadsheets, and are much happier with hard copies. If you are one of these people, you can:

- use different-coloured boxes and files to store information on different subjects;
- highlight photocopies or print-outs in different colours for specific reasons, for example, green for 'theme', yellow for 'important', blue for 'possible quote' and red for 'key message';
- categorise your documents with different-coloured stars for different levels of relevance, for example, gold for very relevant, silver for quite relevant and blue for some relevant sections (which you could then mark with Post-it notes);
- use different-coloured Post-it notes to mark different types of passage.

Again, you will need to devise your own system that suits your approach, resources and topic.

 Post-it notes are ideal for marking passages in books that need to be returned to the library.

There are also computer software packages that can help you manage your references. Dedicated applications such as EndNote will help you to keep track of your references and compile the reference list for your report, dissertation or thesis. Online research services, such as Zotero and Mendeley, also include this function (see later in this chapter for more information about these).

Critical and strategic reading

If you're doing research, the odds are that you can read English fluently and have been reading for a long time. However, reading for research is different from other kinds of reading, and I think it's worth taking a moment to define and consider that difference.

There is a common perception that the process of reading involves ideas from the writer's brain, communicated via the writer's hands into words on a page, which are then transmitted through the reader's eyes into the reader's brain. With some types of writing, this is more or less true, but with research, the process is much more like the illustration in Box 7.1:

Box 7.1: Process of written communication

Writer has idea.

Writer filters their idea through their past experience and present emotions.
↓

Writer chooses language, grammar, structure, and so on to express their idea.
↓

Editor intervenes to alter language, grammar, structure, and so on
(and sometimes even content, for example, if word count needs to be reduced).
↓

Final version is published.
↓

Reader reads writer's idea.
↓

Reader filters writer's idea through their own past experience and present emotions.
↓

Reader considers writer's idea.
↓

Reader reaches some level of understanding of writer's idea.

One way to summarise this might be: I write in my terms and you read in yours. There are two main reasons for this.

The first is emotion. There are times when I've been reading for research and I've come across a chapter or article that has made me so cross that I can't bear to finish reading it, let alone give dispassionate consideration to the point it makes. There are other times when I read something that excites me, I think it's marvellous and the writer becomes my new hero.

The second is the richness of the English language. Writers frequently have to choose from a wide range of synonymous words, each with a slightly different meaning and resonance. Readers bring their own understanding to the chosen words. For example, one person's 'careful' might be another's 'cautious' or 'wary' or 'vigilant'. Choices writers make about grammar, syntax, structure, and so on also interact with readers' understandings in unpredictable ways.

So the emotions of writers and readers, the choices made by writers and editors, and the understanding of readers can all lead to misunderstanding when reading for research, even when written work is comparatively clear and coherent. And some of it isn't. Some documents and academic texts are abstruse and difficult, whether because they are poorly written, or poorly edited, or the authors are grappling with complex concepts. But the good news is, there's so much literature available that you don't have to read the unreadable. If you're finding a piece of writing too difficult to read, stop trying, and find another relevant document instead.

 If you're reading a complicated piece of writing, and you're struggling to understand, try reading it out loud.

So what is the best way to manage this potential for misunderstanding? I would recommend careful, critical reading. You need to read carefully enough to understand what the writer is saying. However, just because somebody has written something down in words and numbers does not mean it is true or useful or correct. Therefore you also need to read critically. This concept comes from critical theory, a formal theory that encourages scepticism and critical reading and thinking across a range of disciplines. Critical reading does not simply mean finding things to criticise; it means analysing the positive and negative aspects of the text (Jesson et al, 2011: 16), and making a careful assessment of the document's value, both to your own research and more widely. In practice, 'critical reading' means assessing what you are reading against a range of parameters including the document's age, relevance to your work, wider relevance, the skills of the author(s), any perceptible political stance, the quality of the explanations and reasoning, and so on. Critical reading requires critical thinking, which, in this context, has been described as the process of identifying another author's position, line of reasoning and conclusions (Cottrell, 2005, quoted in Jesson et al, 2011: 48). One way of learning to think critically is always to ask yourself: Could there be another explanation? Could a different conclusion be reached?

You should also 'determine … the authenticity and usefulness of particular documents, taking into account the original purpose of each document, the context in which it was produced, and the intended audience' (Bowen, 2009: 38). When research is being reported, it is important to assess the quality of the report and sometimes of the research. If it is a second-hand report, like the last citation in the previous paragraph, the reporter should cite their source in full (in this case, Jesson et al, 2011: 48), which should, in turn, cite the original source in full (that is, Cottrell, 2005, with the relevant page number if given), so that, if you wish, you can make a full assessment of Cottrell's work. It is helpful to include page numbers to make this process easier for those who read your work. (There is more information about citation in Chapter 13.)

If you are reading a researcher's own report of their work, you should be able to understand what they have done, why they have done it, how they did it and why they drew the conclusions they reached. This doesn't mean you have to agree with their conclusions; just that you need to be able to understand where those conclusions have come from. If you have read their report carefully, and you do not understand it fully, there may be a fault in their reporting and/or in their research. Your skills in critical reading and critical thinking will help you to work out where the fault lies.

It is easy to read carefully from the start. Reading and thinking critically is more difficult at the beginning, although it becomes easier with practice. As you begin to read for your research, be as critical as you can, but don't worry if you feel as if you're reading in a vacuum with no context within which to make sense of your learning. As you continue, you will start to make connections between theories, concepts, findings and ideas, and this will help you to develop your critical faculties.

 For a masterclass in critical reading, read *Bad science* by Ben Goldacre (2009).

You can read strategically to save time. So if you find an article with a promising title, read the abstract first. Does it still seem relevant? If not, discard it. If it does, then read the introduction and the conclusion and, if it still seems relevant, begin to read the rest:

> I've become very good at scanning texts quickly. This gets easier the more experienced you become. You get to learn which articles are worth spending more time on, which you don't need at all, and which have got good or useful references for you to backtrack on and dig a bit deeper.

The same applies with book chapters: read the first paragraph or two of each chapter, and skim the headings, to see what's relevant. With whole books, read the contents list, and perhaps part of the preface or introduction, to decide which chapters you need to read. Then you can read more thoroughly where necessary.

 If you want to get a quick overview of a book's approach to its subject, read the first and last paragraphs of each chapter.

Don't ignore basic works of reference such as dictionaries and encyclopaedias. These can both be found online as well as in print. Two of the best known and most reliable are dictionary.com, which has been around since 1995, and the online encyclopaedia Wikipedia, which was founded in 2001. Both are free to use (although Wikipedia appreciates donations from its users), and both are invaluable resources for researchers.

Dictionary.com draws on 15 different high-quality dictionaries to provide a range of definitions for each word. It is very useful to look through when you need to define a term you are using, or when you're unsure about the meaning of a word, or when you need to choose a word to help you make a point (its sister thesaurus.com site can also be helpful here). The site is run by a private corporation and funded by advertising.

Wikipedia is a collaborative encyclopaedia, developed and maintained by tens of thousands of volunteer contributors from around the world, and run as a non-profit organisation. At the time of writing the third edition of this book, Wikipedia had over 57 million articles, in 325 languages, covering most subjects. Over 6.4 million of its articles are in English. Some regard Wikipedia as insufficiently authoritative because the articles are written and edited by volunteers, and some content is highly disputed between different contributors. It is certainly not good practice to use Wikipedia itself as a reference, for these reasons and also because its content may change, although it is most useful as a starting point for investigation.

Interestingly, in 2005, research showed that the level of errors in Wikipedia was similar to the level of errors in printed encyclopaedias (Giles, 2005). This is an important point. It's easy to forget to read critically when you're looking at a dictionary or an encyclopaedia, whether online or in print. However, humans produce encyclopaedias and dictionaries, so there is scope for human error, bias and even misinformation. Also, the publishers of dictionaries have a history of including fake definitions to prevent plagiarism.[2] So it is essential to read critically at all times, even when you're searching for information in an encyclopaedia or dictionary.

Finding academic journal articles

Journal articles, particularly those that have been peer reviewed, are an important source of information for researchers. Tens of thousands of articles are published each year, but they can be surprisingly difficult to find, particularly if you don't belong to a university:

> If you're not part of academia, where do you even look? I'm thinking specifically now around the academic research project we had to do, oh my God, where do you look?

> If you're in practice, bang goes your Athens password, how do you access some of this stuff?

Access to many academic journals is restricted to individual or organisational subscribers. Most of these journals are accessed electronically through the Athens service, which can be joined only by institutions (which pay the subscription costs) and which issues passwords to individual members of those institutions (for whom access is free). This was originally just for students and staff in academic institutions, but has slowly widened to include, at the time of writing, staff in health services in many countries, including the UK, Australia, Canada, New Zealand and the USA, and staff in some public sector organisations in the UK, Canada, Australia and the USA. Nevertheless, access is still barred to most non-profit, education and criminal justice professionals, and to independent researchers.

There is a growing movement to provide open access to academic journal articles. Researchers from Finland and Iceland found that, in 2008, approximately 20% of all academic literature was openly accessible (Björk et al, 2010). By 2015 this had increased to 28% overall, and 45% of literature published in 2015 was open access (Piwowar et al, 2018). Since the first edition of this book was published, there has been a range of mandates from research funders around the world, requiring research funded with public money to be made open access, either immediately or within 6 or 12 months. However, at the time of writing the third edition, this is not universal. Also, existing open access journal articles are still not easy to find, because access is provided in several different ways, and there is (at the time of writing) no single searchable database. The main ways in which access is provided are:

- in open access journals, that is, those that are entirely free to everyone;
- in subscription journals, which make their electronic versions free after a delay;
- as individual open articles in otherwise fee-paying subscription journals;
- in subject-based online repositories;
- in institution-based online repositories;
- on the authors' websites;
- on the websites of the authors' employers;
- on research funders' websites.

So how do you find these resources? Some of the largest open access journals are published by the Public Library of Science (PLOS) in the USA, BMC, which is part of Springer Nature, and Hindawi in Egypt. However, these are heavily weighted towards medicine and laboratory science, with only a small number of social science journals published by Hindawi. The Directory of Open Access Journals (DOAJ) includes listings of peer-reviewed or editorially quality-controlled journals that are openly accessible. Most of these are in English and cover other areas. At the time of writing the third edition of this book (2022), the Directory included 2,472 journals for education, 100 for criminology, 144 for social work and 67 for government. (The equivalent figures as I wrote the first edition, 10 years previously, were: education 627, criminology 19, social work 22, government 24 – which demonstrates the rise in open access.)

 When using the DOAJ, try as many search terms as you can.

Two further useful websites, which list a range of free resources by subject including open access journals, are the Open University Library Services, based in the UK, and the University of California Libraries, from the USA (use the advanced search function to select free resources).

 You may be able to find other useful websites by using search engines to look for 'open access journals'.

Finding open access articles from subscription journals is harder as there is no equivalent of the DOAJ for these publications. The best way is to use Google Scholar to search for the articles you would like to read, and then check whether they are freely available anywhere on the web. This will also help you to find them on the websites of the authors, their employers or their funders, if they are held in those places. Another option is to track down journals covering the subjects that interest you, and then check the website of each journal to see which articles are available for free. You can also follow publishers on Twitter (or check their timelines there) as they usually tweet when they are making articles open access, whether temporarily or permanently.

 You can set up citation alerts for key academic articles, so you will automatically be notified when there is a new citation.

Subject-based online repositories can also be difficult to find. For example, they are not all indexed by Google Scholar. However, you can find them through the online Ranking Web of Repositories, listing thousands of repositories from all around the world. This is an authoritative resource, updated twice a year. You may also be able to find other subject-based online repositories by using search engines.

For institution-based online repositories, a useful place to start is the Registry of Open Access Repositories (ROAR), based in the UK. ROAR holds information about institution-based repositories, from all over the world, of journals and other academic literature including Master's dissertations and PhD theses. New repositories are being created and registered with ROAR all the time. At the time of writing this third edition, there were 895 from the USA, 262 from the UK, 97 from Canada, 84 from Australia and 22 from New Zealand. (Again, this shows the increase in open access in the last 10 years, as the figures for the first edition of this book were US 400, UK 219, Canada 70, Australia 66 and New Zealand 16.) The site isn't very user-friendly – for example, you can search by type of software, but not by academic discipline or subject. I would suggest that you use it to find a repository that looks as though it might meet your needs, then click through to the repository itself to search in more detail.

It can also be useful to look at online research portals such as ResearchGate, Academia.edu and Mendeley. Authors can deposit their work on these websites, which are accessible to scholars who do not belong (or who do not currently belong) to an institution, so they may contain work that institutional repositories do not hold. These portals also enable people to share information about the literature they are using, and therefore help others to find literature that is new to them. The open source reference manager software Zotero also has this capability, and allows you to add notes to references as well as tags. All are free to use – although ResearchGate and Academia.edu are for-profit, so some people are less inclined to use them. There are hundreds of such portals from around the world, covering research in many languages; the Ranking Web of Repositories keeps a useful list.[3] If you are reasonably computer-literate, it would be worth investigating these resources, and if you like social networking you will probably adore them.

Wherever you are searching, you may be able to use advanced web-searching techniques. These are not universal but operate differently on different websites. Many websites, including (to the best of my knowledge) all search engines, have a page of information about their advanced search functions and how they work. There may be a button you can click on the home page or the search page. If not, you should be able to find the advanced search page from any search engine by searching for the name of the search engine/journal/repository/research portal plus 'advanced search'.

However you find your literature, do remember that you need to read it critically and assess its weight through features such as the presence or absence of peer review (although some commentators are also critical of the benefits of peer review) or the clarity of methods used.

How to conduct a document review

If you are doing a document review for a piece of workplace research such as an evaluation, you are likely to have quite a clear idea of the kind of information you want to find. As most, if not all, of the documents you will review are available in electronic form, you can search them using key terms to find the parts you need to read. This is particularly helpful with long policy documents or reports where only a page or two may be directly relevant. So, for the example used earlier in this chapter, our initial key terms might be 'mental health', 'best practice' and 'service user'. Searching a document electronically with these terms doesn't take long. Then you can copy and paste any relevant sections that you find into a new document, perhaps giving it a number from your spreadsheet if you're storing information electronically, or printing it out and colour-coding it if you prefer to work that way.

As you search the first few documents, you might notice writers using other, similar key terms that you want to add to your list. For example, 'mental illness' and 'service delivery' might be relevant. The more key terms you have, the longer searching takes, but you can also be more confident that you're finding everything of relevance to your research or evaluation.

Remember that for any research project, 'documents' may cover a huge variety of material including letters, diaries, publicity materials such as brochures and leaflets, webpages, newspaper or magazine articles and extracts from social media sites.

Some documents will be relevant in their entirety. When you have identified all of these, and have taken extracts from all the documents you can find that are partially relevant, you are ready to start your analysis. This involves careful reading, note-making and thought. It's similar to the analysis of textual data, which is covered in Chapter 12 of this book, although it doesn't involve detailed coding of the data. You will be looking for content and themes to help you develop your ideas, and quotations to use in your report, and you will need to make notes as you go along. The process of note-making is the same for document and literature reviews, and is covered later in this chapter.

 If you have made a thorough search and you can find few or no relevant documents, this is a finding in itself, so explain your search methods and techniques to show what you were looking for and how.

Document review is primarily a qualitative technique, but in some cases it may be helpful to include a quantitative element. For example, if you have a series of meeting minutes, you might want to count the number of times each person attended a meeting, or the number of times each topic was raised. If you are looking at a set of diaries, it might be useful to count the number of entries made in each diary or within a specific period of time. This kind of quantitative information can add a useful dimension to some document reviews by helping you to think in a different way about what the documents can tell you.

How to conduct a literature review

An academic literature review is not like a review of a book or a concert, written by a critic whose role is to inform a potential audience and entertain readers. Your role as a researcher is to show that you have read, considered, understood and made connections with the academic literature in your field. When academics want to talk about this, they often say someone has 'engaged with the literature'. You literally need to 're-view' the literature (Jesson et al, 2011: 10): to look at it again, with fresh eyes, and bring your unique perspective to the process to create an original review.

Students often ask how many references they need to include, but it's not a numbers game (Jesson et al, 2011: 31). 'More' does not equal 'better'. You need to identify and engage with key texts, which in some cases will have been written several decades ago, and with recent developments in the literature, including academic journal articles (where the latest thinking is often found) that have been published within the last year or two. Then you need some texts in between to show how thinking developed.

If you are researching a very broad and long-standing topic, such as motivation, the literature can stretch back over a century or more, so you will need to be selective. In this case, you should define your selection criteria (Jesson et al, 2011: 30), and explain them to your reader. For example, you might use your research question to help you decide that you want to restrict your initial reading to texts covering both motivation and contact with the criminal justice system. Or you might use other criteria such as time (for example, including only texts from the last five years, unless they are key texts) or research method (for example, including only texts based on interview data, if you are planning a series of interviews yourself). You are the only person who can decide what your selection criteria should be, and these examples should help you to do that piece of thinking.

On the other hand, if you are researching a narrower or newer topic, such as a recently identified illness or disability, there will be less literature to draw on. This will probably mean that you need to think more laterally and read further beyond the boundaries of your topic. Either way, once again you are the only person who can decide whether a particular text is relevant for your document review or literature review (Jesson et al, 2011: 23).

Using libraries

Many universities have research libraries, and if you have access to one of those, that will make your life easier – but if not, don't despair; a lot of help is available for you from other libraries and librarians. Don't think your local lending library is too small to be of use. I live in a town with a population of around 15,000, and our library produced several useful books for me as I was writing the first edition of this book. The librarians there, like librarians everywhere, are always ready to help if help is needed, and to advise on ways to find information.

> The other thing around accessing information, as an absolute non-academic, is thinking, 'Oh yes, the British Library, that's where all the books go, isn't it?' and not knowing how to access that resource, and in the end we never did because we couldn't work it out, sad to say.

 University and other librarians are experts in finding information. It is well worth making contact with them, because they will be happy to help you, and their expertise can save you a great deal of time and effort.

National library websites hold a great deal of useful information, and are putting more online all the time. They all have 'ask a librarian' features – although not all are called that. For example, on the British Library website you need to search for the relevant 'reference team'. All offer specific help for researchers and evaluators, and have a variety of ways for you to get in touch: email is the most common, then post, phone, online chat, and so on. These libraries also have digital collections from which you can request copies of documents to be sent to you online, although there is usually a charge for this to cover copyright and other fees. And each library has special features, with new features being developed all the time. An example is the Social Welfare Portal.[4] This is a single point of access to the British Library's huge print and digital collections of research and information on all aspects of social welfare, which went live in mid-2012. It is free to use and provides access to a lot of free information, although there is still a charge for some academic journal articles.

 Invest a little time in checking out the resources for researchers on your national library's website.

Generally speaking, national libraries will not want to hear from you until you have exhausted the available local and regional resources. Most national libraries will not lend books or other documents to individuals; your local library usually has to request anything you need, on your behalf, for you to read, which, as a rule, has to be done on library premises. Do bear in mind that these inter-library loans can take some time to arrange, and work out what you're likely to need early in your research process, or you run the risk of missing out or missing deadlines.

The British Library was set up to keep a copy of every publication from the UK and Ireland (although this is dependent on publishing organisations lodging copies of the documents they produce, which doesn't always happen – but the collection is fairly comprehensive nonetheless). The national research library in the USA is the Library of Congress, which claims to be the largest library in the world. In Canada, the national library is Libraries and Archives Canada (LAC), which focuses on collecting Canadian publications and materials published elsewhere which are about, or relevant to, Canada. The National Library of Australia and the National Library of New Zealand take a similar approach to LAC. Other countries have national libraries with websites you can access if you speak the language. All national libraries will accept requests for information, from people in other countries, about the collections they hold.

Don't be afraid to contact librarians and ask questions, whether at local, regional or national level. Librarians are experts in finding and using information, and it is part of their job to help researchers (Robson and McCartan, 2016: 53), so do make use of them. If they don't hold the information you need in their own library, they will know where to direct you.

Making notes

Whether you are reading for a document review or a literature review, you will need to make notes. This is not just a recording task; writing your own notes will help you to work out what you think (Becker, 2007: xi). Reading, note-making and writing is an iterative process that is both underpinned by, and supports, the development of your thinking (Jesson et al, 2011: 58–9).

If you have good keyboard skills or your computer supports voice recognition, I would suggest making notes electronically. You are likely to end up with copious notes and electronic storage makes them easy to search. This is a bonus when you're in the middle of writing up your research or evaluation, and something triggers a memory of a really useful paragraph you saw somewhere that would be relevant to the section you're writing now. As long as you can remember a key word or phrase, you can find the paragraph you want in seconds, even if you have hundreds of pages of notes – if they're stored electronically. Doing the same search manually, however good your colour-coding system may be, would take much longer.

Alternatively, if you are a visual learner, you may prefer to make your notes in visual form, perhaps as mind maps or flow charts (Jesson et al, 2011: 61). Some computer applications enable this kind of visual modelling, such as FreeMind and NVivo, or you can use large sheets of paper and add Post-it notes, stickers, and so on to help you visualise and record your reading and ideas.

 In reading for research, there may be times when you lose track of what you're supposed to be doing and why. If this happens, go back to your research questions to help you refocus.

As you make notes, it is useful to categorise your sources. This can be done using tags in Zotero or Mendeley, with attributes in NVivo, similarly in other computer software applications, or by hand on your electronic or hard copy notes. You can define the categories as you please, depending on your subject, but I would like to suggest a couple of categories that might be useful: the author's location and the document's time. The author's location is not restricted to geography; it may be equally or more important to log their political or theoretical location, their location in terms of experience, and so on. Both location and time are useful for grouping literature and documents. It is always interesting to see what a range of authors from a similar location has to say on a subject. Equally, it is useful to arrange your notes on a particular subject in time sequence from earliest to most recent, to show how thinking in that field has developed. Either of these approaches will help you to look at your literature more analytically. I hope these examples will help you to identify other categories that may be useful in your own project.

 Keep meticulous records of document names and page numbers with your notes – it will save you time in the long run.

The iterative process of reading, writing and thinking will also help you to identify your own location. Some aspects of your location may be immediately obvious to you: your gender, perhaps, or your social class, or your political views. Other aspects may become apparent only as you test yourself against the work of others. You will need to be able to identify your own location in your review, to position your own line of reasoning within the wider body of literature you are reviewing, so it will be useful to bear this in mind.

You will need to write more notes about the findings from your source categorisations, and at some point you will have to start writing up your literature review or document review. Advice on writing for research can be found in Chapter 13 of this book, but for now, please just bear in mind that you are aiming for a synthesis which is 'as rigorous and as transparent as possible' (Bowen, 2009: 38).

Knowing when to stop

> Some areas of research, there are vast amounts of information, where do you stop? How do you know when it's enough?

Although you are likely to do the bulk of your reading at the start of your research, you will probably continue reading all the way through your project, and you are unlikely to finish until you have almost finished writing up. This can make it particularly difficult to know when to stop. However, you should eventually reach a place where you find that the same points are being made, the same key texts being cited, and you feel as if you know what's going on (Jesson et al, 2011: 30). This is a sign that you are approaching the end of your reading.

In reading for a research proposal, you can stop when you are confident that you have identified the key texts for your subject, and are clear about how the thinking in the field has developed between the date of the first key text and the present time. For a literature or document review, where possible you need to find and read all the relevant literature and documents. Usually there are too many for you to read them all, in which case you need to read enough to develop your own view of the subject (that is, your location) and know where it sits within the existing views.

It is useful to remember that there is no such thing as the perfect document or literature review (Barker, 2014: 68). Any piece of writing can always be revised, polished and improved, but doing this endlessly will not help you or your research. The important thing is to produce a piece of writing that is good enough and fit for purpose. For this to be the case, your review will need a structure in which information given to the reader flows logically from one point to the next. Within that, it will need:

- a short introduction outlining what the review will cover;
- discussion of all key texts or documents;

- citation of some other relevant, but perhaps more peripheral, texts or documents (see Chapter 13 for methods of citation);
- a report of the ways in which thinking around the topic has developed over the time between the earliest texts or documents and the present day;
- location of your own position in the context of your review;
- details of your own line of reasoning, linked with the evidence from which this grew;
- explanation of how this fills a gap in knowledge or understanding;
- a short conclusion summarising the key points of the review.

There is one most important 'do' and there is one most important 'don't'. Do write as clearly and simply as you can (Barker, 2014: 72). And don't just describe the literature or documents that you read, but extract the arguments from the texts and reflect on those arguments to create your own interpretation and analysis (Jesson et al, 2011: 66).

It is very hard to read your own work critically, so seek and use feedback from others – colleagues, tutors, supervisors, peers – to help you assess the quality of your work. And when it is good enough, that's when you can stop.

Conclusion

Whether you review documents or literature, whether you include quantitative data or your background research is entirely qualitative, the same principles apply. Keep good records of what you use and how and where you found it. Read critically and thoroughly. Think carefully as you make connections. Make notes that will be helpful for your future self, in whatever format works best for you. Write clearly, and ensure that your writing is analytic and interpretative, not simply descriptive. This chapter has offered guidance on how to ensure you work to these principles.

Remember, however, that the divisions between the chapters in this book do not imply discrete stages of the research process. You may well need to add to your background research at various points during your research, even quite close to the end.

> ### CASE STUDIES
> Ana needs to use academic literature to contextualise her work. She searches Google Scholar and discovers a small body of literature on non-heterosexual families and the media, with around 300 items listed. She decides to work through these items strategically to begin with, collecting those which seem relevant and which she can access. This yields 35 items of literature, mostly journal articles, which Ana then reads critically and records carefully. Ana finds that most of the articles are interesting. Also, the process of reading through them helps her understand some aspects of her topic more clearly.

Ali wants to conduct a document analysis including departmental records and some quantitative data on numbers and types of unpaid family carers. All the documents and data he needs are available from within his organisation. When Ali has collected everything together he makes a record of all the documents first. Then he does some initial calculations with the quantitative data to get an overview, and then reads the departmental records in chronological order, picking out key points, before summarising everything to present to his co-researchers. Ali finds that this process gives him a good understanding of the work of the department.

EXERCISES

1. Devise a system for storing and retrieving your documents and literature.

2. Search the Directory of Open Access Journals (DOAJ) for journals in your field.

3. Search the Ranking Web of World Repositories for subject-based online repositories in your field.

4. Search the Registry of Open Access Repositories (ROAR) for institutional repositories in your country.

5. Look at the website of your national library (or nearest equivalent), and figure out how you can make use of the resources it offers for your research.

Discussion questions

1. Why is it helpful to learn to read in different ways?
2. How can you choose what to use to set your research in context when there are so many options?
3. What is the best way to make notes?

Debate topic

Background research is irrelevant.

8

Secondary data

Chapter summary

This chapter includes:

- Online secondary data sources
- Secondary qualitative data and where to find it
- Archival data and what it might be useful for
- Information about open data worldwide
- Application programming interfaces (APIs)
- Large-scale surveys, with examples
- International surveys, with examples
- Some advice on working with secondary data

Introduction

Secondary data is data that has been collected by someone else, for a purpose other than your research or evaluation project, and has been made available for reuse. Most of this is in digital form. Each individual collection of digital research data is known as a 'dataset'; these can include numbers, texts, images, blog posts, and so on. Due to great efforts to open up data to the public, there is now a huge amount of secondary data freely available on the internet, and more is being added all the time. Secondary data is also held in libraries, museums and archives. Examples of quantitative secondary data are government statistics and census data. Examples of qualitative secondary data are criminological data, health data, web archive data and oral history data:

> I use secondary data to evaluate health-related services. They collect information and outcome-related data from their clients for their own purposes, which I then use to evaluate service effectiveness.

Freely available secondary data is a tremendous resource for any research or evaluation project. However, only two of the people I interviewed for this book mentioned secondary data. This chimes with findings from the research literature that state that secondary data is generally under-used (Lewis and McNaughton Nicholls, 2013: 53). Yet secondary data has a great deal to offer to researchers.

Use secondary data wherever possible, especially data that is freely available online, as this can save you a great deal of time.

Although there are several advantages to using secondary data, there are also some disadvantages. Both are summarised in Table 8.1.

Table 8.1: Pros and cons of using secondary data

Pros	Cons
Quick, easy, free access to datasets, with far more data than you could ever collect yourself	So much data available that it can be hard to find what you need
Opportunities to identify gaps in data that your own project might help to fill	Secondary data will have been collected and presented by people with different priorities from yours
The ability to compare your primary data with local, regional and national equivalents	Data from different sources may use different categories, such as different age bands or different socioeconomic classifications, which can make comparison difficult or meaningless
The option of a historical, longitudinal or cross-cultural perspective	Data from different sources may be collected differently, for example, in some countries it is a legal requirement to participate in national surveys while in others it is not, which can make comparison difficult or meaningless
Often collected and presented by professional research teams with high-level expertise	Not infallible – even professional and expert teams can, and do, make mistakes in data entry and analysis
Reusing existing data is good ethical practice, to minimise the burden on research participants	It can be more difficult to understand data you have not collected yourself, especially when it's in large complicated datasets
Data collection can be much quicker than with primary data	Secondary data may be old and out of date, and so less relevant
Less time spent on data collection means more time for data analysis	Some people find secondary data so fascinating that it becomes a time eater
Scope for enormous creativity	It can be hard to find out why and how secondary data was collected and analysed, which can leave you unsure of its quality

Despite the disadvantages, I would recommend the use of secondary data where possible, particularly at the start of a project. It's an excellent way of exploring a research question and finding background information to give context, evidence and rationale for your own work. But, as with everything else in research, it is important to look at secondary data with a critical eye.

Where possible, you need to ask questions to assess the integrity of the data as well as interrogating the data itself. Useful questions include:

- Why was this data collected?
- Who financed the data collection?
- Who collected the data?
- How did they collect the data?
- When was the data collected?
- What kind of sampling was used?
- What variables were included?
- How were those variables categorised?
- How was the data prepared for analysis?
- How was the data analysed?

Some datasets will include answers to these questions, perhaps on a 'frequently asked questions' or FAQ page, and sometimes with other useful information such as response rates for questionnaires. Other datasets will not offer this kind of information, although in some cases answers may be found or deduced through careful exploration of the website concerned or wider searches of the internet. Overall, the less you can discover about the background to a dataset, the less trust you should place in its findings.

You also need to use your critical eye on the data itself. Useful questions here include:

- How has the data been presented?
- Has any of the data collected been left out of the presentation? If so, are the reasons for exclusions made clear?
- Can you see any evidence of bias in the way the data has been presented?
- Is the data raw (that is, every piece of data collected is presented separately) or aggregated? If the latter, which analytic methods have been chosen? Do you think those methods are appropriate, given the nature of the data? Why?

If you can conclude from the evidence available that the researchers asked sensible questions, and used robust methodology to collect, analyse and present the data, you can place a high degree of trust in their findings. If your conclusion is any less confident, then the level of trust you place in the findings should decrease accordingly:

> We wanted to establish the extent to which health study samples represented women from different groups in the general population.

The advantage was that we could look at the existing situation for research and we could explore a range of other studies using slightly different designs to identify possible routes to improve sample representativeness. The main disadvantage was that not all data was readily available to us, and because we had not collected it, at times there was insufficient information to allow us to compare studies or the measures used were not comparable across studies.

Some types of official data are notorious for problems with their accuracy and thoroughness. The main example is crime statistics (Bryman, 2016: 319) due to under-reporting of crime and to the number of judgements that go into each statistic that does become part of a dataset (Westmarland, 2011: 64–5). Westmarland points out that before any event can officially be called a 'crime', discretionary decisions are taken by at least three people: the person who decides whether or not to make an arrest, the person who decides whether and how to record that arrest, and the person who decides whether and how to prosecute the arrested person. Therefore, as Westmarland says, it is essential to question the integrity of crime data (2011: 81).

Secondary data can offer a great deal of reward for a surprisingly small investment of time, especially if you know where to start. The rest of this chapter contains information about the main sources of openly accessible secondary data worldwide.

Online secondary data sources

Online social science data archives are held by many countries around the world. In the USA, there are several, including:

- Sociometrics[1] at Princeton University Library, New Jersey;
- Roper Center for Public Opinion Research, Connecticut;
- Stanford Center for Population Health Sciences, California;
- ICPSR (Inter-university Consortium for Political and Social Research) based in Ann Arbor, Michigan;
- DISC (Data & Information Services Center), Wisconsin;
- Social Science Data Archive, UCLA, California.

Harvard University Graduate School of Design has a useful webpage of worldwide geospatial and statistical data resources.[2]

There are also numerous data centres in Canada, which are all part of Canada's Research Data Centre Network.

Europe has a Consortium of European Social Science Data Archives (CESSDA) which lists over 20 individual members. Australia has the Australian Data Archive, based in Canberra. The New Zealand Social Science Data Service is based in Auckland. No doubt there are also online data archives based in other countries; you should be able to find out by searching the internet.

Secondary qualitative data

Most of the data in the archives already mentioned is quantitative, but there is also a growing interest in online data archives for qualitative social science. Again, their names and locations should enable you to find them on the internet. The first online qualitative data archive, Qualidata, was established in the UK in 1994, and at the time of writing the first edition of this book it held over 350 qualitative datasets. Since then it has moved to the UK Data Service along with other qualitative data collections. Other archives that hold qualitative data, sometimes alongside quantitative data, include:

• The Henry A. Murray Research Archive in the USA;
• ADA Qualitative in Australia;
• The Irish Qualitative Data Archive in Ireland;
• FORS in Switzerland.

There are some specific ethical concerns about reusing qualitative data. When quantitative data is collected at national or local governmental level, it is usually understood that the aggregated findings will be made public and called 'data'. In most quantitative datasets, the data has been prepared and analysed into categories, so there is no chance of anyone using it to identify individuals. Qualitative data, however, is a different matter. Participants in qualitative research often speak openly, trusting the researcher to omit any identifying details from their analysis and reporting. Also, it is rare for qualitative researchers to seek consent from their participants to the use of the data they provide for anything beyond the project in hand. Where consent has not been obtained, and/or details that could identify an individual have not been removed, it would be highly unethical to share qualitative data.

Some online commentators have expressed concerns that the reuse of qualitative data could be hampered by the reuser's lack of knowledge of the context and drivers for the original research. Other people see this as a positive advantage. Either way, the UK Data Service has identified six ways of reusing qualitative data:

1. Description: of the original participants at the time of the project.
2. Comparison: over time, between social groups, between geographic locations, etc.
3. Reanalysis: to see what the data will yield to a new researcher, at a later time, who may be using different analytic methods or asking different research questions.
4. Research design: studying existing data enables assessment of the research design used in the light of the quality of the data it yielded, and the ability to draw conclusions to inform future research designs.
5. Methodological advancement: study of methods used and the resulting data can enable existing methods to be improved and new methods to be devised.

6. Teaching and learning: genuine data is an excellent aid to the study of research methods and individual social science disciplines.

Archival data

Archival data is a subset of secondary data made up of historical records. These may be very recent or from long ago. They are held by organisations, and may be in print, digitised or digital text, audio and video recordings, photographs, and even records on fabric or tree bark.

It is not only historians who find archival data useful. Other researchers and evaluators can use archival data to:

- gain a better understanding of the context for research or evaluation;
- shed new light on other secondary or primary data;
- identify relationships or patterns they might not otherwise find;
- formulate a baseline for comparison with other secondary or primary data;
- look at changes or trends over time;
- compare data with information from other organisations, districts or countries.

However, archival data isn't always easy to find or use. Some is online, but you may have to travel. Archival data is often held in huge quantities, which can make it hard to find the information you want. And when you finally do track it down, it may not be in a helpful format.

Many countries have national archives. Examples include:

- UK: The National Archives;
- USA: National Archives and Records Administration;
- Canada: Library and Archives Canada;
- Australia: National Archives of Australia;
- New Zealand: Archives New Zealand.

National archives are staffed by experts who can help you find your way around. Many national archives also have online catalogues.

Open data

The open data movement is lobbying for more data to be freely available to the public. This has led to many governments making national non-personal data freely available via the internet. For example, in 2013, the USA created a policy requiring all newly created government data to be made openly and freely available. The UK open data website contains data on health, social care, crime and education, as well as transport, housing, and so on. There are also regional and local government open data websites such as, in the UK, the London Datastore and Manchester Open Data, which covers Greater Manchester. Other countries work in a similar way. The open data websites of the main English-speaking countries are listed here with, where available, information about the numbers of datasets they held on 2 December 2021:

- USA: Data.gov, 334,208 datasets (not including geospatial data, which is held by various federal agencies);
- Canada: Open Government, 30,000 'open data and information assets';
- UK: Data.gov.uk (no information about number of datasets);
- New Zealand: Data.govt.nz, over 30,000 datasets;
- Australia: Data.gov.au, over 30,000 datasets.

At the time of writing the third edition of this book, the Open Government Partnership (OGP) had 78 participating countries and almost 100 local governing bodies from around the world. Launched 10 years earlier with just eight founding governments, the OGP is committed to making government data accessible for the benefit of all citizens.

There is also a movement to make datasets as easy to find, identify and cite as books or journal articles (see Chapter 13 for more on citation). This is being spearheaded by an international group called DataCite, which supports a system for identifying datasets reliably on the internet even if they move from one web page to another. This system is called the digital object identifier, or DOI. The DOI for a dataset is permanent – a bit like an article's title, or a book's ISBN – so it can lead people to the dataset itself, not just to the place on the internet where that dataset is (or was) located. This also means that the researcher or researchers who collected the data can be credited every time it is reused. (Journal articles are also now given DOIs, as you will see in this book's References.)

There are academic repositories of data, known as Dataverses, associated with universities worldwide. These enable you to upload your own data and receive a formal scholarly citation for that data, either a DOI or Handle (another form of 'global persistent identifier'). Although the stated aims of the Dataverses are to 'share, preserve, cite, explore, and analyze research data',[3] at present it seems much easier to share your own data than to access other people's data. Also, the Dataverses seem primarily designed by and for quantitative researchers. However, it seems likely that exploration and analysis of data will become easier, and that more qualitative data will be included, with time.

Application programming interfaces[4]

Application programming interfaces, or APIs, are used to release some open data. An API is a piece of source code that provides a mechanism by which external applications can communicate with it and access or exchange data. Sites such as Google and Facebook use APIs to keep their stream of data and content coming at you through applications, so they can be very powerful tools. Many companies and organisations are making data available like this for free, but you need to know how to use APIs to access their content. If you're interested, The Programmable Web is a good place to start. This user-friendly site provides lists of APIs and information on ways to interact with and use them, including the 'data mashup' or mixture of data from two or more APIs that can offer different perspectives on that data. This sounds complicated, but the mashup tools are often surprisingly simple, for example mapping the data on top of Google Maps, requiring no great level of technical skill to use.

There are countless APIs providing data globally, and more are being created all the time. Examples of some APIs that could be useful to researchers are:

- The World Bank has five different APIs[5] for datasets on indicators (that is, time series data), data catalog (that is, development-relevant datasets), projects (that is, the Bank's operations), financial data and climate data.
- Ordnance Survey has released geographic data via API,[6] as have projects such as Google Maps and Open Street Map.
- The National Library of Australia, Jisc Library Hub Discover (combined catalogues of major UK and Irish libraries, including academic and research libraries), Crossref and DataCite have released their catalogue information and/or metadata via open APIs. National libraries and library consortia in other countries may also have APIs.
- Transport APIs: for example, Transport for London has a unified API[7] to release live data on all forms of transport in the city. There are equivalents in other countries.
- If you are interested in researching social networks, Twitter data is available through three APIs,[8] one for Twitter itself, one for Twitter advertisements and one for Twitter on websites.
- The UK National Archives has a Discovery API,[9] which allows searching of archival metadata. Other countries may have equivalents.

If you are interested in finding more APIs, there is a helpful API Directory[10] on The Programmable Web, which holds over 24,000 APIs at the time of writing (December 2021). However, given the speed at which APIs are developed worldwide, this directory is unlikely to be exhaustive. If you're interested in the APIs for a specific organisation or type of organisation, it's best to use a search engine to look for that organisation's name or type, plus 'API'.

Some computer programming skills are usually required to connect to an API and make it work, but as web development is becoming more accessible these skills are coming within the reach of researchers. There is more information about these skills at the API University[11] on The Programmable Web. There is a huge amount of free data available via APIs, and they offer an easy way of keeping data up to date – often in real time. So, for anyone who isn't too daunted by the technical aspects, this is a research method worth investigating.

Large-scale surveys

Most countries now regularly carry out large-scale surveys of the population on subjects such as health, crime, education, and so on. The census is one of the best known, and is carried out every five years in some countries, such as Australia, and every 10 years in others, such as the UK. However, there are many other surveys that may be of interest to social researchers. For example, in the UK, some of these include:

- Annual Population Survey: a survey introduced in the mid-2000s, providing information on a range of topics, such as health and education, between the 10-yearly censuses.
- Crime Survey for England & Wales: carried out biennially from 1982 and then annually from 2001, focusing on people's experience of crime rather than reported crime, and one of the largest social surveys conducted in the UK.
- British Social Attitudes: annual since 1983, covering attitudes to a range of subjects including health and social care, education, and social inequality.
- Family Resources Survey: annual since 1992, covering family resources including welfare benefits, savings, and housing costs.
- General Lifestyle Survey (formerly the General Household Survey): annual since 1971, covering a range of topics including health and education. A longitudinal design component was introduced in the mid-2000s, the survey closed in its current format in January 2012, and is now part of the Integrated Household Survey.
- Health Survey for England: annual since 1994.
- Integrated Household Survey, also known as the Continuous Population Survey: a new approach that began in 2009 and will encompass the General Lifestyle Survey, the Expenditure and Food Survey, and three other large-scale surveys.
- Labour Force Survey: biennial from 1973, quarterly from 1992, covering employment and earnings.
- Life Opportunities Survey: a longitudinal survey, started in June 2009, exploring disability in terms of social barriers.
- Living Costs and Food Survey (formerly the Expenditure and Food Survey, which included the National Food Survey set up in 1940): annual since 1957, covering family incomes and domestic spending. Part of the Integrated Household Survey since 2008.
- National Travel Survey: carried out periodically from the mid-1960s to the mid-1980s, and continuously since mid-1988, to assess people's travelling choices.
- English Housing Survey: annual and in its current form since April 2008, when it was formed by a merger between the Survey of English Housing (annual from 1993) and the English House Condition Survey.
- Scottish Health Survey: carried out in 1995, 1998, 2003 and annually from 2008.
- Welsh Health Survey: conducted periodically since the mid-1980s.

Much of this data collection is now being standardised across Europe through Eurostat, which is the Statistical Office of the European Communities, based in Luxembourg.

Surveys in the USA include:

- American Community Survey: a monthly survey that has been conducted since 1940 and includes labour force and earnings data.
- General Social Survey: an annual survey conducted since 1972 that covers a wide range of topics and attitudes, and has had an international component since 1982 (there is more information on international surveys later in this chapter).
- National Crime Victimization Survey: a bi-annual survey, similar to the British Crime Survey, which has been conducted since 1973.
- National Health Interview Survey: annual since 1957.

Surveys in Canada include:

- General Social Survey: a five-yearly survey conducted since 1985 covering a range of topics including population, health, time use, victimisation (similar to the British Crime Survey), education, work, family, housing, ageing and social engagement.

Surveys in Australia include:

- Australian Health Survey: five-yearly from 1977 to 2001, then three-yearly, most recent results available (at the time of writing) from 2017–18.
- Longitudinal Surveys of Australian Youth: began in 1995, designed to track young people through the transitions in their lives.

Surveys in New Zealand include:

- Household Economic Survey: conducted annually since 1973, the full survey has run every three years since 1998 with smaller versions each year in between; includes population and income/spending.
- Household Labour Force Survey: conducted quarterly since October 1985.
- New Zealand Crime & Safety Survey: every three years since 2003 (formerly the National Survey of Crime Victims, conducted in 1996 and 2001).
- New Zealand Health Survey: every five years since 1992, continuous since 2011.

International surveys

There are a number of international groups that collect and disseminate potentially useful data. For example, the Organisation for Economic Co-operation and Development (OECD) is an international alliance of, at the time of writing the third edition of this book, 38 member countries representing over two-thirds of the world's goods and services. The OECD collects and disseminates data on education, social expenditure and the labour force, among other things.

Also at the time of writing, the International Social Survey Programme (ISSP) has 42 member countries and works on cross-national collaboration in general social surveys. Even more impressively, the United Nations website provides access to a free database, UN data,[12] which includes data from many countries on population, education, health, labour force, crime, social and economic issues.

Working with secondary data

Many other websites hold, or act as portals for, secondary data. These include census websites, local government websites at city, county and regional/state levels, health service websites and even national newspaper websites. Faced with this immense wealth of data, it can be hard to find data that is directly relevant to your own research questions; it is a bit like looking for the proverbial needle in a haystack. The best way to look for useful data is to take a step-by-step approach:

1. Identify a website that seems likely to hold data that is relevant to your research.
2. Read the website's FAQs – if only the headlines – to ensure you know enough about how the site works for your purposes.
3. Search the site, using appropriate search terms.
4. Save any data you find which looks useful (if you can't download the data, then save the URL by using a 'bookmark' or 'favourite' in your web browser, or copying-and-pasting the URL into a document with a note of where it leads).
5. When you have finished searching, assess your saved data more thoroughly to establish how useful it can be for your research.

You can repeat this process until you have enough secondary data for your needs.

You will then be able to analyse the data using the same analytic techniques you would use for primary data. These methods are covered in Chapters 11 and 12.

Conclusion

Secondary data has a great deal to offer researchers. So much, in fact, that researchers are increasingly doing projects using secondary data alone. There are good ethical reasons for this so, if it is feasible, it makes great sense to use just secondary data.

There are also disadvantages and barriers to using secondary data: it may not truly answer your research questions, it may not be readily comparable, and it may not be accessible in the first place. This means some researchers will need to collect primary data. A range of methods for doing this is set out in the following two chapters.

CASE STUDIES

Ana wants to find some secondary data to show how many families are non-heterosexual, to help her contextualise her work. However, this proves difficult because official agencies don't collect any relevant information. Many don't collect information about sexual orientation at all, and those that do, collect data about individuals, not about families. This puzzle will take time for Ana to solve.

Ali realises there is a gap in his research design: he and his co-researchers have not considered talking to staff, to find out what they think about how the service they provide could be improved. He discusses this with his co-researchers, and they think first of interviews, but they are all concerned about how busy the staff are. So they consider other ways to investigate this, and decide to ask for anonymised case records and meeting minutes, which they can analyse to find out more about the service. They will then present their draft findings and recommendations to the department's staff for discussion before the work is finalised.

EXERCISES

1. Visit the website of a national archive and spend some time exploring the online resources in your subject area.

2. Find a large-scale survey that could contextualise some research you are doing or would like to do. Explore the survey's findings and write a contextual paragraph for that research.

3. Design a research project that could be carried out using only secondary data.

Discussion questions

1. What are the ethical reasons for using secondary data?
2. What ethical problems might you face when using secondary data?
3. Why might a researcher not make their data available for others to use?

Debate topic

Secondary data is too unreliable to be of use in research.

9

Primary data collection: conventional methods

Chapter summary

This chapter includes:

- Quantitative data collection:
  - Counting
  - Measuring
  - Questionnaires
- Qualitative data collection:
  - Interviews
  - Focus groups
  - Documents
  - Observation

Introduction

The collection of data is often the first thing people think of in connection with research or evaluation. A common misconception is that more data always leads to better research. As we saw in Chapter 5, this is not the case:

> There's a danger of people burying themselves in data. Don't ask too many research questions. Set the agenda firmly at the beginning and find out only what you need to know, or you will be drowning in numbers and information, which is nice to have, but not necessary.

Too much data, particularly qualitative data or data in a variety of formats, can become unwieldy and difficult to analyse:

> When it came to analysing data I think I dumped about a third of the questions that were asked that weren't relevant to what we were doing.

Collecting data that you don't use is unethical because it places an unnecessary burden on participants. However, insufficient data will definitely lead to poorer quality research. It isn't always easy to figure out how much data you need.

 When you're planning your data collection, try to work out the smallest amount of data you can collect that is likely to provide an adequate answer to your research questions.

You don't have to collect data using one method alone. In fact, using more than one method can be helpful, and this is known as 'triangulation'. The term has its origins in physical sciences, such as land surveying and water navigation, where two known points are used to find the location of a third. In social research, collecting data using two or more different methods can help you to look at your research topic in different ways. Triangulation doesn't apply only to primary data collection. Depending on your research question, you may be able to use more than one theory to underpin your work, collect more than one kind of document or literature, analyse your data in different ways, and so on. I am not suggesting that you should try to do all of this, or even any of it if it is not relevant to your research or evaluation. However, it is important for you to know that it is an option, and to do the necessary thinking to decide whether or not you want to take it up. If you are interested, see the section on mixed methods research in Chapter 4.

Data collection is the most visible part of research, and often the most fun. Almost half of the interviewees for this book said data collection was their favourite part of the research process – not necessarily the easiest part (although it was for some), but definitely the most enjoyable.

Collecting quantitative data

Some research questions lend themselves to the collection of quantitative data. In particular, questions of 'how many' or 'how much' require numerical answers. Much quantitative data can be collected from existing sources such as organisational monitoring information, or national statistics such as those discussed in Chapter 8. For now, we're looking at quantitative data that you need to collect yourself.

Your research may be entirely quantitative, entirely qualitative, or a mixture of the two. Mixed methods research is becoming more and more common. Even research that is essentially quantitative, such as drug trials, is now likely to include a qualitative element, such as patients' self-reports of possible side effects. And even research that is mostly qualitative, such as an investigation of users' and carers' views of a service for people with learning disabilities, will include a quantitative element, such as the number of people who use the service.

It may be that you need to collect only a little quantitative data, and all you have to do is ask for it. But if you are conducting, say, a needs assessment, or an evaluation in which you want to compare baseline data with outcome measures, you will have to collect a sizeable amount of quantitative data.

There are three main methods of collecting quantitative data: counting, measuring and using questionnaires.

Counting

Collection of primary data by counting is not used often in social research, but it does have a role to play. For example, in the transport survey discussed in Chapter 5 of this book, the researcher might count the number of buses that arrive in a given time period.

Counting itself is often used in social research, but mostly in the context of secondary data (as we saw in Chapter 8). Nevertheless, when you are planning your research or evaluation project, it is worth giving a little thought to whether there is anything you can usefully count, and if so, what that is and how it can best be counted.

Measuring

Some practitioners will be familiar with scales used to measure certain variables in people's lives. Health professionals may use scales to assess, for example, the severity of a patient's depression or their quality of life. People who work in Human Resources (HR) will know of personality profiling tools that aim to measure someone's personality type. This kind of measuring instrument is also widely used in research (Pallant, 2010: 5).

If you are interested in a specific variable of individual people, such as motivation, intelligence or spiritual beliefs, you will find it useful to know that many devices exist to measure these kinds of variable. Such a device may be called a scale, tool, inventory or instrument. They consist of a series of questions that are designed to measure the variable. Some of these measuring instruments include several hundred questions, while others are of a more manageable size. If you want to use one of the more complex measuring instruments, you are likely to need training first, while the simpler ones can be used straight away.

Most measuring instruments will have been tested to ensure that they work and that they are reliable, generalisable and valid. In this context, 'reliable' means that a device will yield consistent results even if it is used by different researchers, in different environments, at different times, or with different groups of participants. 'Generalisable' means that findings from the use of a device can be generalised from your sample to the population.

There are several types of validity. For example, face validity (also known as content validity) refers to whether the device actually measures what it is supposed to measure. Internal validity assesses whether every item in the device is clearly related to the overall aim of the device. External validity checks that the overall aim of the device is closely related to other indicators of the variable.

 Use a measuring instrument that has been thoroughly tested for reliability, generalisability and validity.

Even though there are hundreds, perhaps thousands, of these devices, finding a suitable measuring instrument for your own research can be a challenge (Pallant, 2010: 5). You may find one that appeals to you through the literature, and a useful resource is given in the 'Further reading' section at the end of this book. If not, the internet is a rich source of measuring instruments, many of which are free to use for non-commercial purposes. For example, the Psychology Tools website includes links to numerous scales and measures. It is worth using a measuring instrument that has been tested thoroughly, because then you will have a range of studies with which to compare your own research.

 Search the internet using the name of the variable you are interested in, plus 'measurement', plus 'scale', 'tool', 'inventory' and 'instrument' in turn. So, if you are researching anxiety, you would search on: 'anxiety measurement scale', 'anxiety measurement tool', 'anxiety measurement inventory' and 'anxiety measurement instrument'.

A device may be completed by the research participant or by the researcher. The researcher can complete a device face-to-face with the participant, over the telephone or using an online communication system such as a chat room, video conferencing or software that lets you make calls over the internet, for example Skype (see Chapter 10 for more on data collection online). Some devices enable a researcher to complete them using observation alone, but this method has more limited application.

It is possible to develop and test your own measuring instrument, but this is a complex and time-consuming process. It is not advisable to attempt this unless you are doing it in the course of your work, with sufficient resources and support from your management, or for more advanced academic work such as doctoral study.

Questionnaires

Questionnaires are primarily instruments for collecting quantitative data. They can also be used to collect qualitative data in the form of open questions with text answers. These enable the person answering the questionnaire to write down their response in their own words, rather than marking one or more options from a list or range. Here is an example:

Please could you tell us what we can do to improve our service? Write your answer in the box in your own words.

```
┌─────────────────────────────────────────────────┐
│                                                 │
│                                                 │
│                                                 │
│                                                 │
│                                                 │
└─────────────────────────────────────────────────┘
```

However, open questions with text answers are not used frequently, for two main reasons. First, they demand more of participants, as they take a comparatively long time to answer and require more literacy and creativity than marking a pre-determined option. This can reduce your response rate. Second, they demand more of researchers, as the data collected from these questions is more complicated to code and analyse than numerical data from questions with pre-defined answer options. If you are designing a questionnaire and you find that you want to include a lot of open questions, you should consider doing interviews instead.

Some people think closed questions just mean binary answers such as 'yes/no' or 'agree/disagree'. In fact, there are several kinds of closed question. For example, you can ask people to choose one from a range of options, several from a range of options, rank their responses or complete rating scales. Here are examples of each of those question types:

Choose one option:
Which activity do you like best from the following list? Please tick one only.

☐ Reading
☐ Gardening
☐ Eating out
☐ Cooking
☐ Visiting museums or art galleries
☐ Going to a performance, eg, play, musical, gig
☐ Listening to music at home
☐ Playing sport
☐ Watching TV
☐ Social networking (Facebook, Twitter etc)
☐ None of the above

Choose more than one option:
Which of these activities have you enjoyed in the past month? Please tick all that apply.

☐ Reading
☐ Gardening

- ❏ Eating out
- ❏ Cooking
- ❏ Visiting museums or art galleries
- ❏ Going to a performance, eg, play, musical, gig
- ❏ Listening to music at home
- ❏ Playing sport
- ❏ Watching TV
- ❏ Social networking (Facebook, Twitter etc)
- ❏ None of the above

Ranked responses:
Please rank these activities in order of preference, starting with 1 for the activity you like best.

- ❏ Reading
- ❏ Gardening
- ❏ Eating out
- ❏ Cooking
- ❏ Visiting museums or art galleries
- ❏ Going to a performance, eg, play, musical, gig
- ❏ Listening to music at home
- ❏ Playing sport
- ❏ Watching TV
- ❏ Social networking (Facebook, Twitter etc)
- ❏ None of the above

Rating scale (sometimes called the Likert scale):
Please circle one number to indicate how satisfied you are with the service you received.

1	2	3	4	5	6	7
Satisfied						*Very dissatisfied*

There are several arguments for and against using questionnaires, which are summarised in Table 9.1.

Anyone can put together a questionnaire that looks convincing, but a questionnaire that will yield useful results needs to be developed carefully. There are some established good practice points in designing questionnaires, and these are covered in the literature recommended in the 'Further reading' section at the end of this book.

Table 9.1: Pros and cons of questionnaires

Pros	Cons
Questionnaires are quick and cheap to develop and administer	Standards of design and development are often so low that the results are not worth having
Email can be used to send questionnaires, with higher response rates than other methods, and to chase up unreturned questionnaires	Email is no use for contacting people who don't have access to computers or the internet, and for those who do, questionnaires can be difficult to open and use if software is incompatible
Participants can complete the questionnaire at their own convenience	Response rates are often low, so results are unrepresentative
Participants have time to think about their answers	Questionnaires assume that people have answers available in an organised way
It is easy to maintain participants' anonymity	It is difficult to motivate potential participants
There is no interaction between researchers and participants to affect participants' answers	The way questions are worded can affect the answers given
It is easy to get information from a lot of people in a short time	Data may be incomplete and/or inaccurate, and misunderstandings cannot be corrected
Each participant is asked exactly the same questions, and can be given exactly the same responses to choose from	Participants have little or no input into the research agenda, and may feel frustrated if the questions or the permitted responses don't fit their view or experience of the subject
Flexibility is available with open-ended or text response options	People with low levels of literacy, or whose first language is not that of the questionnaire, are unlikely to be able to respond at all
Questionnaire data can enable you to test a hypothesis	There is no way to check the honesty or accuracy of the responses
Data analysis is, in general, quicker and easier than analysis of other types of data	There is no way of knowing what lies behind the responses given, or what participants might have contributed if they had been able to choose how they responded, so interpreting the analysed data can be problematic
With a big enough response rate from a representative sample and careful statistical analysis, results can be robust	Questionnaires are more liable to superficial questions than other methods, which can lead to irrelevant or unhelpful results (particularly if the questions are prepared by researchers who have little or no experience of the subject)

Ask closed questions wherever possible, because this will lead to higher response rates and make analysis easier.

 Only use open questions when you don't know enough about the subject to write appropriate options for people to choose from; you are asking about particularly sensitive issues; or you want to give the participant the opportunity to contribute to the research agenda.

 Pilot a draft version of the questionnaire with people from outside your target group, to check the questions and layout for any problems. Then revise and refine the questionnaire on the basis of your participants' feedback. Piloting may seem like extra work, but finding and fixing any problems with your questionnaire at an early stage can save you a huge amount of time later in the research process.

 If you are comfortable with technology, set up a questionnaire online. There is free and user-friendly software to help you do this such as SurveyMonkey, which will give you a unique survey link that you can use to reach people by email, on web pages, in Facebook links, through a blog, via Twitter, and so on. This has three main advantages over paper questionnaires. First, it is more flexible and less prone to errors than sending out questionnaires by email or post. Second, you can create quite complex questionnaires that would look off-puttingly long and complicated on paper, but online respondents will only see the questions that are relevant to them based on their answers. For example, say question 1 is a 'yes/no', if the answer is 'no' the respondent is instructed to go to question 7. On paper, they would have to read through the questionnaire to find question 7, whereas online, they wouldn't even see questions 2–6, so the questionnaire would seem shorter and easier. Third, online questionnaires prevent mistakes at the data-inputting stage, because that is done automatically. (If you use SurveyMonkey, you will need to pay a small fee, but it is well worth the cost.) However, again, you won't be able to use online questionnaires if your target group includes people who don't readily use computers and the internet.

Collecting qualitative data

Qualitative data is any data that is not in the form of numbers. This data is often in the form of words, but also includes audio data, video data, photographs, artwork, and so on. There is a wide range of methods for collecting qualitative data. These include interviews, focus groups, collecting documents, observation and collecting visual data.

Interviews

If you enjoy talking to people and hearing their stories, you will probably enjoy doing some interviews for your research. Interviews were very popular with the interviewees for this book:

> I love listening to people's stories, and I find it so rewarding and such a gift that people are willing to sit down and tell you about themselves. People you've never met, you ring them up, with addiction recovery they're telling you their major epiphanies and people are so generous, I get a lot from that, it feels like a privilege.

If you are planning to conduct interviews, I have a few recommendations. First, wherever possible, don't use the word 'interview' when communicating with potential interviewees. It is the technical term in research and evaluation, but for many people, 'interview' has negative connotations of being tested against covert standards through job interviews, university interviews, disciplinary interviews, and so on. I tend to say things like, 'I'd like to hear what you think of X for my research', or 'Could we have a chat about X for the evaluation I'm doing?' rather than 'Can I interview you?'

Second, people must be able to give free and informed consent to taking part in a research interview (Davies, 2007: 101). 'Informed consent' is another technical term in research, which means that someone must be able to understand why the research is being done, by whom, how any information they give you will be used, and so on. 'Free' means they must not be forced or coerced into taking part, as that would be highly unethical. It's fine to ask, even to be a little bit persuasive, but nothing more than that, and you must always take 'no' for an answer. People are not repositories of data for researchers to download at will; they are human beings with complex lives to manage. Everyone has the right to say 'no' to voluntary work – and taking part in research, unpaid, is voluntary work. A reward such as a gift voucher for interviewees or focus group members is a nice gesture, if you have the budget, but should be given as a 'thank you' rather than used as a lure. Furthermore, you should make it clear to anyone you interview that they have the right to stop the interview at any point and to have their data withdrawn from your research, either then, or later, if they wish. It is helpful to give a cut–off point after which this won't be possible because, as you get into the data analysis and writing, it becomes more and more difficult to extract the contribution of one individual's data from your interpretations.

Third, please make sure you look after your own safety – and, by implication, that of your interviewees – when conducting research interviews (Davies, 2007: 101). Try to choose a location where there are other people around, such as a room in a community centre, workplace or college, or any public place where confidentiality would not be compromised. Don't invite people to your home, or go to theirs, unless you're absolutely sure it would be safe to do so. (See Chapter 3 for more on researcher safety and wellbeing.)

Interviews are a great exercise in listening. This is an undervalued skill in our society, where we teach children how to talk but we don't teach them how to listen. When you are doing a research interview, try to listen actively, that is, to hear and understand not only the person's words but also their whole message. To do this, you need to:

- pay attention to the interviewee's body language and facial expression;
- make sure your own body language is conveying receptive attentiveness (open relaxed posture, appropriate facial expressions in response to their words);
- encourage the interviewee to keep talking – nodding your head and short utterances like 'yeah' and 'mm–hm' are helpful here;
- be comfortable with silence when an interviewee needs time to think or reflect;
- check you understand what they are saying by asking questions about anything you're not sure you understand fully, and taking the time to summarise their comments;
- react and show emotion if they tell you something shocking or upsetting – don't be afraid to do this; the interviewee will be reassured by your humanity.

Most importantly, you need to concentrate on whatever the interviewee is telling you. As far as possible, don't let yourself get distracted by noise and movement around you, or by your own thoughts of appointments you need to make and what you should pick up at the supermarket on your way home. Focusing on someone else's opinions for a while is often a surprisingly therapeutic experience for the researcher as well as for the interviewee. You will find that interviewees tell you they value the experience.

There are several arguments for and against using interviews, which are summarised in Table 9.2.

 Send your questions to participants in advance. This is good ethical research practice, as it shows participants exactly what you're interested in and reassures them that they will be able to contribute. This also enables participants to prepare if they wish. Not all will take up the opportunity, but the interviews will often be quicker when they do.

 You can interview people in pairs, thereby getting two views in approximately the time it would otherwise take to get one. The participants would need to be from the same target group and happy to be interviewed together. People in pairs are less likely to indulge in small talk or start telling you their life story. However, there is a risk that one may inhibit the other to some extent.

Table 9.2: Pros and cons of interviews

Pros	Cons
Interviews yield rich data	Interviews are time-consuming for researchers and participants
Face-to-face interviews let the interviewer include observational elements, such as from the participant's appearance or body language, that are not available with other methods	The researcher's interpretation of the data from a face-to-face interview may be affected by the quality of the rapport they developed with their participant
Interviews can be conducted by telephone, which saves time and costs and increases anonymity	Not everyone is comfortable using the telephone, and it can be harder to create a rapport over the phone than in person
An interview equivalent can be conducted by email, which avoids transcription and so saves time and money; this also helps in reaching some groups of people, for example, those with severe hearing impairment	Conducting an 'interview' by email can make it more difficult to follow up interesting answers with supplementary questions
Interviewers can follow up interesting answers with supplementary questions	Interviewers' input can influence participants' answers
Unstructured interviews can be particularly useful at the exploratory stage of a research project	Unstructured interviews run the risk of missing important issues or degenerating into a general chat
Semi-structured interviews allow participants to participate in setting the research agenda, which may be more politically acceptable, lead to more useful data, or both	Semi-structured interviews make it harder to compare data from different individuals or groups
Structured interviews enable clearer comparison of data from different individuals or groups	Structured interviews require the question designer to be able to consider all the issues that are relevant to the participants
Recording data enables exact reproduction of someone's words and pauses	Transcribing interview data is time-consuming and expensive

If you can touch-type at a reasonable speed, you can record interview data straight onto a laptop or desktop computer. You need a headset for telephone interviews, but these are readily available and cheap. Your data won't be as exact as recorded and transcribed data, but it will be close, especially if you leave out people's speech tics (for example, 'you know' and 'I mean'), fillers ('er', 'um') and repetitions. Also, you can use all sorts of acronyms and abbreviations, and ignore any spelling mistakes, because you can tidy up your data straight after the interview. (And I do mean *straight* after – otherwise you'll forget what those abbreviations meant.)

There is more information about how to conduct interviews in the 'Further reading' section at the end of this book.

Focus groups

A focus group is, in fact, a type of interview, but conducted with a group rather than an individual or a pair of people (Robson and McCartan, 2016: 298). However, while one person having a chat with one or two other people is a fairly normal social situation, one person facilitating a group discussion is quite unusual. Therefore, running a focus group will generally demand more skills and energy from you, as a researcher, than conducting an interview.

Several interviewees expressed an awareness of and interest in focus groups, but few people actually used them for collecting data, and those who did found that the process was full of pitfalls:

> I don't think I fully anticipated how long it would take to get people and to get everything organised. To work out where the focus groups were going to be, and when, and start recruiting people. I think you also need to look at what communities you're trying to engage; some will take longer than others. Two focus groups filled quite quickly, two others that were specifically for the BME [black and minority ethnic] community, they took time. So it's not just about what you're doing, but how long it's going to take you, and don't underestimate that.

There are several arguments for and against using focus groups, which are summarised in Table 9.3.

Instead of setting up a focus group especially for your research, think about whether there are existing groups you can use to make contact with potential participants. For example, you can reach teenagers through youth clubs, students via student unions, parents of young children at toddler groups, drug users through support groups, and so on. Negotiating contact with an existing group will save you all the time it would take to set up a group of your own, find a venue, and so on. You will need to negotiate this with the group's 'gatekeeper', that is, the person who can help you reach your potential participants. This is usually the person who organises or runs the group. Make sure the gatekeeper understands what you need, and that you can have an appropriate amount of time with the group's members. It's frustrating to sit through someone else's meeting and then be allocated five minutes at the end just as everyone is putting on their coat to leave.

Table 9.3: Pros and cons of focus groups

Pros	Cons
Focus groups can yield rich data	To be conducted effectively, traditional focus groups need two moderators, one to facilitate and one to take notes
Focus groups enable you to get the views of several people at once	Focus groups can be time-consuming to arrange
Some people are more relaxed in groups than one-to-one	Not everyone is comfortable speaking in a group
Focus group moderators can follow up interesting answers with supplementary questions	Moderators' input can influence participants' answers
Unstructured focus groups can be particularly useful at the exploratory stage of a research project	Unstructured focus groups run the risk of missing important issues or degenerating into a general chat
Semi-structured focus groups allow participants to participate in setting the research agenda, which may be more politically acceptable, lead to more useful data, or both	Semi-structured focus groups make it harder to compare data from different groups
Structured focus groups enable clearer comparison of data from different individuals or groups	Structured focus groups require the question designer to be able to consider all the issues that are relevant to the participants
A single moderator can use participatory action research techniques (see Chapter 4 for more on this) to enable focus group participants to construct research data	Research data constructed through participatory action research techniques is not as rich as recorded verbal data
Recording focus group data enables a fairly exact reproduction of what was said	Transcribing focus group data is time-consuming and expensive. Also, it is sometimes difficult to identify the different speakers, and often impossible to understand what is said if more than one person is speaking at the same time

 TIP Email focus group questions to potential participants or gatekeepers in advance (or, if necessary, post them). This is good ethical research practice, as it shows potential participants exactly what you're interested in and reassures them that they will be able to contribute. It also enables people to prepare. Not all will take the opportunity, but if at least some do, the group is likely to run more smoothly.

If you can touch-type at a reasonable speed, you can record focus group data straight onto a laptop computer. Your data won't be as exact as recorded and transcribed data, but it will be close, especially if you leave out people's speech tics (for example, 'you know' and 'I mean'), fillers ('er', 'um') and repetitions. Also, you can use all sorts of acronyms and abbreviations, and ignore any spelling mistakes, because you can tidy up your data straight after the interview. (And I do mean *straight* after – otherwise you'll forget what those abbreviations meant.)

If you decide to use focus groups, you can find more information about how to do this in the 'Further reading' section at the end of the book.

Collecting documents

In Chapter 7 I wrote about how you can use documents to give background and context to your research. Using documents as data is subtly different. When you're using documents for background and context, you are primarily interested in the content of those documents. Of course you need to read critically, and take into account relevant aspects such as the author's location and perhaps the source of funding for the work you're reading. But when you're using documents as data, the identity of the document is also relevant.

A document is not just a container for content (Prior, 2011: 95). Documents are also tools for people to use as they act in the world. For example, one of the negotiating techniques suggested by Professor Stuart Diamond in *Getting more* is to use organisational standards to help you get what you want. So if you receive poor service from a business, instead of ranting and raving, you could find its customer service standards on the internet and then calmly quote the obligations stated in that document. Diamond suggests that using documents as tools, in this kind of way, can have astonishing results (2010: 83–112).

Some documents have a wider impact on society. Government enactments and legal judgments fall into this category. Other documents hold people's instructions and wishes, whether a child's letter to Santa or an adult's last will and testament, and so are, in a sense, an extension of the writer. A document may be anywhere on the spectrum from intensely private, such as a diary that was only ever intended for the writer to read, to very public, such as a newspaper article published on the internet.

As we saw in Chapter 7, when you use documents for background, you need to read and think critically to help you select and evaluate documents. Using documents as data requires you to develop your skills in critical reading and thinking further, so that you can also categorise, compare and contrast documents, find patterns, identify interesting phenomena and recognise items of significance (Cottrell, 2005: 17).

As with other methods of data collection, there are pros and cons to using documents. These are set out in Table 9.4.

Table 9.4: Pros and cons of using documents as data

Pros	Cons
Huge quantities of documents are freely available in libraries and on the internet	The sheer number of documents available can make it difficult to find and select those that will be most relevant for your research
Documents at the private end of the spectrum can offer fascinating insights into people's lives and social topics	Documents at the private end of the spectrum can be difficult to obtain, and to get consent to use in research
Newspapers and magazines offer contemporaneous data	Newspapers and magazines have an 'angle' that is designed to please their readers, because their main concern is sales (which also means they cost money)
Newspaper and magazine journalists can often interview people who researchers would find difficult to access	Newspaper and magazine journalists are unlikely to ask questions about everything that would interest a researcher
Documents can contain information that is not accessible in any other way	Some documents are written in languages and/or styles that make them difficult to understand
Documents can contain a great deal of rich and detailed information	Researchers have no control over the structure or content of documents which may not address research questions directly
The use of documents as data can make research more accessible for people who find it difficult to interact with others	Documents alone may not provide all the information needed to answer the research questions

 Where possible, collect digital documents, because they are easy to search electronically.

 Keep careful records of the metadata from the documents you have collected (see Chapter 12 for more about metadata records).

There are no particular shortcuts when it comes to using documents apart from those already covered in Chapter 7. If you decide to use documents, you can find more information about how to do this in the 'Further reading' section at the end of the book.

Observation

This is data recorded by a researcher from their observations of an event or phenomenon. The observations may be conducted in real time, or the event may be filmed and the resulting video data converted into text. This process is similar to transcribing recorded audio data, but with extra complexity because of the need to record both visible and audible information. As a result, it is even more time-consuming than transcribing recorded data, and should be used sparingly, if at all.

It can seem simple just to go and watch people at a business meeting, or a police station custody suite, or a children's playground. But as soon as you try it, you will realise that there is a lot going on (Robson and McCartan, 2016: 322). Comings and goings, interactions, facial expressions, body contact, gestures, speech – what can it all tell you? There is no way you can record everything, so you need to decide what you're interested in and create a recording system, such as a list or grid, to act as an aide-memoire and enable you to record observations of interest quickly and easily. For example, if you were going to observe people with advanced dementia in a nursing home, you might choose to record:

- Independent action: hand gestures, body movement, vocalisation, eating, drinking, sleep.
- Dependent action: receiving food, drinks, personal care, medication.
- Interaction: with other residents, with staff, with family/friends, with other visitors.

You could use these to create a grid, with each form of action listed in a column on the left, time periods of 10 minutes across the top, and cells large enough to enter a number of minutes (or simply a tick, if someone is doing an action for the whole 10-minute period), with a few words of explanation if necessary. You might also want to leave a few blank rows for recording observations that were not pre-determined, such as the particular behaviour of one individual, or simply something you didn't think of in advance.

Observation may be unstructured, where you simply record whatever you notice; semi-structured, where you have a recording system that also allows you the freedom to record other items of interest; or structured, where you record only what you previously decided to record. There is a role for each type of observation, at different stages of research projects and in answering different research questions.

You may have heard of a specific type of observational data collection known as 'participant observation', which was briefly touched on in Chapter 2. This technique was developed by anthropologists and involves observing a defined group of people very closely over a considerable period of time. For example, a participant observer might go to live in a community far from their own home, or be taken on by an organisation as a full-time worker, or go to several religious services per day – often for many months or even years. While participant observation is fascinating to do, and yields rich findings when conducted by doctoral students or experienced researchers, it is difficult for novices and far too time-consuming for busy students and practitioners.

As with the transport survey discussed earlier in this chapter and in Chapter 5, observational data can yield quantitative as well as qualitative data. However, it is primarily a qualitative method.

There are several arguments for and against using observational data, which are summarised in Table 9.5.

Table 9.5: Pros and cons of observational data

Pros	Cons
Observational data can be rich and specific	Observational data recorded by hand may be very subjective, as it is not usually possible to record everything that is said and done
Two researchers, observing the same situation or group, can compare their data after the event to reduce subjectivity	It is not always possible to use two researchers
One researcher can check their data with some or all of the participants after an event to reduce subjectivity	It can be difficult to check data with participants if they are not willing to help, or if different participants have different views of the event, or if a participant feels unfairly represented
Observational data can be useful to confirm (or deny) findings from other methods, for example, questionnaires or interviews	The presence of the observer may affect the behaviour of the people being observed, and there is no way to know whether or not this is the case
Observation is a direct technique that can be useful in situations where other techniques are difficult to use, such as prison visiting rooms, school gates and hospital reception areas	Observation raises difficult ethical issues: how detached or involved should the researcher be? How can consent be obtained from participants?
Covert observation of people in public places – hospitals, cemeteries, courts, streets – avoids the need to negotiate access through a gatekeeper	The covert observation of people for research purposes is ethically dubious
Unstructured observation, where a researcher records whatever catches their eye, can be useful at the exploratory stage of a project	Unstructured observation may produce data that is not easily comparable with data from other observations
Semi-structured observation, where a researcher takes notes on a grid and records whatever else catches their eye, can help in picking up aspects of a situation that might otherwise have been missed	If the situation being observed is very complex or busy, there may be no time for the researcher to do anything other than take notes on the grid
Structured observation, using a grid alone, may be easier for the researcher to manage and produce data that is more comparable, reliable and valid	Data from structured observation may not represent the full complexity of the situation being observed
If recording observational data by hand, thinking through what you want to record and preparing a grid can help you to clarify your research question and themes	Recording observational data by hand can be slow and the researcher may miss things in the situation while they're writing
Video can be used to record observational data at an event where a researcher also needs to participate	A researcher won't be able to record observational data by hand at an event where they also need to participate
Recording observational data using video enables a fairly exact reproduction of what was said and done	Transcribing recorded observational data from video is very time-consuming and expensive

Unstructured observation is quicker than semi-structured or structured observation because you don't have to spend time thinking through what you want to record and preparing a grid. But this is a false economy of time if it doesn't yield the results you need.

 Whatever kind of observation you want to do, always pilot your method in the setting where you plan to collect your data, or (if that is not possible) somewhere similar. This will enable you either to make sure your method is workable or to revise your method until it works.

 Observational data rarely forms the basis for a whole research project. Observation is more often used as one of a pair or set of data collection methods.

Really, there are no effective shortcuts when it comes to observational data, so I would recommend that you use it sparingly, and only when your research question(s) cannot be answered in any other way. If you do decide to use observational data, you can find out more about it through the 'Further reading' section at the end of this book.

Conclusion

If you have used a method of collecting data in previous research or evaluation, it can be tempting to use that method again because you know how it works. It is better research practice, however, to use the method that is most likely to help you answer your research question(s). This may be among the conventional methods of collecting data in this chapter, or the creative methods outlined in the next chapter.

CASE STUDIES

Ana has already decided to collect primary data using interviews. Learning about other methods has strengthened her view that interviews are the most appropriate method for her research.

In conjunction with his co-researchers, Ali has already decided to use a questionnaire followed by interviews with people who receive a service from the department he is evaluating. He has also decided to analyse departmental documents to find out as much as he can about how well the service works. Now he is confident that these decisions were good ones.

EXERCISES

1. Imagine you are designing some research into how to reduce loneliness among older people in a rural area. Think of at least one advantage, and at least one disadvantage, of collecting data through:

   a. Questionnaires

   b. Interviews

   c. Focus groups

   d. Documents

   e. Observation

2. Which method or methods would you choose for the research, and why?

Discussion questions

1. Which of the methods in this chapter appeals to you most, and why?
2. What are the ethical implications of your answer to question 1?
3. If you were sure your research required you to collect detailed data directly from people, what circumstances would lead you to choose interviews rather than focus groups, or vice versa?

Debate topic

Too much research is done in the world today.

10

Primary data collection: creative methods

Chapter summary

This chapter includes:

- Selected examples of creative data collection methods:
  - Collecting data online
  - Smartphones
  - Enhanced interviews and focus groups
  - Diaries, field notes, journals and logs
  - Visual data
  - Mapping
  - Mobile methods
  - Case studies
  - Collaborative methods

Introduction

Creative methods of collecting data draw on the imagination of participants and researchers. There are myriad options available, and as this chapter can only cover a few, I have tried to demonstrate the diversity on offer by presenting a range of examples. See the 'Further reading' section at the end of the book if you are interested in finding out more.

Looked at one way, all methods of collecting research data were once considered creative, and not so very long ago. Questionnaires were invented in 1838 by the London Statistical Society (now the Royal Statistical Society), researchers borrowed interviews from journalism in the early 20th century, and focus groups were first used in the 1940s. Until the 1960s, research was the preserve of white, able-bodied men, but then the diversity in methods, and those using them, began to expand. Now, the variety of research methods has reached an astonishing level, and is still extending further. Perhaps this chapter will inspire you to devise your own research method, as many others have done before you.

A word of caution, however. It is easy to be seduced by new and innovative methods and forget that your choice needs to be based on those most likely to help you answer the research question. The use of creative research methods should not conflict with the principles of good research practice (Kara, 2020: 8–9).

Do not push yourself more than a step outside your comfort zone when using creative methods because if you do, you risk having a more difficult time.

Participants are not always willing or able to engage with creative methods, so offer them a choice of methods or have a Plan B up your sleeve in case of need.

The rest of this chapter introduces various creative methods for collecting research data. This is not a comprehensive list; in fact, such a list would not be possible to compile, as new methods are being devised all the time.

Collecting data online

Long before the global COVID-19 pandemic, the internet had increased researchers' choices about how to collect quantitative and qualitative data. Every internet user will be familiar with online and emailed surveys and interviews, but it may be less obvious that focus groups, observation and more creative methods of collecting data can also be used online. In the pandemic we learned a great deal about doing research online (Kara and Khoo, 2020a, b, c).

Before the pandemic, market researchers led the way in collecting primary data online through dedicated 'access panels' of people who volunteered to be involved, usually in return for a small 'reward' every so often, such as a gift voucher or some air miles. If you want to find out more about access panels, or experience them as a participant, sites like Ipsos i-Say and Toluna are good places to start. Primary and secondary data can also be collected from existing sites such as social media sites (Twitter, Facebook and so on), blogs, forums or other interactive sites such as newspaper comment boards (Poynter, 2010: 163–6).

There are specific and complicated ethical issues involved in online data collection. The boundaries of public and private space are not always clear; anonymity cannot be guaranteed; and it is not always possible to identify and safeguard vulnerable participants (Markham, 2011: 122–3). The Association of Internet Researchers, an international body, has produced a useful set of guidelines for ethical internet research.[1]

As well as the ethical dilemmas, there are other pros and cons of conducting research in virtual environments. These are summarised in Table 10.1.

Table 10.1: Pros and cons of online data collection

Pros	Cons
Online data collection enables you to reach more people	You may not be able to verify that your participants are who they say they are
Online data collection is often free of cost	Online data collection requires a degree of technical know-how
Observational research can be carried out in public and semi-public areas of the internet	It may be difficult or impossible to obtain full informed consent from all potential participants in public or semi-public areas of the internet
Interviews can be conducted online, via Facebook, Twitter, in chat rooms, etc	Participants recruited online often use pseudonyms that may conceal their gender, ethnicity, disability, etc – and there is no way to assess the credibility of the data collected
Interviews can be conducted by telephone worldwide, with software and apps that let you make calls over the internet, such as Skype and WhatsApp	Not all potential participants will be able and willing to use the internet in the same way as you, which can be a barrier
Chat rooms, video-conferencing, etc enable focus groups to be conducted online	It can be difficult to persuade people to participate in online research
Focus groups can be conducted online via chat rooms or conferencing software, which only needs one moderator, is useful where potential participants are not co-located and provides instant textual data	It can be difficult to moderate a group with no non-verbal cues. Also, there is no guarantee that the person responding is who you think they are. And this method will not reach people on the wrong side of the digital divide
Many creative methods of data collection can be used, or adapted for use, online	Some creative methods of data collection can only be used in person
Good relationships can be created and developed online	It is often hard to perceive emotion accurately in online communication
With some online data collection methods, data arrives ready-prepared for coding and analysis	You will need a system for storing data securely and backing it up frequently

As the internet develops, so do the associated research methods. There is huge scope for creativity, and the constraints of the pandemic encouraged researchers to produce some very innovative practice (Kara and Khoo, 2020a, b, c). However, there are also many ways for problems to arise. If you think your research questions can best be answered through data collected online, you will need to think very carefully about how to collect that data.

More information about collecting data online can be found in the 'Further reading' section at the end of this book. However, as this is such a fast–moving field, I would also recommend searching for information online.

For any method of data collection, always run a pilot.

For online data collection, as with all the other methods outlined in this chapter, I can't emphasise enough that you should always run a pilot (Robson and McCartan, 2016: 400–1). This means testing the method you have adopted or devised with a small number of people from the target group, to find out how well it works. Then revise and refine your method on the basis of your participants' feedback and/or your own observations before doing the bulk of your data collection. This can seem like extra work, but it will save you time later in the process, and will also help to ensure that your research is as good as it can be.

Smartphones

Smartphones can be a great asset for collecting data. They can be used to remind us about appointments, record interviews, take photographs, communicate with participants and make notes. However, there can also be problems as a result of battery run-down or failure, file corruption, virus hacks or being lost or stolen. Also, you cannot assume that participants will have smartphones or, if they do have a smartphone or access to a smartphone, that they are willing or able to use it for research. Some people have other kinds of phones by choice, and some people share their smartphone with others for financial reasons. Also, the use of a smartphone depends on a good connection or internet access, which are not universally available. And the battery needs to be charged, and the smartphone needs to be in credit. Overall, aiming to use smartphones as research tools may not simply be helpful; it may also change the nature of your research (van Doorn, 2013: 392).

Smartphones enable the use of apps to gather quantitative or qualitative data, or both. This can make research more accessible for people who own smartphones and like using apps. It can also offer the immediacy of a diary or journal. However, app developers charge high fees, and it is difficult to create an app that works on all kinds of smartphones. If an app only works on, say, Android phones, this limits the potential participant group in a way that may have implications for the research findings. It may be necessary to provide alternative equipment, such as cameras or voice recorders, for participants who have a different kind of phone or an inadequate connection, or are unable or unwilling to use an app (García et al, 2016: 517). And this can incur even more costs for the researcher.

There are a lot of variables that can affect smartphone use, and the technology is developing rapidly. This means it is difficult to be more specific about how you might or might not be able to use smartphones in your research. The broad pros and cons of using smartphones in research are summarised in Table 10.2.

Table 10.2: Pros and cons of using smartphones

Pros	Cons
For people who have smartphones, they are easy to use for research at no extra cost	Not everyone has, or can use, a smartphone
Smartphones are flexible and powerful tools that can help researchers in various ways	Smartphones can go wrong in a variety of ways, which may cause big problems for research
Smartphones enable the use of apps for collecting data	Not everyone is willing or able to use apps
Data from apps comes ready-prepared	Expertise is needed to create an app for research – and this can be expensive

Enhanced interviews and focus groups

These are interviews and focus groups where objects or creations are present for participants and researchers to focus on during their conversations. One of the early kinds of enhanced interview is known as 'photo-elicitation', where the participant takes photos on a theme from the research before the interview. Then, during the interview, the participant shows their photos to the researcher, who looks, asks questions and listens. This method can be very useful for researching experiences in an environment where the researcher cannot easily be present, such as a holiday or childbirth. Another option would be for the participant to find relevant images in newspapers, magazines or online. This could be useful for historical research. A third option would be for the researcher to collect a set of photos or other images to use with participants. This was done by Catrien Notermans and Heleen Kommers, researchers from the Netherlands, who wanted to know about Catholics' relationships with the Virgin Mary, a very important saint in the Catholic religion. They collected around 30 cards with different iconographic representations of the Virgin Mary – some old, some more modern, some local, some from further afield, and so on. They showed the cards to the participants and asked them to pick the icons they liked and disliked, and then to use those images to explain how they would describe the Virgin Mary. This method proved very useful in enabling the researchers to gain insight into Catholics' relationships with this important saint (Notermans and Kommers, 2012: 615).

Other objects that are used to enhance interviews may be brought to the interview by researcher, participant, or both. Maged Zakher and Hoda Wassif studied happiness in lockdown during the COVID-19 pandemic. They conducted their interviews online and asked each participant to bring with them an object of personal value. People brought a wide range of objects, including a LEGO® model, gardening tools and children's books

(Zakher and Wassif, 2022: 146). They found that this created a sense of anticipation, with both participants and researchers looking forward to the research encounter. It also gave participants more control over the interview, which was beneficial because it allowed for 'more naturally occurring discussions around their choices' (Zakher and Wassif, 2022: 149).

Participants, with or without the involvement of researchers, can make collages, models or other such artworks during interviews or focus groups. Suzanne Culshaw encouraged experienced teachers to make collages during interviews to explore their struggles in the workplace (2019: 268). Julie Dalton asked trainee teachers to make and discuss models in focus groups to investigate how mental health problems could affect their teaching and learning (2020: 35). Other researchers have used LEGO®, Play-Doh, drawing, diaries and journals, and various other creative enhancements. All of the researchers who use enhancements in their interviews or focus groups – many more than those cited here – report collecting more and richer data than they would from standard interviews alone.

 If you want to use enhanced interviews or focus groups, be sure to give very clear instructions to your participants.

I loved conducting the interviews during the research. It wasn't as easy as I thought it was going to be but the views and insights shared by the participants were truly fascinating. They brought ideas that I would never have considered and humbling to have practitioners share thoughts about practice that I would never have heard without the research. The skills that I developed to hear all perspectives, to fully listen and to think about what else is going on in the interaction including myself, are something I use regularly now.

 Be ready to embrace the unexpected, and keep the conversation moving with an open, inquisitive mind.

[I am indebted to Maged Zakher and Hoda Wassif (2022: 153) for the tips in this section.]

Like all research methods, enhanced interviews and focus groups have pros and cons. These are summarised in Table 10.3.

Table 10.3: Pros and cons of enhanced interviews and focus groups

Pros	Cons
Generate richer, more detailed data than standard interviews and focus groups	Takes more time to prepare and more effort during the process
Participants can have more control over the research encounter	Participants may struggle to understand what is expected of them
Enhancements can be used with online interviews as well as in person	Participants may feel uncomfortable with an unfamiliar task
Asking participants to bring objects is usually easy in countries where most people own many things	Some people own little or nothing, through choice or circumstance
Photos can be taken and shared freely using smartphones and tablets	Not everyone has access to suitable hardware, or the skills or abilities to use it
Arts-based methods such as collage and modelling allow participants to express themselves freely	Materials for these methods can be expensive

Diaries, field notes, journals and logs

These are mostly documents generated by researchers, although in some cases researchers may use other people's diaries, field notes, journals and logs as secondary data. The terminology is inconsistent: some people talk of field journals rather than field notes, or divide diaries into 'solicited' for primary data and 'unsolicited' for secondary data. Disciplines and professions have an impact here: one person's reflective journal may be someone else's learning log (see Chapter 6 for more on researchers' own diaries and journals). Barbara Bassot offers a useful distinction: logs are for recording facts such as who did what and when, diaries are for recording what has happened on a given date, and journals are for researchers to write in as they please (2020: 12–13). Field notes are used by researchers to record their observations and thoughts, particularly while they are collecting data (or 'in the field', as it is sometimes called). These can be made in any form.

Diaries are most commonly used for collecting primary data. Researchers from a wide range of disciplines have asked participants to keep a regular record of their experiences, feelings, thoughts or observations, for use as data. This can be useful for a number of reasons. First, it allows participants to make records at or close to the time of an event, which can lead to more accurate data. Second, it is possible to collect data over a period of time, such as by asking participants to keep a weekly diary for a few weeks or months. Third, it can be a useful way of collecting data on personal or sensitive topics (Bartlett and Milligan, 2021: 8–9). And diaries also have an ethical aspect, because participants can take the time to think about how they want to respond to the researcher's prompts or questions.

TIP **If you are going to solicit diaries from participants, think carefully about how to pose your questions or prompts.**

These methods, too, have pros and cons, which are summarised in Table 10.4.

Table 10.4: Pros and cons of diaries, field notes, journals and logs

Pros	Cons
Data recorded at or close to the time of an event may be more accurate	These methods can be onerous for participants
Data can be recorded in writing or by voice, or video, or drawing, or even through stitching	It can be difficult to decide what information to ask for, and in which format or formats
Researchers can use these methods themselves to collect data	These methods can be onerous for researchers
Data can be collected online or even through a dedicated app	Creating apps for research is time-consuming and expensive
These methods can provide usefully comparable data	Participants may not complete records in the ways researchers asked them to
Regular contact with participants can encourage them to use the method	Keeping in touch with participants can be time-consuming for researchers

Visual data

Visual data includes photographs, drawings, collages, paintings, diagrams, and so on. Visual data may be collected from existing sources, such as magazines, the internet or art exhibitions, or created specifically for your research, perhaps through techniques such as photo–elicitation or 'draw and write'.

If you want to collect visual images from existing sources to use as data, there are a huge number of places you can look (Rose, 2012: 47). Examples include:

- image collections on the internet, such as Google Images;
- art galleries;
- museums;
- libraries;
- books;
- magazines;
- catalogues;
- web pages;
- screenshots, for example, of particular moments in video games;
- posters;
- leaflets;
- street advertisements.

You can view some images in a range of ways (Rose, 2012: 48), and this is another form of triangulation. For example, you might see a painting in an art gallery, buy a postcard of it in the gallery shop, view an online reproduction on screen, and print out that reproduction to look at on paper. You might see an advertisement on a hoarding in the street, take a photo with your phone to help you remember, and later find the same advertisement in a magazine. Using different media to view the same image can help to enrich your experience of that image, as we perceive images differently in different contexts. Where there is a unique image that you want to use, such as a specific artwork, do try to see the original if you can.

Photo-elicitation may involve participants' existing photos, or photos created specifically for the research, either by participants or the researcher or both (Prosser and Schwartz, 1998: 123). The rather impenetrable academic term 'photo-elicitation' conceals an everyday activity for people in many parts of the world: one person showing another their photos and telling them about the context for each picture and the histories and relationships of people in them. This everyday activity can be fun for participants and for researchers, and can yield rich data. For example, some years ago, I conducted an evaluation project in which I asked parents and carers of pre-school children to take some photos, as they went about their daily lives, of things that helped or hindered them in looking after their children. As this was in the days before camera phones, they were each given a disposable camera. The participants were encouraged to use some of the film in taking photos for the research and the rest in taking photos for themselves, and were given a set of prints to keep as a thank you for helping with the research. One photo was of a little girl sleeping, and the notes I took as her carer told me about the picture are as follows:

> That was giving me a break, she went to sleep on the settee. She's just so active and into everything I seem to need that little break. I know I try to keep young but you do get tired, when you're, not getting on, but I mean I'm 67 now, so you do get tired. She's so active during the day. I have her from 9 till 3 so it's quite a full day really.

This shows how much information can be elicited from just a few comments on one photo.

The 'draw and write' technique was devised in Nottingham, England, in the 1970s to enable children to express their views and opinions in their own terms (Wetton and McWhirter, 1998: 273). Again, it is based on an everyday activity, drawing, which most children enjoy. The children are given simple and age-appropriate questions and asked to draw their answer, and then add a few words of explanation and/or a title (this can be done by an adult helper, under a child's instruction, if any child's writing skills are not yet up to the task). This also elicits surprisingly rich and fascinating data.

There are some specific ethical issues that you need to consider if you want to use visual data. Images in the public domain may be under copyright.

Photographers and artists earn their livings from making and selling these images, and might take a dim view to a researcher using one without permission. One way around this is for a researcher, or their participants, to create images specifically for the research, but this raises another ethical problem: consent. If created images include any recognisable people, they should be asked to give written agreement to their images being used for research (or, if they were unable to consent for themselves, for example, because they were too young, consent should be given by an appropriate person). The images themselves may be ethically questionable, particularly if they are potentially shocking for readers, such as images depicting gruesome medical matters, violence or pornography.

In some cases, the use of visual data can save you time at the data collection stage, because participants will do most of the work. Sometimes this can happen without you even having to be present, for example, by arranging for the art coordinator of a project for ex-offenders to help their service users to produce work around a particular theme for your research.

However, with visual data, you may need to spend more time on data interpretation and analysis than with other forms of data. This depends on the amount and complexity of the data, and the nature of the client group. For example, data can be collected using the 'draw and write' technique outlined earlier. This can be speedy to collect if you can persuade schools to help you, and can be relatively quick to analyse – but the results yielded are likely to be quite brief. Conversely, collages created by non-English-speaking refugees from conflict zones may yield rich data, but may also be very difficult for an English-speaking researcher from a peaceful country to interpret and analyse. So you will have to balance the type of data you need with the amount of time you have available for data analysis.

There are several arguments for and against using visual data, which are summarised in Table 10.5. More information about the use of visual data can be found in the 'Further reading' section at the end of this book.

Table 10.5: Pros and cons of visual data

Pros	Cons
Visual data is useful in contexts where literacy levels, difficulty in speaking English, learning disability or sensitivities mean that collecting spoken or written data is impossible or unhelpful	Interpreting visual data can be challenging, particularly where there are language barriers
Participants can create much of the data themselves, through photography, painting, collage, etc	You have to convert any visual data into text before it can be fully analysed
Some visual techniques, such as the use of digital cameras and the draw-and-write technique, are suitable for use with young children	Photography of people, for use in research, requires written consent, which may make this method impractical in practice
Visual data can enable participants to convey experiences that are difficult or impossible for them to put into words	Visual data needs to be carefully analysed and then checked against a range of other sources to ensure it is not being interpreted to fit your theories
Visual data collection can be useful when working with disparate groups, as the shared activity can help to bring people together	Some people are not comfortable with visual techniques and may feel their skills in painting, photography, etc are 'not good enough'
Visual data can add an extra dimension to research reports, dissertations, theses, etc	Visual data alone is very unlikely to provide robust answers to complex research questions

Mapping

You probably think of a particular kind of map: perhaps a road map if you are a driver, or an Ordnance Survey or similar map if you like to hike or climb, or a weather map if you are a keen gardener. But there are many different kinds of map that can be used for collecting data. These can be very simple. Market researchers often use concentric circles with a brand or product in the centre, and ask participants to indicate how close they feel to the brand or product by placing a mark somewhere within the concentric circles. Sara Eldén adapted this approach with children aged 5–12. She used five concentric circles on a sheet of paper, with the participant in the centre, and asked them to map their personal networks of care and support (Eldén, 2013: 71).

Maps can also be quite complex. Here are some of the kinds of maps that can be used in research:

• Cognitive maps: show people's perceptions of place and distance.
• Concept maps: show links between ideas.

- Social maps: show relationships between people and communities, networks, organisations, and so on.
- Thematic maps: show variations on a social theme between geographic areas, such as wealth/poverty.
- Transect maps: show the location and distribution of resources and the uses of land or space.
- Floor plans of buildings, ships or other constructions: show what happens where.
- Body maps: life-sized outlines, which can show all sorts of things such as stereotypes and ideals, feelings about physical experiences, aspirations.

Maps can be drawn or annotated by participants, or by participants and researchers together. They can generate quantitative data, or qualitative data, or both. And they can provide a useful visual component to your data.

 Think ahead about how to protect participants' anonymity and confidentiality when using maps to collect data, because you may want to include the maps in your research outputs.

The pros and cons of using maps and mapping in research are summarised in Table 10.6.

Table 10.6: Pros and cons of maps and mapping

Pros	Cons
Maps can help you to collect data that could not be collected in any other way	There are many different kinds of maps, and it can be difficult to know which one to use
Maps provide visual representations that are helpful for some people	Maps can be hard to draw or annotate effectively
Maps can be fun to create and use	Some people are unfamiliar with, or unable to read and use, maps
Maps can be a useful addition to research reports and presentations	Maps can be difficult to analyse

Mobile methods

In some research contexts it is useful, perhaps even necessary, to collect data while moving around. Fieldwork in geography and anthropology has always involved mobile elements. Specific mobile methods have been developed in a variety of academic and professional contexts, and no doubt more will be developed in future. Examples include walking interviews, guided tours and shadowing.

Walking interviews are just that, interviews held while walking (Ellingson, 2017: 120). This method allows participants to have more input into the process, perhaps by choosing the route, or by deciding which aspects of the environment to comment on. Walking interviews can be particularly useful where place is relevant to the research topic, such as in community-based research. A guided tour is a particular kind of walking interview where the participant is in full control of the process, showing the researcher around a place in whatever way they choose. Guided tours can be very helpful for finding out about how other people use and perceive a place, and about their lives and priorities. And shadowing involves following a single person around for a period of time, to find out as much as possible about their experiences and motivations. Shadowing can provide in-depth insights into people's lives, professional and/or domestic work, hobbies and other leisure activities, and so on (Bartkowiak-Theron and Sappey, 2012: 8).

Mobile methods can even be used with groups (O'Neill, 2018). And in the COVID-19 pandemic, I heard of a researcher doing walking interviews remotely over WhatsApp. So there is a great deal of flexibility. These methods enable researchers to collect data in real-world settings. They can generate rich and useful data. They are also quite demanding for the researcher, who has to literally think on their feet in response to a wide variety of stimuli and unexpected events. Perhaps at least partly for this reason, mobile methods are rarely used as the only method of collecting data in a research project. However, they can provide data that would not be accessible through other methods. And they may be particularly useful within methodologies that prioritise participants, such as participatory methodology.

 If you plan to use a mobile method, think carefully about what you will record, and how. You may wish to use a variety of methods: audio recording, voice notes, photographs, and so on.

The pros and cons of mobile methods are summarised in Table 10.7.

Table 10.7: Pros and cons of mobile methods

Pros	Cons
Mobile methods can be helpful when place is relevant to your research	Mobile methods can be demanding for the researcher
Mobile methods allow participants more control within the research encounter	Mobile methods can be time-consuming for researcher and participant
Mobile methods can generate rich, useful data, that could not be generated in any other way	Recording data while mobile can be difficult
Mobile methods are accessible for most people	Some people cannot use mobile methods due to illness or disability

Case studies

A case study is not really a method in itself; it's a way of using a range of methods to look at a single case (Thomas, 2015: 9). That case may be a person, an organisation, a sporting event – any single thing. Case study research may be exploratory, descriptive or explanatory (Yin, 2018: 8). Case study research is different from most other kinds of research because you don't try to generalise from it; you are interested in a holistic, 360° complete view of the case in all its uniqueness (Thomas, 2015: 5). To gain such a complete view, you would need to look at the case in several different ways, using a variety of conventional and/or creative methods with rigorous analysis to obtain new insights about the case under scrutiny (Thomas, 2015: 67).

A research case study is different from a journalistic case study, in which an individual example is used to illustrate more general points in a newspaper or magazine article (Yin, 2018: 19). Doing case study research, you would need to make decisions about what kinds of data to collect, how much data to collect, how to analyse your data, how to manage ethical issues, and so on, just as you would for any other type of research (Thomas, 2015: 112). And as with any other type of research, the quality of a case study will depend on how well you have thought through your key decisions.

The pros and cons of case studies are set out in Table 10.8. More information about conducting case studies can be found via the 'Further reading' section at the end of this book.

Table 10.8: Pros and cons of case studies

Pros	Cons
Case studies are particularly useful for researching things that are unusual or unique	People confuse research case studies with journalistic case studies
Case studies are good for finding out about something in great detail	It can be difficult to work out what kinds of data to collect

Collaborative methods

All the above methods can be used collaboratively. There are also some specific methods that can be useful for people using participatory methodologies (see Chapter 4 for more on these). These can also be useful in organisational or other settings where you want a group of people to work together as part of your research. Here are a few examples:

- Spidergram: everyone has a pen and access to a large sheet of paper where they can write or draw whatever they wish in response to a question or problem written in the middle of the paper.

- Timeline: everyone has a pen and access to a long sheet of paper with a defined timeline (which may extend into the past, or the future, or both) where they can write or draw whatever they wish about events, experiences, wishes or plans at particular times or over given time periods.
- Map: everyone has a pen and access to a large sheet of paper with an outline map, perhaps of a local area or of a publicly accessible building, where they can write or draw whatever they wish about specific locations on that map.
- Ranking matrix: people work together to define options, say for solving a problem, and then to define criteria for selecting an option, before ranking options against criteria to identify priorities for action.

Ranking matrices can be difficult to visualise, so here is an example. A small town community wanted to solve the problem of young people having few activities available to them outside school and home. This problem led to groups of young people congregating in the town centre, which made older people perceive them as anti-social (even though they were, in fact, perfectly well behaved). When young people were asked what activities they would like, they came up with several options, but the town couldn't afford to provide them all, so a ranking matrix was used to prioritise the young people's ideas against available resources. People of all ages worked together to define criteria for selection, and the options and criteria were made into a matrix, as shown in Table 10.9.

Table 10.9: Ranking matrix

		Criteria for selection				
Options	Cost	Construction needed?	Accessibility (age, ability, etc)	Staff needed?	Venue available?	Total
Skateboard park	5	5	1	0	1	12
Youth club with games	4	1	2	5	3	15
Cookery courses	3	1	1	3	1	9
Dance studio	2	1	4	4	4	15
Music club with DJ	2	1	3	4	4	14

The group decided to mark each cell from 1 to 5 on the basis of discussion, with the marks running from 5 for undesirable criteria (high cost, construction needed, low accessibility, staff needed and no venue available) to 1 for their opposites. Scores would then be added together such that the maximum possible score would be 25 and the minimum would be 5, with the lowest-scoring option being the best. The outcome of the discussions was that cookery courses scored 9, the skateboard park scored 12, and the other options all scored more highly. (The cookery courses could be run by volunteers at a local school; the skateboard park would be expensive to build but would have minimal running costs and no staff requirements.) The group decided that cookery courses could start straight away. They would also begin raising funds to build the skateboard park, and would start work on the other options once funds for the skateboard park had been secured.

 If you want to use collaborative methods, make sure you have enough space and materials.

 Participants may have difficulty accessing collaborative methods for any number of reasons – dyslexia, dyscalculia, arthritis making it difficult to use a pen, and so on – so offer different options to help everyone join in.

The pros and cons of collaborative methods are summarised in Table 10.10.

Table 10.10: Pros and cons of collaborative methods

Pros	Cons
Collaborative methods can be more egalitarian than most	Collaborative methods can create or reveal friction or factions within a group or team
The resources needed are generally inexpensive	Collaboration between researchers increases project costs
Collaborative methods can generate rich data from a variety of perspectives	It can be difficult to integrate varied data into coherent findings

Conclusion

Creative methods of collecting primary data can be interesting and fun to use for researchers and for participants. However, they also present challenges. Most of the methods in this chapter are rarely used alone. Some yield data that is time-consuming and difficult to analyse. And when data collection is interesting and fun, it can be tempting to collect lots of data, which also sets up difficulties at the analysis stage.

Creative methods are not better than conventional methods; they are useful to know about because then you have more options. The best research method or methods are those that give you the best chance of answering your research question, within any constraints such as budget or timescale. And the more you know about methods, the more likely you are to make a sensible choice.

CASE STUDIES

Ana had already decided to use media stories to enhance her interviews. Again, learning about other methods has strengthened her conviction that this is the best method for her research.

Ali discusses creative research methods with his co-researchers, and they decide to add mapping to help them work out whether the service covers all geographic areas equally and evenly.

EXERCISES

1. Go back to the research questions you constructed for the exercises in Chapter 5. What kind(s) of data would you collect to answer those questions? How would you collect that data?

2. Find a report of a research case study and read it critically. Would you have made the same or different choices about the methods used? Why?

Discussion questions

1. Which of the methods in this chapter appeals to you most, and why?
2. What are the ethical implications of your answer to question 1?
3. What do you see as the pros and cons of creative methods of data collection in general?

Debate topic

Using creative methods to gather data is just playing; it is not proper research.

11

Quantitative data analysis

Chapter summary

This chapter includes:

- Advice on preparing quantitative data
- Information about coding quantitative data
- Ways of analysing quantitative data including descriptive and inferential statistics

Introduction

When you have collected all your data, you need to analyse it, to find a way to understand what it can tell you. This is both one of the most challenging and one of the most rewarding parts of the research or evaluation process.

One of the people I interviewed for this book said they found data analysis to be the easiest part of the research process. Another said quantitative data analysis was the easiest. On the other hand, four said that for them, data analysis was the hardest part of the research process. Also, two of the interviewees who teach novice researchers commented that new researchers often find data analysis to be one of the most difficult parts of the process.

Even if your own data is mostly quantitative, you need to understand the principles of data analysis for both types of research. This chapter will cover quantitative data preparation and analysis, and the next chapter will cover qualitative data preparation and analysis, looking at how to cross-analyse and synthesise different datasets. I would urge you to read both chapters, even if you feel a definite antipathy to one or the other. This is because you will need to understand both kinds of data analysis to be able to read critically reports of quantitative, qualitative and mixed methods research. Also, some of the advice and information applies to data analysis in general, and this has been split between the chapters.

Preparing quantitative data

Before you can analyse your data, you will need to prepare it for analysis. How you do this depends on the form of your data. For example, data from a pile of handwritten questionnaires with numeric answers, such as from rating scales, would need to be collated by hand or entered into a computer application such as Microsoft Excel, StatsDirect or SPSS:

> Data preparation can be surprisingly time-consuming.

 TIP   **As far as possible, prepare your data as you collect it.**

Although it is time-consuming, data preparation can easily be done in small bite-sized chunks. Even five spare minutes can be usefully spent in collating figures or entering data onto a spreadsheet. Also, data preparation is one of the most boring parts of any research project, so setting aside a whole day for it can leave you feeling ready to jump off the nearest cliff by lunchtime. Boredom leaves you vulnerable to making mistakes or poor decisions, so try to interleave your data preparation with more interesting tasks. And remember, the end result will be worth the effort.

It is essential to be meticulous about the accuracy of your data preparation. To err is human, so it is worth putting in place some safeguards. However you prepare your data, you need an easy way to trace your collated data back to the source. One implication of this is the need to preserve your original data, in its original form, at least until your research or evaluation project is finished. Then, when you are analysing your data, if you think you may have found an error, you can go back to the original data and check. Of course, how you do this will depend on the type of data you have collected. For example, if you have questionnaires, number each one before you start collating your data, and make sure each entry in your handwritten lists or spreadsheet rows is linked to the number of the individual questionnaire.

It can also be helpful to be aware of the types of error you might make. Some common errors that occur when preparing quantitative data are:

- Errors of omission: leaving something out.
- Errors of commission: putting something in which shouldn't be there.
- Errors of transposition: putting two numbers, letters, or words in the wrong order.

In an extreme scenario a single error could completely change your findings. For example, a misplaced zero can cause a factor of 10 error. Putting the decimal point in the wrong place can also be a very big mistake. With handwritten numbers, it can be easy to confuse a 1 with a 7; with typewritten numbers, it can be easy to misread, say, 78332 as 78832.

 Take great care to be accurate when preparing your data – it will save you time in the end.

Because data preparation is so boring and therefore prone to errors, it is worth proactively checking a selection of your data for any mistakes when you have finished the preparation. You can do this by taking a random selection of your original data and checking that it has all been entered correctly. If you find no mistakes, you can be reasonably confident that the whole dataset is error-free. If you find a few mistakes, correct them as you go and keep checking until you are sure you have found them all. If you find a lot of errors, you will need to start again and re-enter the data, being much more careful this time around.

Coding quantitative data

When you are working with quantitative data, coding happens very early in the process. For example, if you are entering questionnaire data into a spreadsheet, you need to convert data into codes before you begin. Let's say your first question was about someone's marital status. The categories you offered were:

- Unmarried
- Married
- Living with partner
- Divorced
- Widowed

A simple way to code these categories is with their initial letters: U, M, L, D and W. So on your spreadsheet, the first row will be numbered '1' to correspond with the first questionnaire, and the first column will be labelled 'Marital status'. You look at your first questionnaire and the participant has indicated that they are living with their partner, so you enter an 'L' in the first cell of your spreadsheet. Another option is to code the categories numerically from 1 to 5. Some people prefer numbers, some prefer letters – either enable you to sort your spreadsheet, so it doesn't matter which you use.

Some quantitative data doesn't need converting into codes. The answers to questions such as 'How many children do you have?', or rating scales where the participant is asked to circle a number from 1 to 7, can be transferred directly on to a spreadsheet as they stand. But most data will need to be coded for ease of analysis.

You may also need to specify a code for missing data, such as XXX, 99999 or −42, or you may choose to leave cells blank where data is missing. There are two kinds of missing data. The first kind is where a participant, whether accidentally or deliberately, has not answered one or more questions. The second kind is where a question is structured such that the participant is unlikely to give all the possible answers. For example, consider this question:

Which of these beverages do you drink every day? Please tick all that apply.
☐   Tea or herbal tea
☐   Coffee
☐   Hot chocolate
☐   Water
☐   Fresh fruit juice
☐   Fruit squash or cordial
☐   Wine
☐   Beer, lager or ale
☐   Spirits
☐   Liqueurs

It is very unlikely that anyone would drink all of those every day, so there will be some 'missing data' in the answers to this question.

As there are two kinds of missing data, you may choose two different codes, one for each kind. For example, you could leave a cell blank for a non-answer to an option in a question like this one, and use the code 99999 where a participant has not answered a question at all.

Quantitative data analysis

As we saw in Chapter 5, when you are working with numerical data, your analytic methods will be partly determined by the sampling technique you use. For any kind of sample, you can use descriptive statistics, such as percentages, averages, medians and ranges, to communicate your findings. If you have used a random sample, you can also use inferential statistics, such as t-tests, analyses of variance, factor analyses or regression analyses, to show how your findings relate to the wider population from which your sample was drawn. Inferential statistics can also be used with purposive or convenience samples, although calculations based on these kinds of sample will be less dependable for generalisation to the wider population. With a random sample, inferential statistics enable you to draw conclusions about the wider population, and to assess how likely or unlikely it is that those conclusions could have arisen by chance alone.

If you are mathematically eager, you may find this an exciting prospect and long to discover more. Conversely, if you are mathematically timid, you may find the prospect alarming. Either way, I have help for you.

I'm not going to go into detail about how to do statistical calculations. There are numerous textbooks on the subject, some of which are listed in the 'Further reading' section at the end of this book, and there is also a good deal of advice online. If you enjoy mathematical activity, you can do the calculations yourself. If you don't, there is software available to do it for you, such as Excel, which has the facility to do many statistical calculations, or SPSS (Statistical Package for Social Scientists), which is specialist software widely used for quantitative data analysis in research and available in most universities (Greasley, 2008: 2). Another option is StatsDirect, which does most of the same things as SPSS but is significantly cheaper and easier to use (Davis, 2010).

One interviewee shared their experience of both SPSS and Excel:

> I love playing with data. I loved looking at SPSS and seeing what we could get out of it. We asked the question 'Would you prefer a same-sex service?' and we found out that most women would prefer a same-sex worker and most men would prefer a woman. That was quite interesting and unexpected. With SPSS you can play with things like that, gender, sexuality. We did have a monitoring section at the end of our questionnaire so we could cross-reference things, and use SPSS to do a bit of the data crunching, also at the same time learning about SPSS. One thing for this is I wouldn't specialise too much on SPSS, it's a very expensive package, and with training I think programs like Excel can do just as much work. SPSS can be about £1,000 a licence; Excel, especially if you're a charity, you can pay £20. Obviously you need training but it can do most of the same things. We only had 80 participants, SPSS was like a sledgehammer to crack a walnut in some ways.

Excel is a Microsoft Windows application so cannot be used by everyone. Also, even a low cost can be prohibitive for some researchers. If you want free spreadsheet capabilities, check out OpenOffice, which is open source cross-platform software. OpenOffice includes a spreadsheet application that is very similar to, and compatible with, Excel. There is also an open source option for full statistical analysis, the R Project for Statistical Computing, commonly known as R.

Although you don't need to be able to do the calculations yourself, in order to analyse your data effectively, you will need to know which calculations are appropriate for your kind(s) of sample, and the rationale behind each calculation (Bryman and Cramer, 2009: 69). Further, when you write up your research or evaluation, you will need to explain the justification for using the calculations you chose. I will give a brief introductory overview here, but if you are intending to analyse quantitative data, and you are not already statistically literate, you will need to read more widely to ensure that you understand what you are doing well enough to explain it to others.

Descriptive statistics

Whatever kind of sample you use, you will need to describe your data for your readers. Descriptive statistics, which can be used for any sample, include ways to summarise parts of your data. For single variables, these are known as 'univariate' statistics (Bryman and Cramer, 2009: 68), and include frequency distributions, measures of central tendency and measures of variability.

Frequency distributions show how many times a particular variable has occurred, of itself and in relation to other variables. These are usually in the form of tables, graphs or pie charts. Table 11.1, and Figures 11.1 and 11.2 show examples.

Table 11.1: Frequency distribution table

Marital status	%
Unmarried	10
Married	25
Living with partner	32
Divorced	28
Widowed	3
Missing	2
Total	100

Figure 11.1: Bar graph

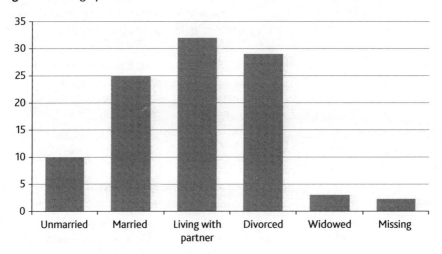

Figure 11.2: Pie chart

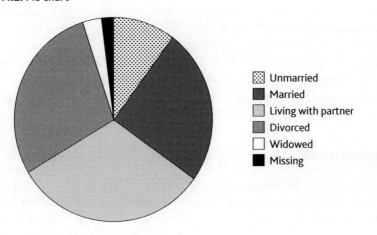

Measures of central tendency include mode, median and mean or average. The mode is the value occurring most commonly, so in this dataset it would be 'Living with partner' at 32%. The median is the middle value in a dataset after it has been ranked in order (or, if there are an even number of values, the average of the two middle ones). This is usually used for ordinal data, and is useful when there are a few extreme scores or the data is skewed. The mean, or average, is the total of all the values divided by the number of values. The mode and the median can be used with any type of data, but because the mean involves calculation, it should only be used with interval data. (See Chapter 5, or the Glossary at the end of this book, for definitions of ordinal, interval and other types of data.)

Let's say you have a dataset of test scores. Your subjects scored 23, 47, 32, 46, 37, 36, 42, 33, 46, 29 and 41. To work out the median, you need to put these scores in order, to find the central score:

23 29 32 33 36 **37** 41 42 46 46 47

The median score is 37. The mode is 46, because it occurs most frequently, but in this dataset that's not very useful because it is so close to the top score. Data like this, where the mode is close to one end of the ranked data, is called 'skewed' data.

We can calculate the mean for this dataset, as test scores are an example of interval data. If we add all the scores together, we find that the total is 412. Then we can divide this by the number of scores, that is, 11:

$$412 \div 11 = 37.5$$

The mean of the dataset is 37.5. This is very close to the median, which is often the case.

Measures of variability show how values vary around the central tendency, and include range and variance. Range is the difference between the smallest and largest values, and can be used with any type of data. So the range for this dataset can be calculated as follows:

$$47 - 23 = 24$$

The range of the dataset is 24.

Variance is an estimate of the average distance of each value from the mean. To calculate this, you first need to work out the mean, then how far away each value is from the mean (ignoring any negative signs), and then take an average of those scores. This is known as the 'average deviation'. Computer statistics software will calculate this for you, or its close relative, the 'standard deviation', which is another way of showing how much variation there is from the mean. Like the mean itself, variance involves calculation, so should only be used with interval data.

As we know the mean of our small dataset, we can calculate its variance. In order, each score's distance from the mean is:

14.5 8.5 5.5 4.5 1.5 0.5 3.5 4.5 8.5 8.5 9.5

If we add all these together, we find that the total is 69.5. Then we divide this by the number of scores, that is, 11:

$$69.5 \div 11 = 6.3$$

The variance of the dataset is 6.3.

There are also descriptive statistics that can be used to describe the relationship between two variables, or 'bivariate' statistics (Bryman and Cramer, 2009: 68). There are two main kinds of these relationships. The first is known as 'covariant', which means the variables change in accordance with each other. An example of this might be a baby's age and weight in its first year of life – weight should increase quite steadily as age increases. Variables are also covariant if one increases as the other decreases. For example, as an adult's food intake increases above the necessary level, their quality of health decreases, so these variables are again covariant. The second kind of relationship between variables is known as 'independent', which means the variables change independently of each other. So, for example, a researcher might hypothesise that women are more left-wing than men, but find that the same number of women and men are left-wing and right-wing, that is, that political affiliation is independent of sex.

As with univariate statistics, bivariate statistics include graphs, tables and statistical calculations. These are scattergraphs, frequency tables, correlation coefficients and the chi-squared test.

Scattergraphs give an overview of the relationship between two variables by constructing a graph with one variable on each axis and plotting each piece of data as a dot or an x. If there is a relationship between the variables, the scattergraph should enable you to identify its direction and its strength. To help with this, you can sometimes draw a line of best fit or 'regression line', with an equal number of dots or x's above and below. If the line is diagonal from bottom left to top right (or thereabouts), there is a positive relationship between your variables; if it is diagonal from somewhere in the top left to somewhere in the bottom right, there is a negative relationship. Where all the dots or x's are close to the line, the relationship is a strong one; if they are widely scattered throughout the graph, the relationship is weak. If the dots or x's are so widely scattered within the graph that your line is horizontal, the variables are independent. Figure 11.3 is an example of a scattergraph with a strong positive relationship between the variables.

Bivariate frequency tables have one variable in a column and the other in rows. So, for example, you could construct a bivariate frequency table to help you look at the relationship between marital status and income. It might look as shown in Table 11.2.

Figure 11.3: Scattergraph showing strong positive relationship

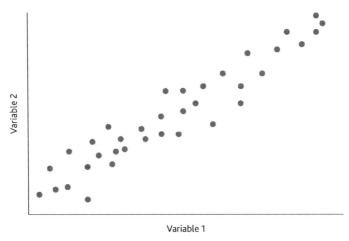

Table 11.2: Bivariate frequency table

Income:	Under £15,000	£15,000 to £29,999	£30,000 to £44,999	£45,000 to £59,999	£60,000 and over
Unmarried					
Married					
Living with partner					
Divorced					
Widowed					

You can enter your data into the table, simply in terms of the number of participants who fall into each category. When all the data has been entered, you will be able to see whether there is any kind of relationship.

Scattergraphs and bivariate frequency tables can be used with any type of data, and are useful for summarising data and giving the overall picture, but they give only a flavour of the relationship between the variables. For a more precise description, you need to use more complex calculations.

The correlation coefficient is similar to variance, giving an estimate of the average distance of each point on a scattergraph from the regression line. Like variance, it should be used only with interval data. All computer statistics software offers ways of calculating correlation coefficients, such as Pearson's r, Spearman's rho and the phi coefficient. The closer the result of the calculation is to 1, the stronger is the correlation between the two variables. However, it is important to note that a correlation does not indicate cause and effect. Think of the baby in its first year of life. It does not gain weight because it increases in age, or vice versa. It gains weight because it is fed; it increases in age because time passes. The variables have a positive relationship but one does not cause the other; the causes of each increase lie outside the relationship between the two variables.

The chi-squared test, written as χ^2, gives us more detail about the relationship between the variables in a bivariate frequency table. It does this by showing whether and how the values differ from those that would exist if the two variables were independent. This calculation yields a probability figure, and the smaller this is, the less likely it is that the values in the table could have occurred by chance. So, for example, if the probability figure is $p<0.05$, there is only a 5% risk that it could have occurred by chance; if the probability figure is $p<0.01$, there is only a 1% risk that it could have occurred by chance. One word of warning, however: while a bivariate frequency table can contain any type of data, the chi-squared test requires nominal (categorical) data (Howitt and Cramer, 2005: 134).

Inferential statistics

Apart from descriptive statistics, the other main type of statistics is known as inferential statistics. These calculations allow us to infer something about a population from a sample. This is where you need a random sample that is large enough, or (in statistical terminology) has the 'power', to allow us to make these inferences. As we saw in Chapter 5, this raises the question, 'How large is large enough?' There are a number of online web pages that offer calculators of statistical power to determine the answer to this question, which is worth doing at an early stage to ensure that you are planning a sample that will give a firm basis to your calculations (Myers et al, 2010: 15).

Even with sufficient statistical power, inferential statistics are not fool-proof. An inference may have a robust rationale, accurate calculations and still be wrong. As with the chi-squared test, inferential statistics use probability figures to estimate how likely it is that the result could have occurred by chance. A convention in inferential statistics is to say that if $p<0.05$, the result is 'statistically significant'. This is an unfortunate use of vocabulary, because people confuse statistical significance with practical and social significance, but, in fact, it means only that the result has a very low risk of having occurred by chance (Bryman and Cramer, 2009: 128).

To confuse things further, some descriptive statistics, such as the mean, correlation coefficient and chi-squared test, can also be used as inferential statistics in contexts where they enable us to infer something about the population.

Perhaps the most commonly used inferential statistics are the t-test, F-test, analysis of variance (ANOVA), cluster analysis, factor analysis and regression analysis. These should be used only with interval data.

The t-test is used to establish whether there is a difference between the means of two different groups. Ideally you need equal sample sizes, although this is not essential. There are two main kinds of t-test. The first is the 'dependent samples t-test' or 'paired two-group t-test', where the scores are linked in some way, such as having been provided by the same person before and after an intervention. The second is the 'independent samples t-test' or 'unpaired two-group t-test', where the scores are not linked, such as having been provided by an experimental and control group.

The F-test, also called the 'variance-ratio test', compares the variability of the scores around the mean across two groups. It is often a helpful calculation to use alongside a t-test, as two groups may have the same mean but different levels of variability.

ANOVA enables the comparison of the variability of the scores around the mean across more than two groups. The simplest kind of ANOVA involves just one independent and one dependent variable. There are more complex ANOVA calculations available for research with more than one independent variable. One example is a multivariate ANOVA (or MANOVA), which can have any number of independent variables, of differing levels, and two or more dependent variables.

Cluster analysis, factor analysis and multiple/hierarchical regression analysis are also multivariate tests. Cluster analysis helps to sort data into categories, and is particularly useful where you have a number of variables and you want to find out whether some kind of classification system can be produced from your data. Factor analysis helps to identify factors that underlie the relationships between variables. Multiple/hierarchical regression analysis works towards prediction: here the independent variable is called the *predictor* variable and the dependent variable is called the *outcome* variable. This kind of regression analysis helps to show how the dependent variable changes as one independent variable changes (while the others are held constant).

All the inferential statistics described in this chapter are parametric, which means that the result of a calculation on the basis of a sample allows us to make an inference about the parameters of the population. They each have non-parametric equivalents, which don't make the same probability-based assumptions as the parametric statistics. These are shown in Table 11.3.

Table 11.3: Parametric tests and non-parametric equivalents

Parametric test	Non-parametric test
Paired two-group t-test	Wilcoxon signed-rank test
Unpaired two-group t-test	Mann-Whitney U test
ANOVA (one independent variable)	Kruskal-Wallis test
ANOVA (more than one independent variable)	Friedman test

There are also non-parametric versions of cluster analysis, factor analysis and regression analysis.

If you want to know more about statistics, there is lots of free advice and a variety of interactive web pages and calculators on the StatPages online.

This chapter merely skims the surface of statistics. There are many more descriptive and inferential, parametric and non-parametric tests available for you to understand and use if you wish. In order to give a critical reading to reports of research including quantitative analysis, you do need to be able to understand the terms used here well enough to be able to use them yourself in conversation and writing. If you are new to statistics, this will almost certainly mean you have to read more widely to deepen your understanding. There are several books that can help you in the 'Further reading' section at the end of this book. You might also find it useful to take some statistics training or consult a statistician.

Allow plenty of time for coding and analysis, whether quantitative or qualitative. There are few short cuts at this stage. It is essential to take the time to figure out what the data has to tell you rather than imposing your own perspectives or, at worst, prejudices on to the analytic process.

Conclusion

The methods for analysing quantitative data are quite straightforward, but this does not mean it is a simple process. The need to prepare data carefully, and choose statistical tests wisely, means a lot of care and thought is needed. This can lead to frustration if your findings are inconclusive, or if they point to a conclusion that is not the one you had hoped to see. Remember, however, that all new knowledge is useful. And sometimes you will find what you had expected or hoped to find. Best of all, sometimes you will find something completely unexpected and thrilling. Analysing data is always an adventure: by turns uncomfortable, exciting, boring and fun.

> **CASE STUDIES**
>
> Ana considers various methods of quantitative analysis for her complex secondary dataset. She ends up making a complex calculation based on numbers of LGBTQIA+ adults, numbers of adults who form partnerships and numbers of adults who have children. This feels unsatisfactory to Ana, who thinks the figures she has found are probably inaccurate and so her calculation will be very approximate, but she knows it is the best she can do.
>
> Ali enters his questionnaire data into Excel and performs descriptive statistical calculations that enable him to describe and begin to interpret the results. He also does a little quantitative analysis of numbers of cases and meeting attendances.

EXERCISE

Pick two of the following datasets and decide how you would prepare, code and analyse the data:

a. Historical bus timetables and fares, to contextualise a present-day evaluation of local bus services.

b. Data on city-wide prevalence of three types of cancer in different age groups, part of a study into the health of that city's population.

c. Information about the number of people who voted for all candidates in the last two general elections, by local government region, to investigate any connection between location and voting behaviour.

d. Number of mentions of men, women, non-binary and trans people in the sports sections of a tabloid and a broadsheet newspaper, as part of a study of gender representations in the media.

Discussion questions

1. How can researchers avoid bias in quantitative data analysis?
2. Do descriptive statistics simply describe, or do they also interpret? Why?
3. What can researchers do to prevent statistics misuse?

Debate topic

Quantitative data is too superficial to be useful.

12

Qualitative data analysis

Chapter summary

This chapter includes:

- Advice on preparing qualitative data
- Information about coding qualitative data
- Ways of analysing qualitative data including content analysis, thematic analysis, discourse analysis and narrative analysis
- A real-life example of qualitative data analysis
- An overview of data synthesis

Introduction

In one respect quantitative data analysis is more straightforward, because the data is always numerical – or in a form that can be converted into numbers, such as questionnaire responses. By contrast, qualitative data comes in a variety of forms: text, images, sound, and so on.

Starting to work with qualitative data can feel quite daunting:

> You've got it all, you've got this great mountain of *stuff* and then it's okay, what do I do with it now? This is all very interesting, but what do you do with it? I didn't have a computer program or anything like that, so it was your highlighter pen and your cut-and-paste to get things into categories. How was I deciding how to get things into categories? Was it what people said? If some of them said 'integrated working', did they all mean the same thing or something different?

However, this big task can be broken down into small manageable steps. The last chapter covered the steps for preparing and analysing quantitative data. This chapter does the same for qualitative data, and also explains how to synthesise findings from two or more datasets.

Preparing qualitative data

Qualitative data also needs to be prepared for analysis, although in different ways from quantitative data. Audio data from interviews or focus groups would need to be transcribed. This is a laborious task, and you could take a short–cut, such as by outsourcing the transcription of your data or using a digital transcription tool. However, I would advise against this. Outsourced transcriptions need careful checking, so they don't save as much time as you might think. Digital transcription tools are not perfect, and again, the transcriptions will need checking. Also, some digital 'tools' are actually services where transcripts are typed by underpaid people overseas. And the process of data preparation, although tedious, helps to familiarise you with your data:

> Be prepared to transcribe the data yourself. It is time-consuming but you will understand the breadth and depth of what is being studied. It's the going back over the interviews when you're listening to them that really helps. That's when you start to pick up on the connections, the differences or similarities, the further questions you want to ask – so in the end, it helps to make it quite interesting.

When transcribing, it helps to have a pedal to operate your audio software, to leave your hands free for typing. There are dozens of options, with many (at the time of writing) priced between US$50–100. If you search the internet for 'foot pedals for transcription' you will find the latest models and prices. Another option is to use voice recognition software such as Dragon or the open source CMU Sphinx. This kind of software will 'train' itself to your voice, although you will need to speak slowly and clearly. This means it will not transcribe accurately from your audio data itself, especially if you have conducted focus groups. However, it does enable you to transcribe by repeating rather than typing the data. If you are a slow typist, or have any problems with your hands, voice recognition software can be a great asset.

Some software products, such as NVivo, let you import your audio files and code them directly. This saves time, but one drawback is that you can't then use text search functions to supplement your coding, which can be very useful during analysis.

Pictorial data would need to be converted into text for thematic analysis, whether by hand or using computer software such as Microsoft Word (for a PC) or Apple Pages (for a Mac). Alternatively, the data could be scanned and loaded into a computer application that facilitates analysis of visual data, such as NVivo. If you are analysing visual data by hand, it may be easier if you can create electronic copies of any images you have only in hard copy, and then enlarge them before printing them out. This will give you more room to code and annotate each image. If your images are very rich in content, you may need two or more printouts of each one, which can then be used to analyse different features of the image. Another helpful tool for analysis by hand is the metadata record, similar to the literature grids discussed in Chapter 7. As with those grids, you would need to devise your own metadata record to meet your particular needs. For example, if you were using photos as data, you might create a metadata record like the one shown in Table 12.1.

Table 12.1: Metadata record for photographic data

Photo number	
Date photo taken	
Location	
People in photo	
Buildings in photo	
Objects in photo	
Landscape in photo	
Other photo content	
Other features (blurred, horizon angled, etc)	
Purpose of photo	
Any other comments	

Then you can use one metadata record for each photo, which will help you to compare and contrast the significant features of your data. You can see that I have left some blank rows at the end of the metadata record, which is good practice as you may think of significant features as you work through your data preparation that you didn't consider at the start. I expect you realise that this system would also work with documents, interviews, and so on.

 Create and use your record sheets electronically to save time at the analysis stage.

You have to spend quite a bit of time getting the data ready for analysis, so you need to build in time for that. The focus groups had to be transcribed, and I didn't get any admin support or resources for that, that was me, and actually transcribing everything took a month. That was a month I didn't anticipate, which is stupid because I should have thought about it.

If you have also read the previous chapter, I offer no apology for repeating the next couple of paragraphs, because this is so important. Despite being time-consuming, data preparation can easily be done in small bite-sized chunks. Even five spare minutes can be usefully spent in transcribing audio data or scanning pictures. Also, data preparation is one of the most boring parts of any research project, so setting aside a whole day for it can leave you feeling as if you would rather be bathing in baked beans by lunchtime. Bored people are more likely to make mistakes or poor decisions, so try to interleave your data preparation with more interesting tasks. And remember, the end result will be worth the effort.

It is essential to be meticulous about the accuracy of your data preparation. Even the most careful researcher can make mistakes, so it is worth putting in place some safeguards. Regardless of how you prepare your data, you need an easy way to trace your transcribed data back to the source. One implication of this is the need to preserve your original data, in its original form, at least until your research or evaluation project is finished. Then, when you are analysing your data, if you think you may have found a mistake, you can go back to the original data and check. Of course how you do this will depend on the type of data you have collected. If you are transcribing audio data, it is helpful to put a note in the transcript at regular intervals, say every one or two minutes, of the amount of the recording you have transcribed. This way, if you need to check for accuracy, you can find the relevant section of the recording quickly and easily.

It can also be helpful to be aware of the types of error you might make. Some common errors that occur when preparing qualitative data are:

- Misreading errors: reading something incorrectly.
- Substitution errors: writing something incorrectly.
- Typographical errors: reading correctly and intending to write it correctly, but accidentally pressing the wrong key on a keyboard.

In an extreme scenario a single error could completely change your findings. When working with textual data, the substitution of just one letter can cause a dramatic change of meaning. Consider this interview excerpt:

> I told my precious wife I loved her.

An error could be made here by misreading, or substitution, or through a 'typo' as the character 'c' is next to the 'v' on a QWERTY keyboard:

> I told my previous wife I loved her.

Or:

> I was only kidding him.

The 'd' is next to the 's'….

> I was only kissing him.

And, of course, these kinds of errors will not be detected by a computer spell-checker. Similar errors can easily be made with handwriting, too, especially when you're reading writing which isn't clear, or if you're writing in a hurry yourself (or if your handwriting, like mine, resembles the scrawl of a demented gibbon).

Because data preparation is so boring and therefore prone to errors, it is worth proactively checking a selection of your data for any mistakes when you have finished the preparation. You can do this by taking a random selection of your original data and checking that it has all been entered correctly. If you find no mistakes, you can be reasonably confident that the whole dataset is error-free. If you find a few mistakes, correct them as you go and keep checking until you are sure you have found them all. If you find a lot of errors, you will need to start again and re-enter the data, being much more careful this time around.

Coding qualitative data

Unlike quantitative data, qualitative data is coded after it has all been prepared. A code, or label, may be applied to a chunk of data of any size from a single word to an entire file or document. With qualitative data, as with quantitative data, you decide what the codes will be, and this can feel quite daunting (Rapley, 2011: 280). There may be almost unlimited ways to code any section of qualitative data, which may be partly why people who are new to research often find this a challenging task. However, many systems have been devised to help with this, and two seem particularly useful.

One approach is to devise a 'coding frame' or a set of words and phrases to guide your coding of the data. For example, if I was doing a piece of research to evaluate the effectiveness of a partnership service, I might decide to use this simple coding frame:

> Partnership working pros (PWP)
> Partnership working cons (PWC)
> Partnership working barriers (PWB)
> Partnership working enablers (PWE)
> Service effective (SE)
> Service effective reasons (SER)
> Service ineffective (SI)
> Service ineffective reasons (SIR)
> Suggestions for improvement (SFI)

Then, as I was coding the data, I would pay attention only to data that related to one of the points in my coding frame. This doesn't mean I would use the wording in the coding frame as my codes, although I would probably use the initials of the coding frame descriptions – PWP, PWC and so on – to link the chosen codes to the coding frame.

To show you how this works in practice, here's a piece of interview data:

> At operational level, we work together well. We know all the social workers and they know us, so we can sort problems quickly. But sometimes, you know you have to go higher for a decision. That slows it down, because the managers, they don't talk to each other.

Using my simple coding frame, I might code this data, as shown in Table 12.2.

Table 12.2: Data coded using a coding frame

Data	Code(s)
At operational level, we work together well.	SE operational level
We know all the social workers and they know us,	SER operational level PWE communication
so we can sort problems quickly.	PWE time SE time
But sometimes, you know you have to go higher for a decision.	PWB decision-making level
That slows it down.	PWB time SI time
because the managers, they don't talk to each other.	SIR strategic level PWB communication

I have added explanatory notes that will be used again, where appropriate, as I work through my data.

Where possible, it is best to devise a coding frame in conjunction with others, such as managers, tutors, commissioners and/or service users.

Where you have to devise a coding frame alone, use background literature to help you identify relevant points to include.

This may look like fairly thorough coding, and indeed it is. But the coding of this piece of data might look very different if I used a different system. The other approach that many people find particularly useful is known as 'emergent coding', or whatever the researcher perceives to be of interest in the data. With this system there is no prior plan. Using this approach, the coding of the same piece of data might look as shown in Table 12.3.

Table 12.3: Data coded using emergent coding

Data	Code
At operational level	Front line
we work together well	Solidarity
We know all the social workers and they know us	Solidarity Reciprocity Us and them
social workers	Social workers
so we can sort problems	Problem-solving
quickly.	Speed Time
But sometimes, you know you have to go higher	Hierarchy
for a decision	Decision-making Problem-solving
That slows it down,	Speed Time
because the managers, they don't talk to each other.	Hierarchy Communication Us and them
managers	Managers

I expect you have noticed some differences between this emergent coding and the previous version using the coding frame. With emergent coding, there are more codes – the coding is denser. Also, the codes are more abstract and exploratory. You may have noticed that on two occasions, I have coded small segments of data using the same word or phrase for the codes as in the data itself: 'social workers' and 'managers'. This is known as 'in-vivo coding' and is useful where there are particular categories that you might want to review at the analysis stage. Table 12.4 summarises the pros and cons of both types of coding.

Table 12.4: Pros and cons of two kinds of coding

Coding frame	Emergent coding
Quick, efficient, targeted	Takes longer, but more thorough
Restrictions may cause researcher to miss points of interest	Researcher should be able to include everything they are able to perceive
Two people coding the same data should produce similar findings	Two people coding the same data may produce quite different findings
Can be seen as more 'valid' or 'reliable' from some standpoints	Can be seen as more 'reflexive' or 'inclusive' from some standpoints

I don't think either type of coding is better than the other. The point is to use the type of coding that is most appropriate for the research you're doing within the timescale you have.

I find it easiest to code qualitative data using a software application called NVivo, which is widely used in social research worldwide and is often available through universities. There are other qualitative data analysis software applications, including Quirkos (the most affordable), MaxQDA and Atlas.ti, and web-based software such as Dedoose. There is also free open source qualitative data analysis software online, although this can change rapidly, so if you are interested, I would recommend making your own search and reading reviews.

> Now that I know how to use NVivo, which I only learned towards the end of doing my research, I would start by understanding a data management package and I would use that from the beginning because I think being systematic about what you're reading, thinking, collecting, it's all part of the same project isn't it? I don't think we often talk to people about it, we say, 'You do your reading and then you collect your data', but actually they should be completely intertwined and I do think the software can help.

Whichever application you choose will take time to learn to use and, if not free open source software, may be expensive if you have to buy it yourself. Also, you need to make sure you can export your coded data if you wish, so that you're not locked in to one type of software.

There are other ways of coding data. For example, coding can be done in word processing software, using tables like those shown earlier, or by using coloured highlighting, comment functions or any combination of these and other features that you wish to devise. Coding can also be done by hand on printouts of your data. If you prefer to use this method, I recommend setting up your data to print out double-spaced, on one side of the paper only, and with wide margins at each side and top and bottom. This will leave you plenty of room to insert codes. I would not recommend coding qualitative data by hand if you have more than a few pages, as although the coding itself is manageable, the analysis can become very difficult.

When you have finished coding, the next step is to establish how many times you have used each code. The codes that are used most often will give you an initial idea of the major themes in your data – and can often be surprising. The codes that are used least often will need to be checked to see whether they are genuinely rare or whether they are examples of unclear thinking and should be combined with other codes. Box 12.1 shows an edited excerpt from the methodology chapter of my doctoral thesis that illustrates how this can work in practice.

Box 12.1: Managing outlying codes in practice

The codes were reviewed. First, each code that had been used only once or twice was checked, to assess whether it was truly a single or double instance of something in the data, or whether it was a subject that had been coded in another way elsewhere in the data so that the coding needed revision. For example, the word 'objectives' had been given a single-word coding once. A text search established that the word did indeed only appear once in the data. Then the paragraph in which it appeared was studied, and showed that it appeared in the phrase 'targets and objectives'. 'Targets' had also been given a single-word coding, which appeared ten times in five stories/discussions. The decision was made to change the coding so that the phrase 'targets and objectives' was coded with 'targets', as the phrase in its context was tautologous, and the code 'objectives' was deleted.

The code 'trapped' had been used twice in two stories/discussions. The code 'constrained' had been used 13 times in six stories/discussions. This led me to wonder whether the text coded as 'trapped' could legitimately be combined with the text coded as 'constrained'. All the text coded with both was carefully re-examined, and I concluded that combining them would detract from their meaning, as the text coded as 'trapped' expressed more helplessness than the text coded as 'constrained'. So in this case the coding was left unchanged.

In NVivo you can find out how many times you have used each code with just a couple of clicks of your mouse. Using word processing software, you can save your data in a new document and then copy and paste each instance of each code onto a separate page to make them easy to count. If you are working by hand, you will have to count and record each code in turn.

Whether you use a coding frame or emergent coding or any other system, qualitative data coding is, like data preparation, a laborious task. When you are coding, you will usually need to go through all your data at least twice to ensure that you haven't missed anything. This can take a long time and feel very onerous, but it will make your analysis much easier and give you more confidence in your findings:

> The transcribing was very difficult because it took so much time, but the thematic analysis was great because it all made sense then.

> I didn't like going through the coding, but I liked reading it after the coding, especially because I found an unexpected theme. I got a fizzy feeling! I'd read about 300 documents and it hadn't come up in any of them. That was incredibly exciting. If I'd skipped it or been half-hearted because I had so much data – it is worth keeping going with the same level of detail, it does pay.

Qualitative data analysis

There is a range of approaches to qualitative data analysis (Robson and McCartan, 2016: 461). This section will cover content analysis, thematic analysis, discourse analysis and narrative analysis.

Content analysis

In content analysis, you need to define categories (or codes) and count the number of instances within each category or code (Denscombe, 2014: 284). This is an interesting example of quantitative-meets-qualitative that is useful in some contexts but can be quite superficial. In particular, it only shows you some of *what* exists in your data; it doesn't explain *why* those phenomena occur. Therefore content analysis is often used alongside other analytic techniques rather than on its own.

Content analysis can be used with textual or visual data (Rose, 2012: 81–104). It is often used with secondary data, such as archival data or media data, as it can be particularly useful where there is a lot of data to explore. This is even more the case where your data is, or can be, made available in digital form, so that you can use computer software for the analysis. However, content analysis is easy enough to do by hand with small datasets.

Thematic analysis

For thematic analysis, you need to identify themes within your coded data. You do this by extracting all the data coded with each code in turn (Robson and McCartan, 2016: 474–5), which is sometimes known as 'slicing' the data, and reading each 'slice' to see what it seems to be telling you. It is sensible to make notes of what you find as you go. Don't worry if your notes seem disjointed; as long as you're getting everything down you can make sense of them later on.

Thematic analysis is not a linear process. The first step is to identify a possible theme and create some kind of grouping within that theme, which may be as simple as pairing two codes together. Then you might:

- compare different segments of the data;
- identify and explore patterns in the data;
- identify and explore connections or relationships between codes or themes;
- look for outliers and work to explain them;
- develop a hierarchy of themes, which may include subthemes, and so on.

As you work on your thematic analysis, you will move back and forth between data, codes and themes. You may find that you want to add new codes during this process. The aim is to find clusters of meaning and patterns in your data, and to be confident that the themes you have identified fully reflect the data.

Discourse analysis

In this context, 'discourse' doesn't just mean language, speech or conversation. It can also encompass visual images, texts or anything else that is intended to communicate. In discourse analysis terms, 'discourse' means 'how people use communication to construct their world'. For discourse analysts, communication forms our thoughts, as much as − if not more than − the other way around. Therefore discourse produces knowledge. This means that discourse analysts believe there is much more going on, when people communicate, than simply the transmission of information. The point of discourse analysis is to find out what else is happening:

> I decided that I was going to go through my data and I was going to do a bit of discourse analysis. So I got my categories, looked to see how much was in them, what were they saying, narrowed it down to what seemed to be the most significant things in terms of the question I'd asked.

If a discourse analyst went to a debate on healthy eating, they might hear two opposing views. The first speaker might say that, for a truly healthy diet, everyone should stop eating sugar. The second speaker might say that a healthy diet is one that allows sweet treats in moderation. The discourse analyst would see these positions as part of two different, existing and broader discourses. One of those discourses regards sugar as toxic; the other recognises people's need for self-nurture through food. The analyst would be interested in *what* each of those discourses is doing, in practice, in the data gathered. For example, in the debating context, each discourse would be trying to gain support and so win the debate. The analyst would also be interested in *how* people are trying to achieve those objectives through discourse. Investigating this through discourse analysis would involve close examination of linguistic and other forms of communication used within each discourse.

Narrative analysis

This is a method for identifying and analysing the stories people tell in textual or video data. People tell stories all the time, although not the traditional kind of 'once upon a time' stories; they may be very short, sometimes just one sentence long. Imagine you are studying the effect of education on employment. One of your participants says, 'When I was at school, we learned all kinds of weird things about equations and glaciers and stuff, which have no relevance at all to my work as a train driver.' That single sentence is a story, with a beginning, a middle and an end.

In conducting narrative analysis, your first step is to find all the stories in your data, and code each one for ease of retrieval. It may be helpful to use an overarching code, such as 'story', so you can retrieve all the stories in one go, and then specific codes to identify different types of story. For example, you might code the story above with 'school' and 'learning' and 'maths' and 'geography'. Then you might interrogate your data with some questions, such as:

- Which subjects generate the most stories? Which the least? Why might that be?
- What periods of time do the stories cover?
- What are the values exemplified by the stories? Are these coherent, or not? What does that tell you?
- What function might these stories serve for your participants and others?
- Are the stories skewed in a particular direction? Do the stories conceal as well as reveal – and, if so, what do they hide?
- Are there stories missing? What other stories could be told?

A real-life example of qualitative data analysis

Data analysis is one of the hardest parts of research to explain, which may be why it is one of the hardest parts to do. A real-life example may help. Here is an edited explanation, from my doctoral thesis, which shows how I used my coding to work through my analysis:

> The codes that appeared most frequently were used to 'slice' through the data, extracting segments from all the documents where that code had been used. For example, in the first coding frame, the code 'power' had been used 128 times and had appeared in all 12 stories/ discussions; the code 'identification' (where an apparently unconscious change of grammatical tense denotes a participant identifying with the story character being discussed) had been used 31 times and had appeared in 11 stories/discussions; and the code 'complexity' had been used 36 times and had appeared in 10 stories/discussions. The data coded with each code was extracted and reviewed to establish what light it could shed on the research questions. This is a constant process of asking questions and finding answers. For example, in the initial consideration of the code 'power', my internal dialogue went something like this:
>
> > The 'power' code was used in each story/discussion. Hmmm, that's interesting. I wonder how many other codes were used in every story/discussion? Let's check … oh, okay, just 'amusement' and 'curiosity'. I wonder whether I should change 'curiosity' to 'questioning', I'm not sure the name of the code describes accurately enough what's going on there. That's not about power, though, so to save going off at a tangent I'll just make a note. There we are. Now, what kind of power are we talking about? Let's extract the data and have

a look. Here we go. Well, it seems to be all about hierarchical power-over. Now that's interesting, too, because I would have said that my participants didn't have a zero-sum approach to power. But maybe they do. Let's read some more. Yes, it is all about power-over. I'd better write something about that in the 'findings' chapter, I'll just make a note of that. Now, I wonder whether something else will demonstrate that the participants don't see power as finite. Or maybe they do; perhaps I just want to believe that they don't because that's the way I think myself. Could I create that in the data just by looking for it? That may be a bit far-fetched, and anyway it's a discussion for the reflexivity section, so I'll just make another note and come back to it at a later date. There. Now, about this 'power' code. I wonder whether the emergent coding could shed any light on it. I remember the code 'control' was high up in that one. I'll go and have a look, and see where that gets me.

This process of 'interrogating the data' went on until no new findings were being drawn from the questioning. Writing about the findings took place concurrently, mostly in disjointed sentences and paragraphs. All codes were double-checked to ensure that they had been considered.

When you are analysing qualitative data, you need to:

- be curious;
- be systematic;
- be open-minded, willing to use ideas from any source;
- follow hunches and gut feelings;
- take frustration in your stride;
- write down all your thoughts during the process;
- explore all the ideas you generate while working with the data (Rapley, 2011: 279–80).

Data synthesis

If you have used several methods of collecting data, it is likely to be easiest for you to analyse each dataset in a different way. For a workplace evaluation, you might have:

- quantitative monitoring data;
- documents such as service plans and meeting minutes;
- questionnaire data with some quantitative and some qualitative elements;
- interview data;
- focus group data.

It would make sense first to analyse each of these separately, so that you can compare findings between methods. This would enable you to check whether any of your findings are specific to one method alone:

> In my research several people described themselves as 'not disabled' when they clearly were, so your questionnaire data might tell you some things while your observations tell you something else.

Once you have done that, you will need to cross-analyse or synthesise your data. You can do this by looking at the results of each of the separate analyses and picking out any similarities and differences for discussion. This process can help you build answers to your research questions.

Sometimes your results refuse to synthesise and remain stubbornly separate. If this happens, don't despair; it is a finding in itself. Also, think about possible reasons for the separateness. Look at your sets of results again and see whether you can find a narrative around them. If you are struggling, discuss the problem with colleagues, other students, supervisors or managers who may be able to throw new light on the conundrum.

Conclusion

It is in the nature of research that answers often throw up more questions. This can feel frustrating and you can find yourself thinking, 'If only I'd known...'. The point here is that you couldn't have known, and if you had known, you wouldn't have needed to do the research in the first place. As individuals and collectively, the more we learn, the more we find out about what we don't know. If you take change into account, this seems likely to be an unstoppable process. So if your answers seem irritatingly partial, rather than satisfyingly complete, don't worry. As you write your report, dissertation or thesis, you will be able to identify what you have found out during the research and what still needs to be investigated. The process of doing that writing is the subject of the next chapter.

CASE STUDIES

Ana decides to transcribe her own interview data and to use narrative analysis as her research is based on stories. She spends many evenings transcribing data and is relieved when she gets it done. The narrative analysis fascinates Ana, and she happily spends much of her free time immersed in stories and finding links and patterns in her data. She is pleased to learn that non-heterosexual families are more sympathetically portrayed in most media representations than she had expected, though there are a few unpleasant exceptions.

Ali is delighted when his co-researchers offer to transcribe their interview data. He uses thematic analysis with the anonymised case records and meeting minutes. Then, working with his co-researchers, they also use thematic analysis with the interview data, and synthesise all their findings. They learn that the service is doing a good job in general. However, there is a particular geographical area that is under-served, and the service is not reaching many carers who are in full-time work. This indicates that some targeted work is needed.

EXERCISES

1. Find a newspaper article about sport, either in print or online. Code the text using this coding frame:

   Team (T)
   Individual player (IP)
   Manager, coach or equivalent (MCE)
   Team achievement (TA)
   Team failure (TF)
   Individual achievement (IA)
   Individual failure (IF)
   Physical fitness (PF)
   Injury (I)
   Money (M)
   Ranking (R)

   Then code the text again using emergent coding. What was different? Why?

2. Pick two of the following datasets and decide how you would prepare, code and analyse the data:

   a. 150 photographs of families celebrating Diwali, Hanukkah and Christmas, to support an investigation of similarities between religions in their winter celebrations.

   b. 10 in-depth interview transcripts from people with early-stage dementia, talking about how they want to be cared for in the future, for research to help plan services.

   c. 10 focus group transcripts from teenagers discussing their experiences of gender and race equality and inequality, five from schools and five from youth groups, for research to support the development of local government equality policies.

   d. 79 copies of a lengthy questionnaire, with some open questions, about people's experiences of a local cinema, for an evaluation of its services and facilities.

Discussion questions

1. How can researchers avoid bias in qualitative data analysis?
2. Is it worth taking the time to make metadata records? Why?
3. What would you see as the pros and cons of collaborating on data analysis?

Debate topic

Qualitative data is too complex to be useful.

13

Writing for research and evaluation

Chapter summary

This chapter includes:

- Some myths about writing, debunked
- Information and advice about the writing process
- Thoughts on how to structure writing
- Plagiarism and how to avoid it
- How to cite others' work
- The difference between research findings and evaluation recommendations
- Advice on editing and polishing your writing

Introduction

Although writing has a chapter all to itself in the second half of this book, it is not a discrete activity that happens late in the research or evaluation process. Writing begins at the very beginning, with notes and plans and lists and, more formally, your written research proposal or plan. It continues throughout as you make records of literature and documents that you read, write a research journal, take notes and code data. And it doesn't finish when your report, dissertation or thesis is complete, because you will continue to write your research as part of presenting your findings at a meeting, conference, viva or other event, or in a newsletter or journal article, or on a web page.

These days research and evaluation are not only reported in writing, but also in videos, podcasts, comics, multimedia blogs, and in all sorts of other ways too (Phillips and Kara, 2021: 138–66). However, this chapter focuses on writing for two main reasons: first, written reports of research and evaluation are still by far the most common, and second, most other reporting methods still require the writing of a script, storyboard or other kind of narrative.

Myths about writing

This chapter aims to debunk some of the main myths about writing. The first myth is that writing happens in the same sequence as reading, that is, you start with the words 'Chapter 1', carry on until you get to 'The End', and then stop. Actually there is plenty of reading that doesn't happen like that; I'll bet most of the people who use this book don't read from the first page all the way through to the last. But some books are read as linear narratives, particularly fiction, and that is probably where the myth developed.

A second myth is that writing is easy and that anyone can write if they feel in the mood. Writing is, in fact, hard graft:

> Writing it all up, that was hard.

Like long-distance running, playing the piano or riding a horse, you need a lot of practice before you can be good at writing. Unlike those activities, however, nobody can say to you, 'Look at me, I'll show you how.' Most writing is a solitary, private activity, much of which happens inside the writer's head. If you watched me writing, all you would see was my fingers tapping on the computer keyboard while I stared at the screen, interspersed with times where my fingers were still and I stared out of the window. Your observations wouldn't tell you anything about how to write.

I suspect the myth that writing is easy arose because people see only the finished product (Becker, 2007: xiii). Because people don't see the process of producing what they read, it seems to have appeared as if by magic. But anyone who writes well will have done lots and lots of practice, just like anyone who is good at sport or music. As with sports players and musicians, different strategies work for different writers. You need to try out different strategies to find out what works for you. While you do that, be aware of the possibility of kidding yourself. If you feel that you have to clean the house for an hour before you can start writing, is that really because the house cleaning provides essential thinking time that helps your writing when you get going, or is it, in fact, a delaying tactic? Only you can know the answer, so be analytical and critical about your own practice.

A third myth is that you need huge chunks of free time to be able to write effectively. For some people, this may be true at some stages of the process:

> How it worked best was when I could carve out weeks at a time – this was in the writing up stage – I really struggled when I couldn't take chunks of time like that, so it didn't work for me when I was doing a few hours every couple of evenings a week, it didn't allow me to build enough momentum. I needed my employer to be flexible with me so I could work a week on and a week off, but it was obviously difficult to get many of those so I ended up using holiday.

However, most inexperienced writers find large chunks of free time more useful for procrastination than for actual writing. More experienced writers know that it's more helpful to 'snack' than to 'binge' (Murray, 2016: 99). It can help to break down your writing work into specific tasks and give each task a specific time. For example, you could decide to write two paragraphs about the research methods you used, and give yourself half an hour to do that, after dinner and before watching TV. Don't fall into the trap of thinking there's no point writing just two paragraphs. If you write two paragraphs, that's probably 200–300 words that you didn't have before:

> Trying to write it up I found laborious. In my head I'd already done it. You don't get taught how to do it. The books are there, but you almost need someone to sit down and go through a structure. I got quite phobic about the red pen, you'd go in and it would be, 'That's great, but...' so there was a bit of regression back to school days, which wasn't comfortable or necessary.

One helpful strategy here is to use Raymond Chandler's technique of 'The Nothing Alternative' (Baumeister and Tierney, 2012: 254). To do this, you set time aside in which you allow yourself either to write or to do nothing. No tidying up or checking email – real nothing. It can be useful, particularly if you're sitting at your computer with your mobile phone by your side, to switch off the sound on both devices. Internet addicts may also benefit from apps such as Freedom, which lets you block specific sites, such as social media, for specific periods of time. You can even block the entire internet, although that's less helpful if you need to do online research as you write. During periods of time when you can only write or do nothing, you are likely to write more to stave off boredom.

A fourth myth is that all writing requires the same kind of skill. This is, of course, true to an extent, because all writing consists of combining words to make meaning. But writing a novel, or copy for the back of a cereal packet, or instructions in a technical manual, or a ghost-written celebrity memoir – each requires some very different skills. And writing for research or evaluation is different again, which can make life even more complicated, particularly for people who are schooled in yet another way of writing:

> The police have this thing of writing, Accuracy, Brevity and Clarity, so if you can write everything very briefly – within the police they have a research forecast, but a paper to the police is something that cuts to the chase and isn't wrapped up in any of the references or proof. You would have to read something, understand it, then write it in one-and-a-half or two pages so that it was understandable to everybody. It's overcoming this very prescribed way of writing that I think a lot of police find a problem.

Some of the myths about writing that have been regularly expressed to me by practitioners and students are set out in Table 13.1, together with the essence of my responses.

Table 13.1: Regularly expressed myths about writing, with my responses

Expressed myth	My response
I'll write when I feel like it	You'll get nothing done
One day I'll be in the right mood for writing	You don't know that for sure, you just have to get on with it
I'll start writing when I know what I want to say	You'll know what you want to say when you've written enough to work it out
My writing will never be good enough	It will if you practise writing
I need to start at the beginning and write through to the end	You need to start in the middle and write in chunks, move sections around, experiment
I must write so well that my work won't need editing	That's impossible, even for experienced professional writers; your work will need to go through several drafts
I can't write unless I have a clear morning/afternoon/day	In just five minutes, you can write 150 words in longhand, or 300 on a keyboard
Everything I write is rubbish	No it's not – although doubtless it can be improved. But so can the work of many published writers
Writing is too hard for me; I can't do it	When did you last write an email? A text message? A status update or comment on a social networking site? They're all writing. You can write. All you have to do is keep going

The good news is that writing is something almost anyone can learn to do, and to do well. This chapter will provide some pointers to help you. If you want to find out more after reading it, there are many excellent how-to books on writing, some of which are in the 'Further reading' section at the end of this book. And if you would prefer to learn from a teacher, there are a number of writing courses available on the open market.

The writing process

Many people, including very experienced writers, find it quite daunting to start a new piece of writing:

> It's the blank sheet of paper. I think the actual sitting down to start writing and the having a blank sheet of paper, it was almost like the piece of paper got bigger and bigger and bigger and bigger, it was almost like a flip chart rather than something on a screen.

Don't wait for the muse. She won't turn up.

It may help you to know that writing often starts in the middle. I began writing the first edition of this book with part of the chapter on data collection. As I drafted this chapter, I had written two-thirds of the Introduction and Chapters 4 and 8, one-third of Chapters 5 and 6, and one-quarter of Chapter 9 – although not in that order. This demonstrates that writing is not a linear process:

> I had to start writing it, and I thought, I don't know how to do this. I think I thought I'd got to write it all as a continuous stream of narrative, but actually it was pointed out to me that you could break it up and talk about the various categories you'd found, and what you thought the significance of these was in relation to one another, and any reading or literature you'd got. Once I'd realised that, it was fine.

Breaking the work down into chunks makes a daunting prospect feel much more manageable:

> I do it by breaking it down into small manageable tasks, so not thinking 'OMG I've got to do a 20,000-word literature review', but thinking 'What are the points I've got to make?' Then writing a section at a time, seeing the small things that will ultimately build into the bigger. Stop thinking about the bigger picture and start looking for the smaller take, whether it's themes or codes, and just keep your eye on the small key points and then write around those and look for the links.

Taking the approach of writing whichever section you feel most inclined to write can help to overcome anxiety. So can letting go of perfectionism. Freewriting can be useful here (Elbow, 1998: 13): set yourself an active, first-person prompt related to your project, and write for 10 minutes (or five if you can type fast) without stopping or censoring yourself. This can be used to problem-solve or just to get you going. The kinds of prompts I use are along these lines:

The main features of my method are…
I want my data analysis to…
I don't want to write because…
I would like my research to achieve…

During the freewriting period, if I find my fingers flagging, I rewrite the prompt and carry on. I recommend trying freewriting if you've never had a go; as well as being helpful for getting your writing underway, it often yields surprisingly useful nuggets that you can transfer to your actual write-up. But if freewriting doesn't work for you, don't worry – the most important thing is to get words down on the page in whatever form comes most easily:

I went back and wrote something that my supervisor, she said she just splurges, writes anything that's to do with whatever it is to get going, get into the flow of putting something on paper. If you don't use it again that's fine, if you do it's great. I used bullet points, wrote lists of bullet points, or I'd deconstruct a quote to work out what I thought about it, and that got me going again.

 The best time-saving tip for writing is: write. Just write it down. Anything relevant, in any order. You can sort out the structure later on.

Writing, however haphazardly, will help you to clarify your thoughts and develop your ideas. Conversely, not writing when you need to write will increase anxiety and reduce self-confidence. My own first draft writing is full of question marks where I can't think of the word or simile that I want, and stern reminders to myself in capitals that say things like 'WRITE MORE HERE' or 'LINK THIS SECTION TO THE NEXT'. Writers often use these kinds of placeholders. One thing I do find is that when I start to feel stuck during the actual process of writing, there's no point trying to get unstuck. It's like the classic scenario of the person who is mired in mud and struggling only gets them in deeper. The best thing to do is add a placeholder and move on. When I come back another day to the part that says 'WRITE MORE HERE', I often find I know what I want to write when previously my mind had been as blank as the page in front of me. And when I reach 'LINK THIS SECTION TO THE NEXT', I can see how to make that link.

 Set yourself a daily or weekly word count – and stick to it.

Make a commitment to yourself that each day, or each week, you will write a certain number of words. That number doesn't have to be very high. If you write 500 words per day, you will have written the first draft of a 15,000-word dissertation in a month. Five hundred words is not very many; it's about a page of A4 typed in 12-point Arial. When I started writing seriously, I found 500 words per day was manageable. These days I find weekly goals easier, and my weekly goal for the first draft of this book was 5,000 words (which is equivalent to 715 words per day, so not that much more).

 Do not try to edit your work while you are writing the first draft.

Being a researcher requires you to have shape-changing abilities. While working with literature and documents, you need meticulous recording skills. When you are collecting primary data, you are likely to need a high level of interpersonal skills as well as a nerdy love of accurate recording. When you are coding data, you need geek-level thoroughness. But all this perfectionism is no use to you as a writer of research. Of course you need to write as accurately as possible and report your findings carefully and honestly. But when it comes to the actual art of writing, perfectionism is not an option.

We began to touch on the reason for this in Chapter 7, which explained about the richness of the English language and the range of synonyms available to writers. It is possible to agonise for hours, even days, about whether a sentence should use the word 'outstanding' or the alternative 'exceptional'. This is a monumental waste of time because there can never be a perfect piece of writing. Even a published book need not be the final version, as this third edition demonstrates. As with doing research or evaluation, there are lots of ways to write badly but also lots of ways to write well.

One way to write well is to keep your reader in mind (Becker, 2007: 18). What does a reader of research need to know? Essentially, they need to know *what you did, why you did it, how you did it, and what you found* as a result (Clark-Carter, 2010: 392). In academic terms, they need you to help them understand your 'argument'. The word 'argument' has a slightly different meaning for researchers than for other people. It doesn't mean a quarrel; it means one side of an intellectual debate that is well reasoned and based on evidence (Jesson et al, 2011: 66). Readers need this debate conveyed to them in clear, readable English, within a structure that is easy for them to navigate. The resources in the 'Further reading' section at the end of this chapter give more detail about how to build and communicate an argument.

Work out who your readers are and keep them in mind as you write. What do they need to know? What is the simplest way you can tell them?

The Plain English Campaign advises all writers to:

- be concise;
- use short words where possible;
- vary sentence length, but aim for an average of 15–20 words;
- avoid jargon;
- if you need to use technical terms, give an explanation of each one;
- use active rather than passive verbs (for example, 'she collected the data' rather than 'the data was collected by her');
- write as if you are speaking to your reader;
- make sure your writing is helpful and polite.

If you want more information about writing in plain English, the Plain English Campaign has a number of free resources.

In some ways, with writing, it's easier to be specific about what you should *not* do than about what you should do. So here are some things to avoid.

- Poor spelling, grammar, punctuation etc: if you have difficulty with this, ask someone to check your writing for errors. Also, there is loads of advice on the internet, so anything you're not sure about, look up. (We all have blind spots. I've lost count of the times I've checked the difference between 'practise' and 'practice'. I'm still not sure, without looking first.)
- Unhelpful structure: it's worth thinking about ways in which your report can be made easy for readers to navigate. Page numbers, headings, chapter titles, the contents list and an index all help readers to find their way around your work. The structure for workplace research or evaluation reports, and for academic dissertations or theses, is not so very different. The standard sections, and the purpose of each, are outlined in Table 13.2.

Table 13.2: Structure for research reports, dissertations and theses

Workplace research/evaluation report structure	Purpose of section	Academic dissertation/ thesis structure	Purpose of section
Executive summary	To tell people about your work in as few words as possible	Abstract	To tell people about your work in as few words as possible
Introduction	Introducing your research and why you're doing it	Introduction	Introducing your research and why you're doing it
Document review	Putting your research into context (optional – otherwise context may be covered in introduction)	Literature review	Putting your research into context
Method	How you did your research	Method	How you did your research
Findings	What you found out	Results	What you found out
Discussion	The implications of your research for practice (may be linked with theory; may include recommendations)	Discussion	What your findings mean – link with theory and, if relevant, practice
Conclusion	Next steps	Conclusion	The implications of your research
Appendices	Relevant supplementary information	Appendices	Relevant supplementary information

These aren't hard-and-fast rules, but in practice, most reports, dissertations and theses follow a similar structure.

- Long sentences: the Plain English Campaign advises using no more than 25 words per sentence. Don't worry about this when you're writing your first draft, but it's useful to keep in mind when editing.
- Long words: while you need to use long words at times, always choose shorter ones if you can. Some people think the use of longer words demonstrates their sophistication and cleverness and makes for impressive writing. In fact, they are likely to make your reader want to stop reading. The word 'sesquipedalian' is a useful example. I'm sure most readers would prefer 'someone who tends to use long words' – which is what 'sesquipedalian' means. It is more difficult to produce clear and concise writing than to be obscure and verbose, but your readers will much prefer the former.
- Research reports, dissertations or theses that are longer than they need to be: there is a famous quotation, which has been attributed to all sorts of people, from Pliny the Younger to Mark Twain, which reads: 'I'm sorry I didn't have time to write you a short letter, so I wrote this long one instead.' In academic research you will have a word count, but it's a maximum rather than a target. You won't lose any marks for saying everything you need to say in fewer words, and you will always gain marks for clarity. This is also good practice in workplace research.
- Unedited work: however skilled you are in using the English language, you will always have to edit your writing if you are going to make it as good as it can be.
- Use of jargon or technical terms: in some cases there may be no alternative, in which case make sure you also include a clear definition of the word.
- Clichés: avoid these like the plague, because familiarity breeds contempt. More to the point, a cliché doesn't have the impact that a fresh turn of phrase will bring to your work.
- Repetition: there are times where you need to reiterate something, for example, a point made in the introduction to a lengthy research report, of which you wish to remind the reader when you reach the conclusion. Reiteration is effective writing to help the reader understand your argument. Repetition, on the other hand, is annoying for readers and should be avoided.
- Trying to write and edit at the same time: the first draft and the final draft require different skills. To begin with, just get the words down in a way that makes sense to you. At this stage, don't worry about whether they will make sense to anyone else. As the well-known novelist Elmore Leonard said: 'The first draft is always shit.' This also applies to non-fiction.
- Trying to edit as soon as you finish writing: this won't work. You need to leave your draft alone for a good chunk of time so you can come back to it with fresh eyes. A week is good, longer is better. If you can't manage a whole week, then take what time you can.
- Proofreading your own work: it's notoriously difficult to spot your own errors. And it's fine to get someone else to proofread your work, even for an

academic qualification, as long as they're only looking for things like typos, grammatical mistakes, numerical errors and omitted references.

- Leaving your writing to the last minute: writing is an iterative process and you need to give it time if you're going to do it well. Most good writing goes through at least three drafts: the first draft, where you churn out the words; the second, where you knock it into shape; and the third, where you review your word choices, grammar and structure. You need to rest your draft between each stage. So leaving your writing to the last minute is a really, really bad idea.

Another reason why it's a good idea to do your writing with plenty of time to spare is that then you can ask someone to give you feedback on your work. Writing is always improved by feedback, but the process may not be easy or comfortable, particularly if you haven't had much – or any – experience of this. It's important not to be protective about your writing, as you need to be willing to accept and use constructive criticism if you're going to produce your best work. Feedback is an invaluable opportunity to learn. There is more about dealing with feedback in the section on editing later in this chapter.

 TIP **Always read your work out loud before you decide it's finished. It's amazing how many typos, grammatical errors and clunky sentences you discover when reading out loud that you couldn't see on the page.**

Structure

As shown in Table 13.2, most research reports, whether workplace or academic, have a similar overarching structure, which is something like: introduction, methods, findings, discussion, conclusions/recommendations, appendices. Within this, the writer needs to use subheadings that enable the reader to find their way around the report. These should be in a logical order. Ideally, if you listed all the subheadings with none of the text, the reader should be able to understand how the information you wish to communicate flows through the report. Doing this as an exercise, at intervals as you write the report, can help you to identify gaps, overlaps and inconsistencies.

Another potentially useful exercise, particularly for dissertations and theses, is to pull out the first and last paragraph of each chapter. Again, the information being conveyed should flow smoothly through these sections of your writing. As with the subheadings, doing this exercise can help you to identify omissions, repetitions and other structural errors.

A contents list will be helpful for your readers, and this is easy to produce with most word processing software. An index is also helpful, but this is more complicated to produce. Word processing software will often create a basic index, but compiling a full index that will be most useful for readers is a specialist job, and therefore costs money. A good compromise may be to generate a basic index using your software, and then have a quick check through to see if there's anything that might be useful to readers that you can add to the basic index. It's not possible for an inexperienced indexer to foresee every item that a reader might wish to look up, but it's still worth doing what you can to improve on the basic index.

 Remember to number your pages.

Some people, perhaps particularly inexperienced writers, need to write first and create their structure later. Others are more comfortable starting with the structure:

> I sit down and construct a framework and then backfill it with references, so you get the idea of what you're going to write. You construct a framework, go and do your reading, and it's just like building a big jigsaw.

If you are going to start with the structure, you either need enough understanding of the subject area to know the main issues that are likely to arise, or enough flexibility to amend your structure as necessary in response to unexpected ideas or connections.

Another thing to consider at this point is whether tables, figures, illustrations, images and other such elements would help in presenting your research or evaluation. And if they would, what to put in, and where. If you have visual data such as artwork, or visual analytic elements such as graphs or charts, these are ideal to include. Alternatively, if you have the relevant skills, you can create your own drawings or photos to illustrate your reports. Illustration is not essential but it can help readers by showing another dimension to your findings.

Plagiarism

Plagiarism means presenting someone else's ideas or words as your own original work. This is a form of theft, because – in the Western world – original ideas and words are regarded as the 'intellectual property' of the person who created them. Plagiarism is also a form of fraud because the plagiariser is lying about the origins of the ideas and/or words they have used. It is a serious academic offence with various penalties for students ranging from the plagiariser receiving a zero mark for the piece of work concerned to expulsion from the entire course. Plagiarism is not a crime in law, although it may involve copyright infringement, if the original source is copyrighted. In most countries copyright infringement is a legal offence that can land the offender in a court of law to face the full might of the judicial system.

Luckily, plagiarism is easy to avoid. Knowing the reasons for plagiarism will help. It is unlikely that many people set out to plagiarise, but some may be tempted due to factors such as:

- pressure, from managers, tutors, families, friends or others, to do well in studies or workplace research;
- peer pressure from other researchers who think plagiarism is a short-cut to success;
- feelings of inadequacy, leading the researcher to feel that they can never produce anything as good as the work of others;
- looming deadlines leaving insufficient time for the careful reading, interpretation and analysis that are essential for good-quality research.

Plagiarism may also occur by accident due to factors such as:

- inadequate record-keeping, which can make it difficult or impossible to find information when it's needed for a reference list or citation;
- errors in paraphrasing, which can lead to someone else's work being interpreted incorrectly in such a way that plagiarism results;
- incorrect citation methods, such as using a quote from someone else's work but forgetting to use quotation marks, or paraphrasing and failing to include the citation.

Even if plagiarism occurs by accident, it is still highly unethical. Remember that accidents can be prevented. As a researcher, 'I didn't mean to' or 'I didn't notice' are not defences against plagiarism. It is your responsibility to do research to high ethical standards. To avoid plagiarism, you need to cite others' work correctly. This means that you must make sure you have enough time to do your research work thoroughly, and you must keep your records accurate and up to date.

You also need to be able to paraphrase, that is, to restate an idea or argument in your own words. This is a skill that is rarely taught, even on research methods courses. And it's not easy. To paraphrase effectively, you need a clear understanding of what you have read, and a good command of English to be able to restate it clearly and accurately in your own words. This also, inevitably, means using a different structure from that chosen by the original author.

Some novice researchers find paraphrasing quite daunting and decide to rely almost entirely on quotes from other people's work. This is understandable, but not a good move, especially in academic research where your tutor or examiner will want to see evidence that you have developed skills in interpreting and analysing text. Paraphrasing is a good way to develop and demonstrate these skills.

Let's look at an example. We'll assume that I am working on a review of the literature about the role of emotion in paid work. I have found an excerpt of text that is relevant:

> For about one in three of all British workers, exhaustion, stress or both have become an inescapable part of their working lives. That is a shocking failure of our imagination and our will to devise a work culture which sustains human well-being rather than erodes it. A job which demands a huge proportion of an individual's energy, time and emotional resources is a job which is unsustainable; it passes the cost on to the worker in terms of their health, and to his or her partner, children, friends and community. (Bunting, 2004: 177)

Here is an inappropriate paraphrase, with the words I have changed in bold:

> Bunting (2004: 177) says that for **1 in 3** workers **in the UK**, exhaustion **and** stress **are** an **inevitable** part of their **work**. **It is** shocking **that we cannot create** a work culture that **supports people's** wellbeing **rather than damaging it**. **If work** demands **most of someone's** energy, time and emotional resources **then that is** unsustainable **because it will damage the worker's** health **and put pressure on** his or her **family and** friends **as well as the wider** community.

This paraphrase is inappropriate because all I have done is change some words and phrases for other, synonymous, words and phrases. The structure of the paraphrase is identical to that of the original, and I have not restated the passage in my own words. This is one form of plagiarism.

Here is a more appropriate paraphrase:

> According to Bunting (2004: 177), exhaustion and stress are an inevitable part of the work of as many as one-third of British workers. Her view is that this is unsustainable because of the damage it causes, not only to the health of those workers, but also in the knock-on effects for their families, their friends, and the wider community.

Here I am crediting Bunting for the fact in the first sentence of the paraphrase and for the opinion in the second sentence. It is also an appropriate paraphrase because I have departed from the structure of the original. I have chosen not to include the more journalistic opinion from the second sentence of the original text because, having read Bunting's work carefully, I don't think leaving it out changes the meaning of her argument. I have restructured the quote and restated it in my own words to give my picture of Bunting's argument, which demonstrates that I can analyse and interpret text written by someone else. Therefore this is not plagiarism.

You will notice that I have included only the author's surname, year of publication and page number within my own text. This enables the reader to turn to my References section, which is in alphabetical order for ease of navigation, and find the full reference:

Bunting, M. (2004) *Willing slaves: How the overwork culture is ruling our lives*, London: HarperCollins.

If original material is difficult to paraphrase for any reason, you can always use a direct quote instead. If you use a quote, you must add a citation with the page number (if there is one).

Citation

'Citation' means stating the details of the source of an idea, fact or opinion that you draw on in your research. 'Source' could be many things: book, article, website, video, dataset, radio programme, personal communication, and so on. In your citation, you should give enough information to enable the reader to track down and read your source if they wish to do so – and if that is possible. In some cases, such as personal communications, pages deleted from the internet or broadcast media, it may not be possible. However, this is no excuse for sloppy citation. All details should be given wherever possible, such as dates, names and page numbers. If you give a web page address or URL as part of a citation, you should also give the date when you looked at the web page, because the content and/or URLs of web pages frequently change. As discussed in Chapter 8, the move towards using DOIs may help to resolve this problem, for some sources, in time.

You do not have to cite sources for every single point you make. If you are referring to common phenomena that are widely known, such as that more men than women are convicted of criminal offences, or that dementia occurs more frequently in older than younger people, you do not have to cite a source. A good rule of thumb is: if in doubt, cite a source.

Broadly, there are two methods of citation: the 'bracket' method and the 'note' method. The bracket method is the one used in this book, where the name of the author(s), the year of publication and sometimes the page number is included within the text in brackets, with the full reference given in a reference list, usually at the end of the document. This system is sometimes known as Harvard referencing. The note method uses consecutive numerical superscript references like this,[1] with the note at the foot of each page, the end of each section or chapter, or the end of the document, where the full reference will be given. This system is sometimes known as Vancouver referencing. There are some established referencing systems to choose from, such as those of the American Psychological Association and the Modern Humanities Research Association. Whatever system you use, it is essential that you use it consistently; you should not mix and match different referencing systems within the same piece of research work.

If you are doing workplace research, you can probably make up your own mind about the referencing system you prefer. Universities usually have a system which their researchers are required to use, so if you're doing academic research, ask your tutor about this or check your university's website.

Citations also allow you to frame your own ideas. So, for example, I might add to the paraphrase given earlier as follows:

> According to Bunting (2004: 177), exhaustion and stress are an inevitable part of the work of as many as one-third of British workers. Her view is that this is unsustainable because of the damage it causes, not only to the health of those workers, but also in the knock-on effects for their families, their friends, and the wider community. On May 16th 2011, a press release from the mental health charity Mind stated that they had commissioned a professional research organisation to survey over 2,000 workers in England and Wales, and it had found that 41% were 'stressed or very stressed in their jobs'. So it seems that workplace stress may have increased between 2004 and 2011.

This includes a second citation (the Mind press release) and a final sentence giving my own idea. You will notice that I have worded it carefully, saying 'it seems that workplace stress may have increased' rather than 'workplace stress has increased'. This is for two reasons. First, despite careful reading, I'm not sure where Bunting got her figure of 'about one in three' workers, so I don't want to rely on it too heavily. Second, Bunting's figure refers to 'British workers', that is, including those in Northern Ireland and Scotland as well as the workers in England and Wales who were surveyed for the Mind research. It may be that workers in Northern Ireland and Scotland experience much less workplace stress than those in England and Wales, which would explain the differences in the figures. My own opinion is that this is unlikely, but I must acknowledge the possibility, hence the cautious wording.

 Look for advice and help for citation online, through citation guides such as the one produced by the Chicago Manual of Style, or citation tools such as Cite This For Me.

All research is part of a massive worldwide expression of humankind's thirst for knowledge. Your research builds on the knowledge created by others, and it generates knowledge for use by those coming afterwards. The proper use of citations demonstrates this in two ways. First, citations acknowledge and show respect for the work of authors who have gone before you. Second, citations show care for the researchers who come after you, by enabling readers to follow your thought processes back to their sources if they wish to do so.

Findings versus recommendations

Findings are simply what you have found out through doing the research. In most academic and some workplace research, a discussion of your findings is all that is needed, although there may be recommendations for future research. In other research, particularly evaluation research, you need to write recommendations for future action. These recommendations should be unmistakably rooted in your findings, and should also be possible to implement (Robson and McCartan, 2016: 499). This requires a good working knowledge of the real-world context for the research. So, for example, an evaluation of an outreach service may find that service users want twice as much contact with the service as they get. While it might seem that a sensible recommendation in this case would be for service users to get twice as much contact as they do at present, the service has neither the capacity nor the funding to provide more contact. So recommendations might include: seeking other sources of funding; increasing the capacity of the service, perhaps through secondments or restructuring; looking at services provided by other organisations to see whether some of the service users' needs could be met by those services; and so on. Writing recommendations can require quite a bit of lateral thinking, and sometimes some last-minute research into feasibility. It is all worthwhile, however, when you see the fruits of your labours in the form of improved provision for service users.

Editing

When your first draft is complete, celebrate! Yes, it's messy and full of holes – but it's also your raw material, the ingredients from which you can craft a perfectly cooked report, dissertation or thesis. It's a massive milestone reached, and you deserve a reward. Leave the draft alone for a while – at least a week, or longer, if time allows. You need to be able to read it with fresh eyes. It is really hard to edit your own work effectively, so feedback from others on the readability of your writing is useful at this stage.

Accepting feedback on writing can be difficult when you've sweated and wept your way to the point you've reached (Becker, 2007: 6). Even very constructive criticism can hurt and leave you feeling defensive. Try to get feedback in writing, and take time to digest and consider it before responding. Remember that the person giving the feedback has voluntarily contributed their time and skills to your project, and aim to respond with your head rather than your heart.

The ability to accept feedback gracefully is essential for a researcher, because your conclusions or recommendations are likely to receive criticism even if your writing is beyond compare. So it helps to start acquiring this skill at the writing stage.

If you are doing workplace research, you will have to decide whether to ask for feedback from a colleague who knows a lot about your work or from one who knows a little. Each approach has advantages and disadvantages. Someone who knows a lot about your work may be able to give more detailed feedback, but may also want to influence your research more than you are comfortable with. Someone who knows a little about your work may be able to give a more balanced perspective on your research, but may not have the in-depth knowledge necessary to give a more thorough response. Only you can decide which will be best, in the light of your needs and the individual personalities involved.

While you can ask for very detailed feedback on workplace research if you wish, the situation is rather different with academic research. Here it is much more important that the work is entirely yours. This does not mean that it is inappropriate to ask for and use feedback from others, but those giving feedback should restrict themselves to commenting on the quality of your writing rather than engaging with the arguments you make. This can be a fine line. For example, where a point is unclear, this may be because of insufficient writing skill or because the subject hasn't been fully thought through. Therefore the person giving feedback should confine themselves to pointing out the lack of clarity, and leave it to you to work out why what you have written is unclear and how you can make it clearer.

When you have your feedback, consider each point carefully. The points made will fall into three categories:

1. The no-brainer, which you will want to implement immediately. Typographical, grammatical and spelling errors fall into this category, as do any more complex suggestions that make immediate sense to you, for example, for simplifying the structure of part or all of your work.
2. The no-thanks, which you will never want to implement. These often occur when the person giving the feedback hasn't entirely grasped the point you're trying to make and thinks the problem lies with the writing. However, these pieces of feedback are a useful indication that a careful review of the relevant section would be a good idea.
3. The in-betweener. These require more thought. They may occur because the person giving feedback has identified a problem (which you agree with) but has been unable to come up with a solution, or has come up with a solution that you don't agree with. In either case, you need to find a solution yourself, hence the need for thought.

When you have received and digested your feedback, reread your draft and make a list of the points you need to address. Then work through the list, systematically, until you have completed all the editing tasks. Now you are ready to polish your writing, and at this stage it is again a good idea to leave it alone for a week or more before starting on the next phase of the work.

Polishing your writing

Polishing involves making sure every detail of your writing is correct. First, you should review the structure of your work at every level: overall document, chapter or section, paragraph and sentence. It may help to repeat the editing exercises of pulling out all the headings and looking through them to make sure the flow of information is logical and complete, and then pulling out all the first and last paragraphs of each chapter or section and reading them in order for the same purpose.

When you are happy with the structure, you need to go through your work line by line, checking your grammar, word choices, spelling and punctuation. As you do this, you can also check that all the references you have cited in the text are in your reference list. I do this by printing out a fresh copy of my reference list and ticking off the references on the list as I go through my writing. This also means that, at the end, I can check that every reference in the list has a tick – if any do not, they should be deleted, as it is not good research etiquette to list references in your reference list if they have not been cited in your writing.

Finally, give your work one last read-through out loud, to pick up any clunky sentences your eyes may have missed.

Polishing is a tedious process but worth doing. You'll be surprised by how many errors and inconsistencies you will pick up. It's best if you can correct these yourself, rather than leaving them for your readers to find.

Conclusion

If you find writing difficult, it is not because you are stupid or no good at writing. It is because writing *is* difficult. It does get a bit less difficult as you gain experience, although I think that at least partly involves becoming more comfortable with its difficulty! The only way forward is to keep on getting the words down, then putting them in the right order, then making them all nice and tidy.

An analogy can be helpful here. Think of a potter making a beautiful ceramic bowl. They can't go straight from clay to finished bowl, can they? In fact, the first thing they have to do is obtain and prepare their clay. In some places that involves digging it out of the ground; in others, buying it from a shop. Either way, the potter has to wedge the clay to remove any air bubbles and ensure a smooth consistency. This is like writing your first draft. Then they make their bowl, using whichever technique they prefer, and fire it. This is like writing your second draft. And the bowl is still not finished, because it needs to be glazed and fired again. This is like writing your third draft. You will find similar staged processes in all sorts of creative work. Writing reports of research or evaluation is a creative process, however factual it may be, because you are writing something that nobody has ever written before. Presenting and disseminating your findings are also creative processes and are covered in the next chapter.

> **CASE STUDIES**
>
> Ana has to write a dissertation for her degree. She finds the process quite daunting, but breaking it down into smaller tasks is helpful. Ana would like to include the photos from the three media reports she used in her research, but she is worried about copyright. Then she has an idea, and traces the outlines from the photos and then shades them in to create artistic representations of the images. Ana thinks this will help her readers to understand the quotes she uses from her interviewees. She also includes some simple graphs to present the statistical information she has found.

Ali has to write an evaluation report with recommendations. His co-researchers want to help him and they divide up the report between them, with each person taking responsibility for part of the report. They each write the first draft of their part, and then give feedback on the others' writing before producing a final draft of the whole report. They use some interview quotes and maps to illustrate their findings, and draft a set of recommendations for discussion.

EXERCISES

1. Try freewriting for five minutes using one of the prompts given in the chapter.

2. Paraphrase this paragraph, which is taken from the chapter:

   You do not have to cite sources for every single point you make. If you are referring to common phenomena that are widely known, such as that more men than women are convicted of criminal offences, or that dementia occurs more frequently in older than younger people, you do not have to cite a source. A good rule of thumb is: if in doubt, cite a source.

Discussion questions

1. What are the best ways to counteract writing myths?
2. Which is easier, writing the first draft or writing the second draft? Why?
3. Who will your readers be? How can you meet their needs?
4. Why is it important to cite others' work carefully?
5. When might a more creative type of report be useful, and why?

Debate topic

Writing is an over-rated method of communication.

14

Disseminating research and evaluation

Chapter summary

This chapter includes:

- Some advice on summarising research or evaluation
- An overview of the barriers to dissemination
- Advice on presenting in person
- Some key points about sharing findings online
- Information about data visualisation
- A review of some common dissemination methods
- Disseminating workplace and academic research
- A brief discussion of dissemination ethics

Introduction

The point of disseminating your research or evaluation is to share the knowledge you have gained through the process. Etymologically, the word 'dissemination' means 'to scatter seeds in every direction'. As gardeners know, not every seed will germinate and take root, but it's important to provide the conditions that will give those seeds the best chance of growth. The same applies with disseminating research.

Dissemination is not easy, and there are usually barriers to overcome. Nevertheless, it is really important, because dissemination is where theory, research and practice meet. Doing research or evaluation is a vital way of gathering evidence about a subject, but there's no point gathering all that lovely evidence if you don't tell people what you've discovered. Your research is not just for you to learn from; it's for other people too.

Summarising research or evaluation

Most research and evaluation outputs are in the form of written reports, dissertations or theses. These are necessary so that research commissioners, managers, tutors and examiners can gain a thorough understanding of what has been done, why and how it has been done, and what the findings are. However, these written outputs are usually long and, even when clearly and concisely written, can be difficult to digest. So, for effective dissemination, the researcher needs to produce a summary, and perhaps convert it into different media such as slides or a poster.

The classic types of summary are an 'executive summary' for workplace research, which is usually between one and four pages long, or an 'abstract' for academic research, usually 250–500 words long. An executive summary or an abstract should give a distillation of the rationale, method and findings of the research. These are not easy to write, and will probably take several drafts, but they are useful for two reasons. First, the process will help you to clarify your own understanding of the key points of the research. Second, they are powerful tools for dissemination. Many more people will be prepared to read an executive summary or an abstract than a whole research report, dissertation or thesis.

Executive summaries and abstracts are quite dry, and there are many other ways to disseminate research. Academic or workplace research may be presented in person at meetings, seminars and conferences. Academic research may be further disseminated through such media as journal articles and book chapters. Workplace research may be further disseminated through a variety of methods including newsletters, exhibitions and websites. There is a movement among some qualitative and mixed methods researchers, both in the workplace and in academia, towards more creative methods of presentation and dissemination, using techniques such as poetry, song, video and storytelling (Kara, 2020: 215):

> I'm just coming to the end of a really interesting research dissemination exercise I've been involved in, it was well funded. They wanted a small substudy filming people about their experiences of having a joint crisis plan, three times over a year-and-a-half, so I've been working with a filmmaker to do this work and it's been really fascinating, a really good way forward.

Barriers to disseminating research and evaluation

Dissemination is subject to the same restraints of cost and time as other aspects of research or evaluation. Also, dissemination involves more work, often at the point when you may be feeling you've had quite enough of your research or evaluation project. You may have to: rewrite your research for different audiences; produce summaries in different media, such as posters or Microsoft PowerPoint presentations; and attend meetings and sound enthusiastic about the findings of a project which is, as far as you're concerned, in the past. And even if you can disseminate your work using only your existing summary or abstract, you may well face other barriers to the process.

If you produce research in the course of your work, your employer is likely to hold the copyright to your report, and will therefore have the right to decide what is done with the findings. Copyright laws vary in different countries. In the UK, the writer of any document holds the copyright to that document unless they have signed some kind of agreement to relinquish their rights over their 'intellectual property' (as creative output is known in legal circles). Research commissioners often demand the right to own the copyright of research that they have paid for, which seems reasonably justifiable. More worryingly, more and more universities are demanding the right to own the copyright of the work of their postgraduate students. The trouble with signing away your rights over your own research is that you lose the power to disseminate your findings. If someone else holds the copyright to your research or evaluation, they may not disseminate the knowledge you have worked so hard to gain, and this can be enormously frustrating. This may be due to lack of time, will or resources:

> People that do research for dissertation, they quite often end up choosing a topic that is work-related but there isn't a proper forum for such work to be disseminated. If you gain access to the dissertation repositories of the different universities, I think that nationwide there would be a considerable amount of research that is done that is never built on or capitalised.

Also, commissioners of research or evaluation may choose to suppress findings they find unpalatable, which can be understandable in terms of managing political pressures, but is nevertheless highly unethical.

Here is an excerpt from a research brief I received as I was writing the first edition of this book. The commissioning organisation is large, publicly funded, and has a good reputation. I'll call it GoodGuys. Its brief said:

> A report presenting an analysis of the research findings will be required from the successful supplier. However, it should be noted that GoodGuys may publish a report under its own name in respect of this research and reserves the right to draw and add in its own conclusions and recommendations. Proper acknowledgement will be given to the supplier in any GoodGuys report.
>
> GoodGuys may decide, for various reasons, to keep some of the research findings internal and not include them in the published report. This will be at GoodGuys' discretion.

The organisation has every right to do this in law, and it is presumably seeking to maintain its good reputation. This is eminently sensible when outsourcing research or evaluation to an unknown supplier who will produce findings and draw conclusions that are also as yet unknown. But my interpretation of GoodGuys' reasoning is also guesswork, as GoodGuys doesn't say why it stipulates these conditions. The part I have most difficulty with is 'for various reasons', particularly as this comes from an organisation that trumpets its commitment to transparency, accountability, honesty and openness all over its website. I think it should be transparent, honest and open about what might cause it to keep some of the research findings internal, and why. The lack of transparency here is unhelpful as it leads to inevitable but fruitless speculation. Will the organisation suppress findings it doesn't like? Will it ignore findings if it doesn't like the *researcher*?

Other potential barriers to dissemination include the willingness and skills of researchers themselves.

Presenting findings in person

Public speaking is many people's worst fear (Al-Naggar, 2012: 115). However, as a researcher, you will almost certainly need to present your findings in person at one time or another. This might involve:

- talking through your findings at a team meeting at work;
- making a class presentation to fellow students;
- holding a community event to present findings to participants;
- presenting your findings at a conference.

If the prospect of doing anything like this makes you cringe, here is some information that may help you.

We saw in Chapter 1 that communication is a key skill for researchers. Presentation is only another form of communication. It's just talking to people. Okay, you're talking to a lot of people at once, which makes it a bit unusual. But focus on the fact that it's simply talking to people, telling them about a topic you know well, and that's something you do every day.

 As you present your work, aim to relax as much as possible, and take your time.

The language and structure you use will be different if you are presenting your research in writing than if you are giving a spoken presentation. Everyone uses language and grammar differently in speech than in writing. This is natural, and unconsciously understood, which explains why two of the biggest blunders you can make are to read a verbal presentation from a written script, or to read your PowerPoint slides word for word. Novice or nervous presenters often do one or other of these, but either approach will come across as stilted and unnatural. They will at best bore, and at worst alienate, your audience.

 Use pictures rather than words on PowerPoint slides, so that your audience can look at the pictures while they listen to your words. There are plenty of free photo libraries on the internet, such as Pixabay and Unsplash, where you can find images to use.

If you need to give a spoken presentation, the key is thorough preparation. Write a full script if you like; the process of writing will help to clarify your thoughts, and producing a full script can be a confidence-boosting exercise. But once you have a script, you need to find a way to commit it to memory. I don't mean learning it word for word, although you can if you want to. However, that would be very time-consuming and I believe there are better ways as recitation of rote learning is almost as boring as listening to someone read their slides. (I once went to a fringe theatre show in which an actor recited one of the books of Milton's *Paradise Lost*. It was an admirable feat of memory, but not in itself very interesting or entertaining; I'm ashamed to admit that my main remembrance of the event was my amusement at the incongruous sounds from the Morris dancing that was taking place just outside the window.)

My own approach to any verbal presentation is to summarise it as a narrative, whether from a full script or from the ideas in my head. I try to reduce the presentation to around five key elements that I can write on a single index card. So, for example, if I were going to present the story of *Little Red Riding Hood*, this is what I might write on the card:

- Little girl lives in forest with mother.
- Girl needs to visit sick grandmother but is in danger from big bad wolf.
- Girl makes it to grandmother's, BUT....
- Sick grandmother turns out to be big bad wolf in disguise, eek!
- Little girl saved at last minute by hunter. Phew.

With that index card in my hand, I could spend several minutes telling the story, with embellishment, description and drama, to bring it to life. Making your presentation into a story is helpful for you, as it is easier to remember what you want to say. It's also helpful for your audience:

> In teaching, I illustrate with stories, and the students respond, it makes sense, it's clear. I use a lot of case studies in assignments and class activities, all of them are from my experience, obviously anonymised but they're real, this is what you're faced with. The feedback I get is that it helps them understand, it makes it real.

The same applies to research and evaluation. It is often possible to talk about and present your work in a story-like way, which is a good idea as people enjoy, remember and learn from stories (Gabriel, 2000: 1). An index card is easy to hold unobtrusively but, if you feel you need more notes, keep them to a page of A4 at most. And do use bullet points rather than paragraphs of prose that might tempt you to read rather than speak. Make sure your bullet points are well spaced and in a large font so that they are easy to read.

Verbal presentations can be nerve-racking even for people who aren't terrified of public speaking. Even more so if you're presenting interim findings, when you may be less confident in your research than at final presentation stage. But remember that people attending interim presentations may give feedback or make suggestions that will prove invaluable to your research and which you couldn't receive in any other way. Of course this is not guaranteed to happen, but by presenting you are creating a new opportunity for your research to improve, which is good research practice.

Invite the audience to question you as you go along if they want you to clarify anything. The prospect of taking questions may seem terrifying, but you need to have confidence in your research and in your own knowledge of your research. The most likely outcome is that the audience will be interested in what you have to say, and will ask questions that you can answer easily. If anyone asks you something you can't answer straight away, say so, get their contact details, and tell them you will find an answer and let them know.

 Discuss your presentation with a colleague or other trusted audience member ahead of time and prime them to ask a question. This breaks the ice and makes you more confident as you already know the answer.

It can be helpful to give people a short handout with the key points from your research. This should include your contact details so that people can get in touch with you later if they think of something else they would like to ask or contribute.

The most formal type of presentation is at a conference. There are two important differences between workplace and academic conference presentations. First, you have to apply to give a presentation at an academic conference, usually by sending an abstract or summary – which can be difficult when you haven't written your presentation yet because the conference is six months away and you're still in the middle of collecting data. Second, if you are accepted for an academic presentation, you may need to write a fully referenced paper, similar to a journal article.

In times gone by everyone was expected to read their papers to the audience. These days this is less often the case, and I think there are two reasons for this. First, people rarely speak faster than 150 words per minute, which means that a 20-minute presentation can only be 2,500 words long – and that is a very short space in which to put forward a rounded and well-reasoned argument (and much shorter than most journal articles, which usually weigh in at around 5,000–8,000 words). Second, listening to an inexperienced and unskilled reader can be unbelievably boring, which makes it hard to engage with their argument.

The best way to give an academic paper is to write the paper and then prepare and deliver a presentation following the advice on workplace presentations given earlier in this chapter. You should provide handouts – either a full copy of your written paper or a summary of the key points with your email address so that anyone who wants the full paper, or more information about your research, can get it from you by email.

Dissemination of research findings is a higher priority in academic research than in other workplaces. This doesn't mean it's easier. Competition for places to present at conferences can be fierce. Also, conference presentations are often concurrent, which means there may be several taking place at the same time, and conference delegates can choose which to attend. It can feel dispiriting when you have worked hard for months to reach the point of presenting your work, and you are faced with six people scattered around a room that could hold 80. But don't be discouraged: those are the six people who are really interested in your work, and may well have useful contributions to offer, both during your presentation and later in the conference as you meet over coffee or lunch.

It is also good practice to present your findings to participants before finalising research, especially in workplace research such as evaluation. As we saw in Chapter 3, this is good ethical practice. It helps people to feel their involvement has been worthwhile, reduces 'research fatigue', and can improve the quality of research findings. What's more, input from participants can even improve the quality of future research:

> We learned a lot this year from the mistakes on last year's training needs analysis. People who took part in the survey highlighted problems with the survey: size of sample, the need to ask more open questions to get qualitative data – we got quite a lot of feedback from our users in the survey which enabled us to expand it and hopefully make it more useful for this year.

Presenting research to participants is also helpful more broadly, in demonstrating the value of participation and the reasons for doing the research:

> There are so many people asking for information, and so little of it is fed back, that people get research fatigue and won't want to get involved.

Sometimes, however, presenting research to participants can be difficult or impossible. For example, if your participants are itinerant homeless people, or people in police custody, you may not be able to bring them together – or even find them again – at a later stage. But where it does work, it has a number of practical and ethical advantages, as this interviewee found:

> We held a feedback session for the patients that took part and invited every single one of them. We presented it to them first before anyone had seen anything. We asked them if it was an accurate reflection of what had been said, told them what was going to form the recommendations. 'What do you think about these? Are they workable? Have you got any better suggestions?' Then we formed our final. I don't think it happens very often. Most of the patients that were involved, a lot of them had been involved with other things before, there were a significant number that expressed surprise at

being invited to come in again at that stage. Most of them said, 'We're an afterthought.' If you're doing research in the community, they shouldn't be an afterthought.

The pros and cons of some common presentation methods are set out in Table 14.1.

Table 14.1: Pros and cons of different presentation methods

Method	Pros	Cons
Informal presentation at a meeting or seminar	Can be useful for reaching a small group of interested people	May get lost or sidelined if other agenda items take precedence
Formal presentation at a meeting or conference	Can be useful for reaching a larger group of people who may be interested	Nerve-racking for some researchers; time-consuming; may involve travel and other costs
Community event	Good way to include research participants; good for local publicity; can be lots of fun	Time-consuming and resource-intensive

Sharing findings online

Findings can be shared online in person, such as through a webinar or online conference, or by uploading a research output to the internet. However, simply uploading a research output is unlikely to ensure it is found and consumed by its intended audience. You would also need to alert people to its existence via email, social media and perhaps also hard copy communication instruments such as leaflets or posters.

If you are only sharing findings online, it is important to be aware of who you will not be able to reach. This will include people who choose not to use the internet and people who are unable to use the internet. It may also include people who do use the internet but choose not to use, or cannot access, the virtual space where you are sharing your findings. For those of us who use the internet daily, it can seem as if 'all human life is there', but it is important to remember that is not the case.

Data visualisation

Data visualisation is the process of displaying data, or information based on data, in graphic form. This can include graphs, charts, diagrams, maps, and so on. Visualising data effectively takes work and, for most people, means acquiring some new skills (Kirk, 2016: 1). It is worth the effort, however, because visualising the key points you want to make helps people to understand and remember what you have said (Evergreen, 2014: 18).

While there are no hard-and-fast rules, on the whole graphs and charts are useful for presenting quantitative data, while diagrams and maps are usually more appropriate for qualitative data. The topic of how to visualise data is too broad to address here, as you need to consider all sorts of questions, such as:

- What do you want to visualise?
- How can you represent that to make the most impact on your audience?
- How should you design that representation?
- What is the best way to arrange the elements of the design?
- Which colours should you use?
- Which fonts should you use?

If you want to investigate data visualisation in more detail, you will find resources to help you in the 'Further reading' section at the end of this book.

Dissemination methods

Dissemination is most effective when it's tailored to the needs of your various audiences (Robson and McCartan, 2016: 488). For example, if you are carrying out an evaluation of a community-based service as part of your work, you might:

- give a full written research report to your manager;
- email the executive summary to your colleagues in partner agencies;
- hold a community event in which research participants help to present the findings to the wider community.

If you are doing postgraduate study, you might:

- present your proposed method verbally in class;
- present initial findings through a Microsoft PowerPoint presentation at a departmental seminar;
- give your written dissertation to examiners;
- publish your final conclusions in a peer-reviewed academic journal article.

Dissemination doesn't only happen when the research is completely finished. Sometimes it's useful to disseminate interim findings:

> I did lots of little dissemination exercises, which didn't take much but kept them in the loop.

There is a wide range of possible methods for disseminating research, each of which has its pros and cons. The pros and cons of the most commonly used methods are summarised in Table 14.2.

Table 14.2: Pros and cons of different dissemination methods

Method	Pros	Cons
Written report or dissertation	Can include full details of the research	Too long for most people to read
Executive summary or abstract	Short length makes it accessible; helps people decide whether to read more	Only gives an overview
Peer-reviewed academic journal article	Good for reaching interested academics; career-enhancing for academics and people wanting to be academics	Researcher has no control over reviewer or editorial input; limited audience, especially if not an open access journal
Article in non-peer-reviewed academic journal or professional journal	Should be easier to achieve than peer-reviewed publication; may reach a wider audience of interested people	Not regarded as highly as publication in peer-reviewed journals by some people
Email	Can reach a lot of people; cheap or free	Recipients may not read it; won't reach everyone
Online	Can, in theory, reach most of the people in the world; cheap or free	Often used as a box-ticking dissemination exercise rather than part of a well thought-out strategy
Creative methods (film, art exhibition, drama etc)	More engaging; improves understanding and retention of information	Time-consuming; you need suitable skills
Mass media (newspapers, magazines, radio, TV, etc)	Can reach a lot of people	Research findings may be misrepresented or taken out of context

When you start thinking about dissemination – which, ideally, should be at an early stage of your research project – you need to consider questions such as:

- Who do I have to tell about my findings?
- Who do I want to tell about my findings?
- Who else might find my research or evaluation useful?

In the same way that research questions help you to identify suitable research methods, the answers to these 'who?' questions can help you to work out how best to disseminate your research. When you have answers to these questions, you will know who your potential audiences are. When you know who your audiences are, you can decide which method or methods are likely to be most effective for each audience.

With audiences from your own profession or academic discipline, you can use professional or academic language without the need to censor or define relevant jargon. With professionals from partner agencies or academics from different disciplines, you can use a fair amount of professional or academic language, with perhaps a definition here and there as you see fit. With professionals from other agencies or non-academics, you will need to keep jargon to a minimum and define any technical terms that you can't avoid using. And with the general public, you will need to use plain English (Clark-Carter, 2010: 392).

Disseminating workplace research

The most common ways in which workplace research is disseminated are:

• by written presentation in a newsletter;
• by email to colleagues;
• on a website.

A written presentation, whether for a newsletter, an email circular to colleagues or a website, should be clear and concise. Again, it should include your contact details so that people can get back to you if they have any questions.

There are more creative ways to disseminate workplace research, such as through a drama performance or an art exhibition (Kara, 2020: 222). Some workplaces take more readily to these than others, schools and museums being two of the main ones in my experience. Using creative methods can stimulate interest from people where it might not otherwise exist. However, it is important not to let the method of dissemination obscure the messages you want to communicate.

Dissemination of research findings is often a low priority in busy public service organisations:

> To be honest, unless it's a major project and there's been a catastrophe, there doesn't seem to be anywhere that the findings go to, from my department.

This is both unfortunate and unethical, because it prevents the learning from that research being shared.

Even where the conditions for dissemination are good, colleagues may be dismissive of research that they feel is telling them something they already know. This happens most often with evaluation research. 'What's the point of doing all that research', they may say, 'to tell us what we knew already?' The answer is that there is now evidence for their assertions, evidence that may be useful as a lever in making necessary changes to the service or obtaining funding. Sometimes 'what everybody knows' is actually wrong. At other times, the conclusion is correct, but the reasoning is incorrect. For example, providers of a service that is in great demand may conclude that their service is well used because it is of good quality. A service evaluation may show that there are many ways in which the quality of the service could be improved, and it is only well used because there is no other similar service within easy reach. This is why managers, funders and so on are reluctant to make decisions on the basis of 'what everyone knows' and much prefer to base their reasoning on evidence.

Disseminating academic research

The most common ways in which academic research is disseminated are:

- through a poster at a conference;
- as an article in an academic journal;
- as a chapter in an academic book.

Academic conferences often have space for posters to be displayed, and these are intended to present a summary of research findings. Like verbal presentations, posters can cover interim or final findings. They are usually large in size, like a flip-chart sheet, or even larger. Visual learners often enjoy making and looking at posters, while others may view the prospect with dread. If you are planning to make a poster, here are a few tips:

- Find out the size of poster preferred by the event organisers, and what kind of fixings they intend to use.
- Don't use large areas of dense text.
- Do use attention-grabbing visuals such as headings, pictures, graphs, cartoons, and so on.
- Don't make it too busy – keep it simple to get your messages across more effectively.
- Do include your contact details.
- Make two copies and transport them separately (ideally in suitably sized cardboard tubes) in case one gets damaged.

Academics, too, may be open to more creative methods of dissemination. I have been to conferences and seminars where research findings have been communicated through song, poetry, storytelling and multimedia presentations.

The advice on writing in Chapter 13 will help if you are aiming at publication in an academic journal or book. However, writing up all or part of your work for professional publication involves some different and specific skills. If you want to write for a journal, you need to decide which journal is most appropriate, and then research that journal to find out as much as you can about its criteria for publication, how its articles are structured, their length, and so on (Murray, 2019: 41). You also need to be prepared to receive and deal with detailed feedback from reviewers, which you may disagree with and which may even be destructive (Murray, 2019: 188). Writing a chapter in an academic book can be an easier process, but you can't simply decide to write a chapter; you need to find a suitable 'call for chapter proposals' or wait for someone who is editing a book to ask you to become involved.

You will find resources to help you write and publish an academic journal article in the 'Further reading' section at the end of this book.

Dissemination ethics

Disseminating research is an ethical act in itself, but only if the research is presented accurately, fully and accessibly to the right people. The question of who 'the right people' are can sometimes be a tricky one to answer. Generally speaking, it is held to be good practice to include all your research participants. However, this can be difficult if your participants are, for example, terminally ill or serving custodial sentences. It can also cause anxiety for the researcher, as this interviewee shows:

> For me, when I do a piece of research, I send it out to all the people who took part in it and that's daunting in case you've misrepresented them.

As well as participants, your dissemination should ideally include everyone else who has an interest in the research. This includes funders, commissioners, tutors, supervisors, people who helped you along the way, people who work with your research participants, and so on. It is not always easy to know how best to approach your potential audiences. Simply putting your research online does not make it accessible unless you tell people where it is. It is equally pointless to send a fat research report to everyone you can think of, because that would be expensive and most of them wouldn't read it. You need a strategy somewhere in between the two options.

Put both a summary and the full report online, and send people a short email describing your research with links they can click on if they want to read more.

Universities may not have the resources or the will to disseminate all the research that is done by their postgraduate students, and may choose to focus on that which will best serve their purposes. This is unethical. All knowledge gained should be shared, however unpleasant or unwelcome it may be. There may also be unethical barriers to the dissemination of workplace research such as evaluation, as this interviewee explains:

> It's a real political issue, dissemination. We're going to be met with a lot of resistance about putting people's opinions on the website. People worry about what if they say something negative? The organisation censors itself very highly. It could be a department like press and marketing commenting on content and programmes because it wants to advertise or give a certain style of voice. I think it should be content-led rather than style-led, in a way; content should inform style. It would

make me respect an organisation if they said what they could learn from this, because it would make me feel like they want to work with people, but if an institution is only blowing its trumpet, it doesn't feel like it's truly participating in a dialogue at all.

As we saw earlier, the barriers to dissemination can include political will. As a result, during my career as an independent researcher, I have had some interesting experiences with the ethics of dissemination. At times I have lost clients by holding fast to my ethical position. By contrast, other clients have told me that they value my input particularly because I work to a high ethical standard. This doesn't mean I'm perfect; in my research and evaluation practice, I have done things that I would now, on reflection and with more experience, judge as unethical. But I have always aimed to consider ethical issues as fully as possible at all stages of every research process, and to act wherever it seems necessary. I think that's all anyone can ask.

Conclusion

There's not much point banging on about the importance of disseminating research and evaluation without some acknowledgement that it's also important to be receptive to research disseminated by others. Whether you ever want to do any more research yourself or not, your experience of conducting research or evaluation should make you a more discerning reader of other people's research. As a minimum, you should read the journal that is most relevant to your practice. However, achieving even this minimum standard isn't always easy for busy people.

Some people choose to keep themselves up to date with relevant reading in their own time. If you're studying on top of work, this is probably your only option. However, if you're doing workplace research, you should have time to do the necessary reading within working hours. If this is not the case, consider using some of the negotiating techniques covered in Chapter 6 to lobby for more time to read the evidence from research and evaluation. This will enable you to use others' findings to improve your own and your colleagues' practice. And putting research into practice is the topic of the next chapter.

> **CASE STUDIES**
> Ana decides to write up her findings for an academic journal. She is pleased to find a suitable open access journal that does not charge writers for publication. Ana researches the journal thoroughly. Then she gets a copy of Wendy Belcher's book on *Writing Your Journal Article in Twelve Weeks* from the library, and follows the guidance set out therein.

Ali and his co-researchers present their draft recommendations to staff of the department for discussion and input before they are finalised. The discussion is useful and they make a few important amendments. They create a colourful illustrated summary of their evaluation that they share with participants and colleagues and place on the organisation's website.

EXERCISES

1. Return to the research questions you devised in Chapter 5 and worked on further in the exercises for Chapter 10. What would be the best ways to present and disseminate that research?

2. Think of 10 methods of dissemination that have not been mentioned in this chapter. Use your imagination – nothing is off limits!

Discussion questions

1. Why is dissemination important?
2. What can you do to ensure a spoken presentation is well received?
3. When might creative methods of dissemination be particularly applicable?
4. How can you help audiences to understand and remember what you tell or show them?
5. What steps can you take to make sure people with an interest in your research get to know about your findings?

Debate topic

Dissemination is just shouting into the void.

15

How can research create positive change?

Chapter summary

This chapter includes:

- An overview of research impact
- A discussion of getting research evidence into policy
- An introduction to research implementation
- An introduction to knowledge exchange
- The recent move to a more holistic approach

Introduction

By this stage I would hope you are clear about what your research is for. You may be doing your research because your employer has told you to, or because you want to get a qualification that will help you in your career. Research can indeed be very useful in your job or career. Nevertheless, you are probably also aiming to do your research well, and to have your findings used in ways that will benefit others as well as yourself. Most people do – or commission, or fund – research because they want to create positive change in the world. This is, ultimately, the point of research: it is what research is for.

As we saw in Chapter 4, there are a number of barriers that can make it difficult to use the knowledge gained by research or evaluation to improve your practice. Practitioners, particularly those who become involved in research or evaluation, often find these barriers intensely frustrating. This is because they can see how theory and findings could benefit their service users in practice, and therefore improve society as a whole:

> There's a belief that research is done by academics, uni people. We need to be bringing that more to the workplace, that's where I see bridging the gap between the theory and practice.

> I wish that more nurses, midwives and health visitors would embrace research and evaluation to improve their practice and develop the

professions. It is a fascinating experience, an achievement and skills that are transferable in a number of practical ways.

What I'd like to see is a real valuing of research in practice and that's got to come from practitioners and employers as well.

The good news is that practitioners who undertake research or evaluation are in a position to help break down these barriers. Practitioners may not have the power to change commissioning or management practices, but they can use their research findings to inform and develop their work (Bloor, 2011: 413).

Research and evaluation conducted by practitioners often addresses real-world, front-line problems. Doing research well, and disseminating it thoroughly, can help to demystify research and increase people's confidence in the process. This chapter discusses how your research can create positive change – a process sometimes known as 'research impact'. We consider how research impact can affect knowledge, practice and/or policy. Also, we outline some steps you can take to help your own research create positive change.

Research impact

All research has some kind of impact. The Global Research Council (GRC, 2019: 1) suggests there are several different kinds of impact, including (but not limited to):

- Scientific impact through the advancement of knowledge.
- Social impact through the development of societies.
- Economic impact through fostering innovation.

Other kinds of impact include professional impact (publications, awards), environmental impact (reduced pollution) or cultural impact (increased tolerance of difference) (Kara, 2020: 232). As these examples suggest, positive impacts are the most desirable and are what researchers usually work towards. However, it is not always possible to predict the impacts of research, which can take a long time to be fully understood or felt. DNA was first discovered in 1869 by Swiss doctor Friedrich Miescher, but researchers did not realise that DNA was the genetic material in the cells of living organisms until 1943. DNA-based identity testing, now the fulcrum of many family and police investigations, began with the discovery of DNA fingerprinting in the mid–1980s (Saad, 2005: 130). And work on modifying DNA to treat diseases has only begun to come to fruition, in the shape of treatments or 'gene therapies' approved for use, in the last few years. The impact of that discovery made over 150 years ago is still reverberating around the world, and DNA research may have more surprises for us in future.

Friedrich Miescher could not possibly have imagined the far-reaching positive consequences of his discovery. However, the unforeseen impacts of research may also be negative (Penfield et al, 2014: 22). This can be the case even if research is high quality and ethically conducted. Conversely, unethical research can have positive impacts. There are horrific examples of medical experiments on humans from Europe and Asia in the 20th century, which caused great harm and were sometimes lethal (Tsuchiya, 2008). More recently, there has been considerable controversy about whether or not the data from this kind of research should be used (Cohen, 1990). Some people say it should not be used because the data was collected in horrific, abhorrent ways. Some say it should not be used because the experiments were not conducted systematically or in accordance with good research practice. Others argue that it should be used because its use can benefit people who are alive today. This is an insoluble argument with a huge emotional dimension – for some people, using this data dishonours the memories of those who were injured and died to provide it; for other people, using this data serves as a form of tribute to those who were injured and died in its collection. I am not taking a position in this debate; the point I wish to make here is that this data, collected in some of the most unethical ways possible, has the potential to lead to positive impacts, including saving lives (Cohen, 1990).

We saw an example of ethical research in Chapter 4, the participatory research conducted with the nomadic Roma people in Europe, who are highly marginalised in European society. The method used was critical communicative methodology, or CCM. This is a form of participatory research in which everyone is held to have relevant expertise – not necessarily in the same areas, but everyone is an expert in some areas, and everyone's expertise can be useful in research. Roma people are frequently discriminated against and have difficulty accessing basic services such as health, education and housing. Spanish researchers used CCM with Roma participants over some years, first building trust and then bringing Roma people in as co-researchers, to investigate what could improve Roma people's life experiences. Roma co-researchers presented the findings at the European Parliament, where policymakers listened and then developed a new European strategy and later, changed laws to give Roma people more rights and so improve their life experiences (Munté et al, 2011: 263). You might think that is a fantastic impact from a piece of research, and I would agree with you. But you also need to know that some other researchers came along 10 years later to find out what difference all this had made to Roma people's life experiences in Europe – and they found it had made very little difference, if any, as Roma people were still highly marginalised (Kende et al, 2020: 1).

These examples are useful in demonstrating the complexity of research impact. Indeed the word 'impact' can be misleading, as it has two meanings. The first is a very brief event in which one object hits another, such as a slap or crash, and the second is a much longer process of influence or effect. Research impact is more likely to align with the second meaning than the first, although the length of time between research and impact can vary a great deal (Penfield et al, 2014: 25). And some research has no impact at all:

> When it comes to writing reports and giving presentations, we're constantly pestered for input about how our participants felt about

getting involved, what the project meant to them. We'll get this about projects we've done two or three years ago, but the analysis has stayed in our department because other departments don't take it on.

Generally speaking, research impact will affect knowledge, practice or policy – or any two, or all three, of those categories. Historically, in Euro-Western academic research, the accumulation of knowledge was seen as a worthwhile end in itself. These days students and practitioners usually want their research to do more than add new knowledge, although that is still important. After all, if we know something already, there is no point investigating it through research. But adding new knowledge is not enough in itself. For new knowledge to have an impact, it needs to be taken up, considered, and used by others. And this does not always happen.

Research into policy

One group of 'others' who regularly take up, consider and use research findings are policymakers. However, researchers and policymakers rarely have a good understanding of the nature and complexity of each other's work. This makes it difficult for researchers to produce outputs that are useful for policymakers (Connelly et al, 2017: 185). Policymakers often have to work to tight deadlines, and will draw on all sorts of evidence, not just research evidence (Kara, 2022). Because of the pressurised nature of their work, policymakers will respond best to short, accessible research outputs, rather than long academic or evaluation research reports (Connelly et al, 2017: 184).

All of this means that student and practitioner research can be, and is, of use to policymakers. We saw in Chapter 4 that the user-led research into the effect of ECT, conducted by Rose, had an impact on health policy. One of the people I interviewed for this book had a similar tale to tell:

> I'd done a Master's. My dissertation for that was about traumatic experiences at work and their impact on fire officers. I'd done a little questionnaire asking people about their experiences. What came across was that there's an assumption that we have a natural ability to deal with these traumatic experiences and a natural ability to absorb their impact. That was about training and education. It led to revising national standards on support for the fire service.

So don't think that because you're 'only' a student, or 'only' a practitioner, your research cannot be used by policymakers. It can, particularly if you present your findings in an easily accessible way. Being a practitioner-student can be frustrating if your workplace doesn't value your research and your university doesn't value your practical experience. But it is precisely the combination of research skills and practical experience that can enable you to make a useful contribution to the world (Read et al, 2013: 35).

Implementation

'Impact' is primarily a noun. It is also sometimes used as a verb, but even then mostly without an object, to mean 'affected': 'rising prices impacted sales figures'. Either way there is no attribution. Implement, however, is most definitely a verb. People implement research findings – or do not – and the extent to which this is, or is not, done affects the impact of the research:

> I think that nationwide there would be a considerable amount of research that is done that is never built on or used. I think research is something that will in years to come take up a higher level. Some countries are far ahead of others in terms of establishing a research culture.

Research findings are implemented by many kinds of people – practitioners, managers, politicians and researchers themselves, among others. However, it is often the case that doing research may be easier than implementing its findings. There are numerous barriers to implementation, such as incompetence, corruption and prejudice (Du Mont and White, 2013), lack of relevant knowledge, skills and confidence (Bauer et al, 2015), and lack of political will or resources. Also, implementation often requires practitioners to make changes to the way they work (Bauer et al, 2015). People are notoriously resistant to this kind of change, so support through training, coaching, incentives and suchlike is often essential for successful implementation (Bauer et al, 2015). Yet this requires more resources – skills, time and therefore money, yet research budgets rarely include an allocation for implementation:

> What I'd like to see is a real valuing of research in practice and that's got to come from practitioners and employers as well. We often joke, can you imagine if you're sitting at your desk in a busy social work office reading the *British Journal of Social Work* and the manager comes out and says, 'What are you doing? We've got 12 cases that need assessment here!' It's flippant, but there is a real link, if you want practitioners that are evidence based you've got to have time to do it, to read, to keep up to date.

Creating an implementation strategy, at a very early stage, can help to overcome some of these barriers. To create a successful implementation strategy, you will need to:

- Pay close attention to the context for the research and its implementation.
- Understand what you want to achieve through the research: raise awareness, improve information, promote action?
- Identify goals that are appropriate to the nature of the research and to your target audiences.

- Work out what each of your audiences needs to know and/or do, and how best to convey these messages.
- Be aware of the possibility of unexpected barriers or enablers to implementation, and aim to address problems and maximise opportunities as soon as possible.
- Define suitable indicators to help you work out whether or when you have reached each of your goals.
- Plan to review and update the strategy on the basis of learning from the research and from the implementation itself.

 Think about implementation early in your research planning process.

Getting research into practice is known as 'implementation' in the UK and Europe. Other countries and continents use different names. For example, US health researchers may use the term 'translational research', which refers to ways of implementing laboratory and clinical research within applied healthcare (Drolet and Lorenzi, 2011). Some Canadian health researchers called this 'knowledge translation' (Straus et al, 2011), although later some Irish health researchers used the same term to refer to accessible dissemination of research (Deliv et al, 2021). There are dozens of other terms with no common definition (Tugwell et al, 2011: 1). However, there is general agreement that implementation is both necessary and complicated. Also, it is rarely covered in the research literature and seems to be poorly understood by most researchers (Deliv et al, 2021).

Knowledge exchange

So far this chapter has assumed a one-way relationship from research to practice. However, practice also informs research, not least by identifying topics for research to explore (Byrne, 2011: 191). And some people see research as an arena where people are continually exchanging knowledge, such that everyone involved learns from some or all of the others (Becker and Bryman, 2012a: 361). This view is most commonly held by people using transformative methodologies, although it is also held by some people using other methodologies.

Knowledge exchange sounds as if it is an event, like currency exchange, but it is, in fact, a process. I expect you have had the common experience of being told something and only realising what it meant, or its full implications, some time later. And changing knowledge at a social level is very time-consuming, as we saw with the example given earlier in this chapter of the research conducted with Roma people in Europe.

Also, knowledge exchange is not something that only happens within a research team, or within the stakeholders of a research project. Knowledge exchange can happen more widely, such as by involving other colleagues, publications or the mainstream or social media.

A holistic approach

Some national and global bodies, most notably in health research, have begun to take a more holistic approach to research impact and implementation, its use in policy and knowledge exchange. For this approach, health researchers are using the term 'knowledge translation' (which we have already met as synonymous with 'implementation' in some contexts). The Canadian Institutes of Health Research offer the following definition of knowledge translation:

> A dynamic and iterative process that includes synthesis, dissemination, exchange and ethically-sound application of knowledge to improve the health of Canadians, provide more effective health services and products and strengthen the health care system.

The World Health Organization offers a similar definition of knowledge translation:

> The synthesis, exchange, and application of knowledge by relevant stakeholders to accelerate the benefits of global and local innovation in strengthening health systems and improving people's health.

However, the Social Sciences and Humanities Research Council of Canada uses the term 'knowledge mobilisation':

> The reciprocal and complementary flow and uptake of research knowledge between researchers, knowledge brokers and knowledge users – both within and beyond academia – in such a way that may benefit users and create positive impacts within Canada and/ or internationally, and, ultimately, has the potential to enhance the profile, reach and impact of social sciences and humanities research.

Looking at these definitions, it seems to me that knowledge translation and knowledge mobilisation are the same thing. All of these definitions usefully encapsulate the fact that there is no clearly shaped relationship between research and its uses. Some people try to claim a linear relationship, as in the theory of change approach to evaluation with its inputs, outputs, outcomes and impacts. Others promote a cyclical relationship, with questions being identified, research conducted to answer those questions, findings implemented, leading to new questions, and so on, in a never-ending dance. These kinds of conceptions can be useful to aid understanding, but they bear very little relation to the untidiness of real life, where the links between research, practice and policy are dynamic and complex (Becker and Bryman, 2012b: 50).

Conclusion

When you start out as a researcher, doing research can seem like a daunting task. When you reach the stage of trying to implement your findings, the research seems like the easy part. If you are struggling with this, remember that's not because you are a novice or incompetent; it's because implementation is often very difficult to achieve. It is important to do all you can to ensure your findings are implemented, while accepting that your work may not make much difference. There is an old saying, 'Hope for the best, plan for the worst'. I would adapt that here to say 'Plan for the best, be prepared to accept the worst' – the 'worst' here being that your research makes no discernible impact.

Whether or not your research makes an impact on the wider world, it will undoubtedly have made an impact on you. Completing a research project will benefit your career in various ways, not least by helping you be a more discerning user of other people's research. So one way or another, your research will have an impact.

CASE STUDIES

Ana would love her findings to have an impact, because she wants the media to be consistent in representing non-heterosexual families in sympathetic ways. She realises that, although an academic journal article will help her career, it is unlikely to be read by many people working in the media, even if it is openly accessible. So she decides to pitch a piece to the *Huffington Post* for wider coverage and in hope of her findings being picked up and implemented.

Ali and his co-researchers hold a meeting with staff from the department whose work they evaluated. The aim is to produce an action plan for implementing the recommendations of the evaluation. Ali asks for the action plan to include SMART milestones, with each having an associated date for completion and name(s) of people responsible. His colleagues agree and, after a productive discussion, the action plan is created.

EXERCISE

What specific actions do you think could be taken to implement the following research findings:

a. A hospital needs to reduce the number of discharged patients who are readmitted within seven days.

b. A sporting facility is under-used by two different minority ethnic groups from its catchment area.

c. A university needs to attract more women and non-binary people to its science and technology courses.

d. A brand of herbal tea needs to increase its market share (but only has a small marketing budget, so cannot afford to pay for much advertising).

e. A home for adults with severe learning disabilities needs to improve the satisfaction levels of its residents' families. The residents are happy, but the families are particularly dissatisfied with the communication they receive from the home.

Discussion questions

1. Why is adding to the body of human knowledge not enough for most research to do?
2. Why isn't all research described as 'knowledge exchange'?
3. Why do you think the topics covered in this chapter are rarely researched or written about?

Debate topic

Knowledge should be collectively owned by everyone.

16

Conclusion

One interviewee for this book, a researcher who is also an experienced tutor and supervisor of practitioners undertaking research, gave me her views about what she thought practitioners coming to research for the first time would find most challenging:

> I think the thing with practitioners is, there are certain things which are straightforward and others which are mystical and magical and difficult. They can formulate really good research questions which are really meaningful in practice, they've got all the skills to make research work: engage people quickly, good communication skills, can explain research in lay terms, they can use all of those personal skills that they've got but the theoretical stuff and the analysis that goes around it tends to be more difficult. It's interesting and relates to everything they do so finding the focus is the hardest bit, especially finding a very small and contained research question that means it's manageable and leads to a small piece of analysis is often the trick. The students who don't do very well often fail to find that focus adequately, they think they've got it going in but it gets a bit flaky when it comes to analysis. They do bring a lot of strengths to the research process, they have to manage the identity of a researcher rather than a practitioner, but it's really the theoretical and analytic bits where they need the input.

Judging by the input from other interviewees, this is an accurate summary of the situation. Another part of the work that has proved to be difficult for beginner researchers is learning to have confidence in your own work and your knowledge. This also applies to both workplace and academic research:

> There is another researcher that works for the organisation and she was available for me to pick brains and she read through things and made comments and stuff. Interestingly, we clashed over a couple of things, and one of my learning points has been to trust my instincts. I went against my instincts because she has more experience than I do, I deferred to her knowledge and in hindsight I shouldn't have. It meant some of our data couldn't be used. If I was giving people advice, I'd say, 'Do listen to what people say that have been involved in research before, but it's your research. If it doesn't sit well with you, take it on board but make your own decision, and don't automatically assume that they will be right just because they have more experience.'

I wish someone had said this to me, you've really got to take responsibility from day one. You've not got to expect the supervisors to have the answers or think other people know better. In that first year you've got to work at developing your own confidence in the field so that you believe the stuff that you're thinking. I do think that was my biggest downfall, not standing up for myself against supervisors, academics who've come from different disciplines.

One essential research skill is the ability to change focus rapidly and frequently. It's a bit like having a zoom lens in your brain. We saw in Chapter 5 that you need to narrow the focus of your research topic as you plan your research. The focus changes I'm talking about here are the ones you need to make as you carry out your research project. You need to be able to shift focus from close-up (for example, to scrutinise one small piece of data, or to write a single paragraph) to mid-range (for example, to review your tasks for completion in the next week or fortnight) to a wide-angle view of the whole project.

Having said that, I wouldn't recommend using the wide-angle view more than you have to, because it can be so daunting. As soon as you've planned and prioritised, you shouldn't need to look at the project as a whole until you're well underway with writing, except briefly from time to time to make sure you're still on track. Keep it in the back of your mind, and focus from mid-range to close-up.

Let's recap the key points made in this book. First, more and more practitioners in public services are being required to carry out research on top of their day jobs. To do research well, you need to:

- plan early, plan thoroughly;
- read, write and think, critically, throughout the research process;
- find people you can talk to about your research;
- stay focused on the likely positive outcomes of your research;
- understand the broad paradigms of quantitative, qualitative and mixed methods research;
- make sure that research ethics underpin all stages of the process;
- look after yourself as well as everyone else;
- accept support from others;
- remember that research, theory and practice are closely linked;
- choose your research topic carefully: keep it small, keep it simple;
- write a proposal or plan at an early stage;
- organise your work – including time for breaks;
- manage your time;
- keep meticulous records;
- collect only as much data as you need;
- prepare your data accurately;
- code your data carefully;
- write clearly and concisely;

- disseminate your work widely and effectively;
- do what you can to ensure your findings are implemented;
- reward yourself when you achieve key milestones.

At times, practitioners may feel that their research is so small and local as to be pointless. There is certainly some odd research in the world, such as that celebrated by the Ig Nobel awards, which includes research into why woodpeckers don't get headaches, how to grow diamonds from tequila or how far penguins can poo (note: I did not make these up). But I think any research that aims to improve conditions for fellow human beings is worth doing, however small and local it may be.

Doing, and using, research is on the increase in public services, so it makes sense to learn the techniques so that you can understand and make effective use of research in your work even if you don't want to conduct research:

> I say as a practitioner, if you're doing an intervention with someone you need to be able to say why, and the answer, 'Because I think it might help', won't cut it. You might be doing it because law or policy dictates, or because it's the procedure of your agency, but that will be because research tells us it works. Or if you're in a commissioning agency, and tasked with commissioning a service for drug and alcohol users, and someone comes to you and says, 'We do this because the research shows it works', and someone else says, 'We do this because we think it helps', it's pretty clear who you're going to give your money to.

On the other hand, you may find that you really enjoy research or evaluation. In that case you may want to consider taking it up as a profession. Researchers and evaluators are employed by all sorts of publicly funded services, such as the police, health services, education services and so on. The larger non-profits often employ researchers. There are dedicated research organisations in most countries. Governments can offer varied and interesting careers for researchers. And, of course, academia has many roles for researchers. There is also the option to become a self-employed independent researcher. Each type of role has different challenges and opportunities. So if you think you'd like to become a professional researcher, it's probably best to start by doing some research!

Whether or not you enjoy carrying out research or evaluation, it is always an uncomfortable business. As a researcher, you're giving the unknown and the uncertain a large role in your life. Some people are at ease with this, but most people find it unpleasantly uncomfortable. Console yourself with this: if you don't feel very comfortable when you're doing research, you're probably doing it right.

I wish you the very best of luck.

Appendix 1
Job titles of interviewees

All the interviewees worked for public services in at least one of their jobs. I asked them to give me their job title(s) in a form that they thought best represented what they did, not necessarily in the form that was used by their employer(s). I was also concerned to protect their anonymity, so I removed any details that might have identified them, such as location. Here is a list of all 20 interviewees:

- Marketing and communications manager (non-profit, cultural)
- Head of early years and childcare (local authority, children's services, education, social care)
- Local involvement network (LINk) community researcher (health)
- Shared service manager (local authority customer services)
- Management and training consultant, associate tutor and honorary senior research fellow (private sector, criminal justice academic)
- Head of bereavement care (health)
- Health protection team – project lead, and midwifery lecturer (health, higher education)
- Third sector programme manager (non-profit)
- University lecturer and tutor, and director of a community interest company (higher education, non-profit)
- Freelance wellbeing and mental health consultant (non-profit, private sector)
- Probation officer and Open University associate lecturer (criminal justice, higher education)
- Senior development manager: children and families commissioner (NHS) (health)
- Senior lecturer and researcher in education (higher education, education)
- Museum outreach officer (non-profit, cultural)
- Mental health user consultant (private sector, health)
- Social worker and social work academic (social care, higher education)
- Reader in entrepreneurship (criminal justice, higher education)
- Counsellor and trainer in private practice, and acting project manager in the voluntary sector (private sector, non-profit, social care)
- Senior lecturer – School of Health and Social Services (higher education, health, social care)
- Middle management in further education college (education).

Appendix 2
Sample record-keeping grid

This grid was used by one of the interviewees for this book, who left in one reference so you can see how it was used.

Author/date/ publisher	Title	Quote/page	Why significant	Where potentially useful
Adair, J., 1988 Pan Books, London	Effective leadership	'There can be no success without working on the edge of failure', p 142	Risk of 'failure' – does this inhibit innovative leadership?	Section on leadership modes

Notes

Chapter 3

[1] See prores-project.eu/ethics-codes-and-guidelines

Chapter 5

[1] www.ipsos-mori.com/newsevents/ca/346/Three-Frequently-Asked-Questions.aspx
[2] https://stattrek.com/statistics/random-number-generator
[3] https://powerandsamplesize.com/Calculators
[4] https://en.wikipedia.org/wiki/Freeganism

Chapter 6

[1] Personal communication, Julie Miller, regularly from sometime in the 1970s until early 2020. Thanks, Mother.

Chapter 7

[1] Documents can be used for background research, as discussed here, and/or as data, which is discussed in Chapter 9.
[2] Mark Miller, former lexicographical proofreader, personal communication, 2011.
[3] https://repositories.webometrics.info/en/top_portals
[4] www.bl.uk/social-welfare

Chapter 8

[1] https://library.princeton.edu/resource/4085
[2] https://guides.library.harvard.edu/gsd/gis
[3] https://dataverse.org/about
[4] I am indebted to John Kaye of Jisc for the first draft of this section.
[5] https://datahelpdesk.worldbank.org/knowledgebase/articles/889386
[6] https://osdatahub.os.uk/docs/wmts/overview
[7] https://tfl.gov.uk/info-for/open-data-users/unified-api
[8] https://developer.twitter.com/en/docs
[9] www.nationalarchives.gov.uk/help/discovery-for-developers-about-the-application-programming-interface-api
[10] www.programmableweb.com/apis/directory
[11] www.programmableweb.com/api-university
[12] https://data.un.org

Chapter 10

[1] https://aoir.org/reports/ethics3.pdf

References

Alaszewski, A. (2006) *Using diaries for social research*, London: SAGE.

Alkin, M. (2013) 'Comparing evaluation points of view', in M. Alkin (ed) *Evaluation roots: A wider perspective of theorists' views and influences* (2nd edn), Thousand Oaks, CA: SAGE, pp 3–10.

Al-Naggar, R. (2012) 'Prevalence and associated factors of phobia and social anxiety among university students', *ASEAN Journal of Psychiatry*, 13(2): 112–21.

Banks, S. and Brydon-Miller, M. (2019) 'Ethics in participatory research', in S. Banks and M. Brydon-Miller (eds) *Ethics in participatory research for health and social well-being: Cases and commentaries*, Abingdon: Routledge, pp 1–30.

Barber, R., Boote, J., Glenys, P., Cooper, C. and Yeeles, P. (2011) 'Evaluating the impact of public involvement on research', in M. Barnes and P. Cotterell (eds) *Critical perspective on user involvement*, Bristol: Policy Press, pp 217–23.

Barker, M. (2014) 'Doing a literature review', in A. Vossler and N. Moller (eds) *The counselling and psychotherapy research handbook*, London: SAGE, pp 61–73.

Barone, T. and Eisner, E. (2012) *Arts based research*, London: SAGE.

Bartkowiak-Theron, I. and Sappey, J. (2012) 'The methodological identity of shadowing in social science research', *Qualitative Research Journal*, 12(1): 7–16.

Bartlett, R. and Milligan, C. (2021) *Diary method*, London: Bloomsbury.

Bassot, B. (2020) *The research journal: A reflective tool for your first independent research project*, Bristol: Policy Press.

Bauer, M., Damschroder, L., Hagedorn, H., Smith, J. and Kilbourne, A. (2015) 'An introduction to implementation science for the non-specialist', *BMC Psychology*, 3(32): 1–12. doi:10.1186/s40359-015-0089-9.

Baumeister, R. and Tierney, J. (2012) *Willpower: Why self-control is the secret to success*, London: Allen Lane.

Becker, H. (2007) *Writing for social scientists: How to start and finish your thesis, book or article*, Chicago, IL: Chicago University Press.

Becker, S. and Bryman, A. (2012a) 'Dissemination and knowledge transfer as part of the research process', in S. Becker, A. Bryman and H. Ferguson (eds) *Understanding research for social policy and social work: Themes, methods and approaches*, Bristol: Policy Press, pp 360–7.

Becker, S. and Bryman, A. (2012b) 'Modelling the research process', in S. Becker, A. Bryman and H. Ferguson (eds) *Understanding research for social policy and social work: Themes, methods and approaches*, Bristol: Policy Press, pp 50–4.

Bhana, A. (2006) 'Participatory action research: A practical guide for realistic radicals', in M. Terre Blanche, K. Durrheim and D. Painter (eds) *Research in practice: Applied methods for the social sciences* (2nd edn), Cape Town: University of Cape Town Press Ltd, pp 429–42.

Björk, B.-C., Welling, P., Laakso, M., Majlender, P., Hedlund, T. and Guðnason, G. (2010) 'Open access to the scientific journal literature: situation 2009', *PLOS ONE*, 5(6): e11273. doi:10.1371/journal.pone.0011273.

Bloor, M. (2011) 'Addressing social problems through qualitative research', in D. Silverman (ed) *Qualitative research: Issues of theory, method and practice*, London: SAGE, pp 399–415.

Booth, W., Colomb, G., Williams, J., Bizup, J. and Fitzgerald, W. (2016) *The craft of research* (4th edn), Chicago, IL: University of Chicago Press.

Bourgois, P. (2002) *In search of respect: Selling crack in El Barrio* (2nd edn), Cambridge: Cambridge University Press.

Bowen, G. (2009) 'Document analysis as a qualitative research method', *Qualitative Research Journal*, 9(2): 27–40.

Branfield, F. (2009) *Developing user involvement in social work education*, Workforce Development Report 29, London: Social Care Institute for Excellence.

Brown, N. (2021) *Making the most of your research journal*, Bristol: Policy Press.

Bryman, A. (2016) *Social research methods* (5th edn), Oxford: Oxford University Press.

Bryman, A. and Cramer, D. (2009) *Quantitative data analysis with SPSS 14, 15 and 16: A guide for social scientists*, London: Routledge.

Bunting, M. (2004) *Willing slaves: How the overwork culture is ruling our lives*, London: HarperCollins.

Byrne, D. (2011) *Applying social science: The role of social research in politics, policy and practice*, Bristol: Policy Press.

Christie, C. and Alkin, M. (2013) 'An evaluation theory tree', in M. Alkin (ed) *Evaluation roots: A wider perspective of theorists' views and influences* (2nd edn) Thousand Oaks, CA: SAGE, pp 11–57.

Cialdini, R.B. (2021) *Influence: The psychology of persuasion* (2nd edn), New York: Harper Business.

Clark-Carter, D. (2010) *Quantitative psychological research: A student's handbook* (3rd edn), Hove: Psychology Press.

Cohen, B.C. (1990) 'Nazi medical experimentation: The ethics of using medical data from Nazi experiments', Jewish Virtual Library, www.jewishvirtuallibrary. org/the-ethics-of-using-medical-data-from-nazi-experiments

Connelly, S., Vanderhoven, D., Durose, C., Matthews, P., Richardson, L. and Rutherfoord, R. (2017) 'Translation across borders: Connecting the academic and policy communities', in K. Facer and K. Pahl (eds) *Valuing interdisciplinary collaborative research: Beyond impact*, Bristol: Policy Press, pp 173–90.

Cottrell, S. (2005) *Critical thinking skills: Developing effective analysis and argument*, Basingstoke: Palgrave Macmillan.

Culshaw, S. (2019) 'The unspoken power of collage? Using an innovative arts-based research method to explore the experience of struggling as a teacher', *London Review of Education*, 17(3): 268–83, https://doi.org/10.18546/LRE.17.3.03

Dalton, J. (2020) 'Model making as a research method', *Studies in the Education of Adults*, 52(1): 35–48, doi:10.1080/02660830.2019.1598605.

Davies, M.B. (2007) *Doing a successful research project using qualitative or quantitative methods*, Basingstoke: Palgrave Macmillan.

Davis, C. (2010) *Statistical testing in practice with StatsDirect*, Tamarac, FL: Lumina Press.

Deleuze, G. and Guattari, F. (1987) *A thousand plateaus: Capitalism and schizophrenia* (translated from the original French by B. Massumi), Minneapolis, MN: University of Minnesota Press.

Deliv, C., Putnam, E., Devane, D., Healy, P., Hall, A., Rosenbaum, S. and Toomey, E. (2021) 'Development of a video-based evidence synthesis knowledge translation resource: applying a user-centred approach', medRxiv preprint, https://doi.org/10.1101/2021.03.19.21253944

Denscombe, M. (2014) *The good research guide: For small-scale social research projects* (5th edn), Maidenhead: Open University Press.

Diamond, S. (2010) *Getting more*, London: Penguin.

Dienstmann, G. (2021) *Mindful self-discipline: Living with purpose and achieving your goals in a world of distraction*, LiveAndDare Publications.

Drolet, B. and Lorenzi, N. (2011) 'Translational research: understanding the continuum from bench to bedside', *Translational Research*, 157(1): 1–5.

Du Mont, J. and White, D. (2013) 'Barriers to the effective use of medico-legal findings in sexual assault cases worldwide', *Qualitative Health Research*, 23(9): 1228–39.

Elbow, P. (1998) *Writing with Power: Techniques for Mastering the Writing Process* (2nd edn), Oxford: Oxford University Press.

Eldén, S. (2013) 'Inviting the messy: drawing methods and "children's voices"', *Childhood*, 20(1): 66–81.

Ellingson, L. (2017) *Embodiment in qualitative research*, Abingdon: Routledge.

Evergreen, S. (2014) *Presenting data effectively: Communicating your findings for maximum impact*, London: SAGE.

Fox, M., Martin, P. and Green, G. (2007) *Doing practitioner research*, London: SAGE.

Gabriel, Y. (2000) *Storytelling in organizations: Facts, fictions and fantasies*, Oxford: Oxford University Press.

García, B., Welford, J., and Smith, B. (2016) 'Using a smartphone app in qualitative research: the good, the bad and the ugly', *Qualitative Research*, 16(5): 508–25. doi:10.1177/1468794115593335.

Giles, J. (2005) 'Internet encyclopaedias go head to head', *Nature*, 438(7070): 900–1.

Glasby, J. (2011) 'From evidence-based to knowledge-based policy and practice', in J. Glasby (ed) *Evidence, policy and practice: Critical perspectives in health and social care*, Bristol: Policy Press, pp 85–98.

Goldacre, B. (2009) *Bad science*, London: Fourth Estate.

GRC (Global Research Council) (2019) 'Global Research Council Statement of Principles: Addressing expectations of societal and economic impact', www.globalresearchcouncil.org/fileadmin/documents/GRC_Publications/GRC_2019_Statement_of_Principles_Expectations_of_Societal_and_Economic_Impact.pdf

Greasley, P. (2008) *Quantitative data analysis using SPSS: An introduction for health and social science*, Maidenhead: Open University Press.

Hart, C. (2018) *Doing a literature review: Releasing the research imagination* (2nd edn), London: SAGE.

Home Office (2011) *User guide to Home Office crime statistics*, https://assets.publishing.service.gov.uk/government/uploads/system/uploads/attachment_data/file/116226/user-guide-crime-statistics.pdf

Howitt, D. and Cramer, D. (2005) *Introduction to research methods in psychology*, Harlow: Pearson Education.

Javits, C. (2008) *REDF's current approach to SRoI*, San Francisco, CA: REDF.

Jesson, J., Matheson, L. and Lacey, F. (2011) *Doing your literature review: Traditional and systematic techniques*, London: SAGE.

Kahneman, D. (2011) *Thinking, fast and slow*, London: Allen Lane.

Kara, H. (2018) *Research ethics in the real world: Euro-Western and Indigenous perspectives*, Bristol: Policy Press.

Kara, H. (2020) *Creative research methods: A practical guide* (2nd edn), Bristol: Policy Press.

Kara, H. (2022) 'What is good evidence?', in R. Iphofen and D. O'Mathúna (eds) *Ethical evidence and policymaking: Interdisciplinary and international research*, Bristol: Policy Press, pp 293–305.

Kara, H. and Khoo, S.-M. (2020a) *Researching in the age of COVID-19: Volume 1, Response and reassessment*, Bristol: Policy Press.

Kara, H. and Khoo, S.-M. (2020b) *Researching in the age of COVID-19: Volume 2, Care and resilience*, Bristol: Policy Press.

Kara, H. and Khoo, S.-M. (2020c) *Researching in the age of COVID-19: Volume 3: Creativity and ethics*, Bristol: Policy Press.

Kemshall, H. and Littlechild, R. (eds) (2000) *User involvement and participation in social care: Research informing practice*, London: Jessica Kingsley Publishers.

Kende, A., Hadarics, M., Bigazzi, S., Boza, M., Kunst, J.R., Lantos, N.A., Lasticova, B., Minescu, A., Pivetti, M. and Urbiola, A. (2020) 'The last acceptable prejudice in Europe? Anti-Gypsyism as the obstacle to Roma inclusion', *Group Processes & Intergroup Relations*, 24(3): 1–23. doi:10.1177/1368430220907701.

Kirk, A. (2016) *Data visualization: A handbook for data driven design*, London: SAGE.

Kramer, A., Guillory, J. and Hancock, J. (2014) 'Experimental evidence of massive-scale emotional contagion through social networks', *Psychological and Cognitive Sciences*, 111(24): 8788–90.

Kumar, R. (2005) *Research methodology: A step-by-step guide for beginners*, London: SAGE.

Langdridge, D. and Hagger-Johnson, G. (2009) *Introduction to research methods and data analysis in psychology* (2nd edn), Harlow: Pearson Education.

Leavy, P. (2015) *Method meets art: Arts-based research practice* (2nd edn), New York: Guilford Press.

Lewis, J. and McNaughton Nicholls, C. (2013) 'Design issues', in J. Ritchie, J. Lewis, C. McNaughton Nicholls and R. Ormston (eds) *Qualitative research practice: A guide for social science students and researchers*, London: SAGE, pp 47–76.

Markham, A. (2011) 'Internet research', in D. Silverman (ed) *Qualitative research: Issues of theory, method and practice*, London: SAGE, pp 110–27.

Mason, J. (2018) *Qualitative researching* (3rd edn), London: SAGE.

Merton, R. (2012 [1949]) 'On sociological theories of the middle range', in C. Calhoun, J. Gerteis, J. Moody, S. Pfaff and I. Virk (eds) *Classical sociological theory*, Chichester: Wiley-Blackwell, pp 531–43.

Munté, A., Serradell, O. and Sordé, T. (2011) 'From research to policy: Roma participation through communicative organization', *Qualitative Inquiry*, 17(3): 256–66.

Murray, R. (2016) *How to write a thesis* (4th edn), Buckingham: Open University Press.

Murray, R. (2019) *Writing for academic journals* (4th edn), Maidenhead: Open University Press.

Myers, J., Well, A. and Lorch, R. (2010) *Research design and statistical analysis* (3rd edn), London: Routledge.

Nicholls, J., Lawlor, E., Neitzert, E. and Goodspeed, T. (2012) *A guide to social return on investment*, London: The SRoI Network.

Notermans, C. and Kommers, H. (2012) 'Researching religion: the iconographic elicitation method', *Qualitative Research*, 13(5): 608–25, doi:10.1177/1468794112459672.

O'Neill, M. (2018) 'Walking, well-being and community: racialized mothers building cultural citizenship using participatory arts and participatory action research', *Ethnic and Racial Studies*, 41(1): 73–97, doi:10.1080/01419870.2017.1313439.

Ormston, R., Spencer, L., Barnard, M. and Snape, D. (2014) 'The foundations of qualitative research', in J. Ritchie, J. Lewis, C. McNaughton Nicholls and R. Ormston (eds) *Qualitative research practice: A guide for social science students and researchers*, London: SAGE, pp 1–26.

Pallant, J. (2010) *SPSS survival manual: A step-by-step guide to data analysis using SPSS* (4th edn), Maidenhead: Open University Press.

Patton, M. (2008) *Utilization-focused evaluation*, Thousand Oaks, CA: SAGE.

Pawson, R. and Tilley, N. (1997) *Realistic evaluation*, London: SAGE.

Penfield, T., Baker, M., Scoble, R. and Wykes, M. (2014) 'Assessment, evaluations, and definitions of research impact: a review', *Research Evaluation*, 23(2014): 21–32, doi:10.1093/reseval/rvt021.

Petticrew, M. and Roberts, H. (2005) *Systematic reviews in the social sciences: A practical guide*, Oxford: Blackwell.

Phillips, R. and Kara, H. (2021) *Creative writing for social research: A practical guide*, Bristol: Policy Press.

Piwowar, H., Priem, J., Larivière, V., Alperin, J., Matthias, L., Norlander, B., Farley, A., West, J. and Haustein, S. (2018) 'The state of OA: a large-scale analysis of the prevalence and impact of Open Access articles', *PeerJ*, 6, e4375, https://doi.org/10.7717/peerj.4375

Poynter, R. (2010) *The handbook of online and social media research: Tools and techniques for market researchers*, Chichester: John Wiley & Sons Ltd.

Prior, L. (2011) 'Using documents in social research', in D. Silverman (ed) *Qualitative research: Issues of theory, method and practice*, London: SAGE, pp 93–110.

Prosser, J. and Schwartz, D. (1998) 'Photographs within the sociological research process', in J. Prosser (ed) *Image-based research: A sourcebook for qualitative researchers*, London: RoutledgeFalmer, pp 115–30.

Punch, K. (2016) *Developing effective research proposals* (3rd edn), London: SAGE.

Rapley, T. (2011) 'Some pragmatics of data analysis', in D. Silverman (ed) *Qualitative research: Issues of theory, method and practice*, London: SAGE, pp 274–90.

Rapport, N. (2008) *Of orderlies and men: Hospital porters achieving wellness at work*, Durham, NC: Carolina Academic Press.

Read, R., Cooper, A., Edelstein, H., Sohn, J. and Levin, B. (2013) 'Knowledge mobilisation and utilisation', in B. Levin, J. Qi, H. Edelstein and J. Sohn (eds) *The impact of research in education: An international perspective*, Bristol: Policy Press, pp 23–40.

Ritchie, J. and Ormston, R. (2014) 'The applications of qualitative methods to social research', in J. Ritchie, J. Lewis, C. McNaughton Nicholls and R. Ormston (eds) *Qualitative research practice: A guide for social science students and researchers*, London: SAGE, pp 27–46.

Robson, C. and McCartan, K. (2016) *Real world research* (4th edn), Chichester: John Wiley & Sons Ltd.

Rose, D., Fleischmann, P., Wykes, T. and Bindman, J. (2002) *Review of consumers' perspectives on electro convulsive therapy*, London: SURE.

Rose, G. (2012) *Visual methodologies* (3rd edn), London: SAGE.

Saad, R. (2005) 'Discovery, development, and current applications of DNA identity testing', *Baylor University Medical Center Proceedings*, 18(2): 130–3.

Sample, I. (2009) 'New year's resolutions doomed to failure, say psychologists', *The Guardian*, 28 December, www.theguardian.com/lifeandstyle/2009/dec/28/new-years-resolutions-doomed-failure

SCIE (Social Care Institute for Excellence) (2007) *Collection of examples of service user and carer participation in systematic reviews*, London: SCIE.

Silverman, D. and Marvasti, A. (2008) *Doing qualitative research: A comprehensive guide*, London: SAGE.

Straus, S., Tetroe, J. and Graham, I. (2011) 'Knowledge translation is the use of knowledge in health care decision making', *Journal of Clinical Epidemiology*, 64(1): 6–10.

Strauss, A. and Corbin, J. (1998) *Basics of qualitative research: Techniques and procedures for developing grounded theory*, Thousand Oaks, CA: SAGE.

SVA Consulting (2012) *Social return on investment: Lessons learned in Australia*, Sydney, NSW: SVA Consulting.

Thomas, G. (2015) *How to do your case study* (2nd edn), London: SAGE.

Tsuchiya, T. (2008) 'The imperial Japanese experiments in China', in E. Emanuel, C. Grady, R. Crouch, R. Lie, F. Miller and W. David (eds) *The Oxford textbook of clinical research ethics*, Oxford: Oxford University Press, pp 31–45.

Tugwell, P., Knottnerus, J. and Idzerda, L. (2011) 'Editorial: Definitions and framework for knowledge translation to continue to evolve', *Journal of Clinical Epidemiology*, 64(1): 1–2.

Turner, M. and Beresford, P. (2005) *User controlled research: Its meanings and potential, Final report*, London: Shaping Our Lives and the Centre for Citizen Participation, Brunel University.

van Doorn, N. (2013) 'Assembling the affective field: how smartphone technology impacts ethnographic research practice', *Qualitative Inquiry*, 19(5): 385–96.

Westmarland, L. (2011) *Researching crime and justice: Tales from the field*, London: Routledge.

Wetton, N. and McWhirter, J. (1998) 'Images and curriculum development in health education', in J. Prosser (ed) *Image-based research: A sourcebook for qualitative researchers*, London: RoutledgeFalmer, pp 263–83.

Whitelaw, S., Beattie, A., Balogh, R. and Watson, J. (2003) *A review of the nature of action research*, Sustainable Health Action Research Programme, Cardiff: Welsh Assembly Government.

Wright Mills, C. (1959) *The sociological imagination*, New York: Oxford University Press, Inc.

Yin, R. (2018) *Case study research and applications: Design and methods* (6th edn), London: SAGE.

Zakher, M. and Wassif, H. (2022) 'The use of objects to enhance online social research interviews', in H. Kara and S.-M. Khoo (eds) *Qualitative and digital methods in times of crisis: Methodology, reflexivity and ethics*, Bristol: Policy Press, pp 143–55.

Further reading

Good introductory books

Oliver, P. (2010) *Understanding the research process*, London: SAGE.
This is a short, accessible book that will help you become familiar with research vocabulary as well as teaching you a lot about how research works.

Fox, M., Martin, P. and Green, G. (2007) *Doing practitioner research*, London: SAGE.
Chapter 4 is about doing evaluation as an insider researcher.

Gauch, H. (2012) *Scientific method in brief*, Cambridge: Cambridge University Press.
This readable book explains the rationale behind quantitative research.

Denscombe, M. (2017) *The good research guide: For small-scale social research projects* (6th edn), Maidenhead: Open University Press.
This book will tell you more about quantitative and qualitative research, and also has a useful chapter on action research.

Mason, J. (2018) *Qualitative researching* (3rd edn), London: SAGE.
This is a classic text and well worth reading if you plan to do qualitative research.

O'Dwyer, L. and Bernauer, J. (2013) *Quantitative research for the qualitative researcher*, London: SAGE.
Kara, H. (2022) *Qualitative research for quantitative researchers*, London: SAGE.
These books do what their titles suggest. Each will be useful if you are one kind of researcher who wants and/or needs to explore the other kind of research.

Dahlberg, L. and McCaig, C. (eds) (2010) *Practical research and evaluation: A start-to-finish guide for practitioners*, London: SAGE.
A helpful how-to book for practice-based researchers.

Research ethics

Iphofen, R. (2011) *Ethical decision-making in social research*, Basingstoke: Palgrave Macmillan.
This is a useful book on ethics in practice, and contains a helpful checklist.

Sieber, J. and Tolich, M. (2013) *Planning ethically responsible research* (2nd edn), London: SAGE.

Particularly Chapter 2 on why we need ethics and Chapter 7 on consent.

Boynton, P. (2017) *The research companion: A practical guide for those in the social sciences, health and development* (2nd edn), Abingdon: Routledge.

This book has an excellent chapter on researcher safety and wellbeing.

Webster, S., Lewis, J. and Brown, A. (2014) 'Ethical considerations in qualitative research', in J. Ritchie, J. Lewis, C. McNaughton Nicholls and R. Ormston (eds) *Qualitative research practice: A guide for social science students and researchers* (2nd edn), London: SAGE, pp 77–110.

Although this chapter focuses on qualitative research, many of the points made are also relevant to quantitative and mixed methods research.

User involvement

Wallcraft, J., Schrank, B. and Amering, M. (eds) (2009) *Handbook of service user involvement in mental health research*, Oxford: Wiley-Blackwell.

This is an international collection and, while its focus is on mental health, many of the points made apply to service user involvement more generally.

Morrow, E., Boaz, A., Brearley, S. and Ross, F. (2012) *Handbook of service user involvement in nursing and healthcare research*, Oxford: Wiley-Blackwell.

Again, while the focus is on nursing and healthcare, many of the points made apply to service user involvement in general.

Barnes, M. and Cotterell, P. (eds) (2013) *Critical perspectives on user involvement*, Bristol: Policy Press.

This useful edited collection covers user involvement in a wide range of settings.

Philosophical underpinnings

Pernecky, T. (2016) *Epistemology and metaphysics for qualitative research*, London: SAGE.

Covers epistemology and ontology, positivism and realism, and, to some extent, constructionism. Despite the title, many of the points made apply to quantitative as well as qualitative research.

Denicolo, P., Long, T. and Bradley-Cole, K. (2016) *Constructivist approaches and research methods: A practical guide to exploring personal meanings*, London: SAGE.

A helpful how-to book for anyone wanting to know more about, or do, constructionist research.

Jolivette, A. (ed) (2015) *Research justice: Methodologies for social change*, Bristol: Policy Press.

An edited collection containing examples of the use of transformative research frameworks in practice.

Action research

McNiff, J. (2013) *Action research* (3rd edn), Abingdon: Routledge.

A really useful introduction to action research.

Evaluation

Fox, C., Grimm, R. and Caldeira, R. (2016) *An introduction to evaluation*, London: SAGE.

A good introductory text, which, unusually, contains a chapter on the ethics of evaluation.

Mixed methods

Creswell, J. and Plano Clark, V. (2017) *Designing and conducting mixed methods research* (3rd edn), London: SAGE.

A readable and easy to use how-to book on mixed methods.

Arts-based research

Barone, T. and Eisner, E. (2012) *Arts based research*, London: SAGE.
Leavy, P. (2020) *Method meets art: Arts-based research practice* (3rd edn), New York: The Guilford Press.

These two books from the USA are useful and readable introductions to arts-based research.

Digital methods

Halfpenny, P. and Procter, R. (eds) (2015) *Innovations in digital research methods*, London: SAGE.

This international collection covers a range of topics such as online surveys, data management, data analysis using computer software and the ethics of digital research.

Salmons, J. (2022) *Doing qualitative research online* (2nd edn), London: SAGE.

This is a very useful how-to book that leads you step by step through the process of doing qualitative research online. (Bryman, below, is useful for collecting quantitative data online.)

Theory

Ransome, P. (2010) *Social theory for beginners*, Bristol: Policy Press.
This is an excellent and accessible introduction to social theory.

Jackson, A. and Mazzei, L. (2012) *Thinking with theory in qualitative research: Viewing data across multiple perspectives*, Abingdon: Routledge.
This book is more advanced but offers a useful demonstration of how theory can be used in practice.

Research design

Creswell, J. and Poth, S.-A. (2017) *Qualitative inquiry and research design: Choosing among five approaches* (4th edn), London: SAGE.
The five approaches are: narrative research, phenomenology, grounded theory, ethnography and case study. The book is well written and worth reading, whether or not you intend to use one of these approaches.

Creswell, J. and Creswell, J. (2018) *Research design: Qualitative, quantitative, and mixed methods approaches* (5th edn), Los Angeles, CA: SAGE.
A very good book on designing research.

Booth, W., Colomb, G., Williams, J., Bizup, J. and Fitzgerald, W. (2016) *The craft of research* (4th edn), Chicago, IL: University of Chicago Press.
Section II of this book, 'Asking Questions, Finding Answers', is particularly useful for the early stages of the research process.

Bryman, A. (2016) *Social research methods* (5th edn), Oxford: Oxford University Press.
There is a useful section on quantitative versus qualitative research (pp 400–3), and detailed chapters on sampling in quantitative research (Chapter 8) and in qualitative research (Chapter 18). Chapters 9–12 give plenty of useful details about quantitative data collection, including advice about collecting data online. (See Salmons, above, if you want to collect qualitative data online.)

Research proposals

Denscombe, M. (2012) *Research proposals: A practical guide*, Maidenhead: Open University Press.
Punch, K. (2016) *Developing effective research proposals* (3rd edn), London: SAGE.
These are both helpful step-by-step guides to preparing a research proposal.

Time management

Johnson, S. (2008) *Personal productivity: How to work effectively and calmly in the midst of chaos*, www.cvdtraining.pitt.edu/docs/Johnson2009_Essays.pdf

Professor Johnson is a medical academic in the USA. This is a collection of very useful essays on time and work management, which were originally published in *Academic Physician & Scientist* in 2004–7.

Research journaling

Brown, N. (2021) *Making the most of your research journal*, Bristol: Policy Press.

A readable, practical book to help people get the most out of their research journal.

Literature review

Barker, M. (2014) 'Doing a literature review', in A. Vossler and N. Moller (eds) *The counselling and psychotherapy research handbook*, London: SAGE, pp 61–73.

This is an excellent brief and clear explanation of how to do a literature review.

Secondary research

Chandola, T. and Booker, C. (2022) *Archival and secondary data*, London: SAGE. Covers quantitative secondary research.

Hughes, K. and Tarrant, A. (eds) (2020) *Qualitative secondary analysis*, London: SAGE.

Covers qualitative secondary research.

Questionnaires

Gillham, B. (2008) *Developing a questionnaire* (2nd edn), London and New York: Continuum.

This is an invaluable little book for anyone who wants to put together a paper questionnaire.

Qualitative methods

Ritchie, J., Lewis, J., McNaughton Nicholls, C. and Ormston, R. (eds) (2014) *Qualitative research practice: A guide for social science students and researchers* (2nd edn), London: SAGE.

This book has useful chapters on interviewing, focus groups and observational methods.

Brinkmann, S. and Kvale, S. (2015) *Interviews: Learning the craft of qualitative research interviewing* (3rd edn), Thousand Oaks, CA: SAGE.

This is a well organised and thorough book on interviewing.

Krueger, R. and Casey, M. (2014) *Focus groups: A practical guide for applied research* (5th edn), London: SAGE.

A very useful guide that includes information about conducting focus groups by telephone or via the internet.

Gillham, B. (2008) *Observation techniques: Structured to unstructured*, London and New York: Continuum.

This is a short accessible book that gives an excellent introduction to observation methods.

Visual methods

Banks, M. and Zeitlyn, D. (2015) *Visual methods in social research* (2nd edn), London: SAGE.

This is a readable, practical book, aimed at people with little or no experience of using visual methods.

Data from social media

Bell, J. and Waters, S. (2014) *Doing your research project: A guide for first-time researchers* (6th edn), Maidenhead: Open University Press.

This has a useful central section on data collection including a chapter on using social media in research.

Case study research

Yin, R. (2015) *Case study research and applications: Design and methods*, London: SAGE.

This is a helpful how-to book for case study researchers.

Creative methods

Kara, H. (2020) *Creative research methods: A practical guide* (2nd edn), Bristol: Policy Press.

A detailed overview of creative research methods in practice.

Documentary research

Tight, M. (2019) *Documentary research in the social sciences*, London: SAGE.
A useful textbook for social science researchers who are using documents.

Grant, A. (2022) *Doing your research project with documents: A step-by-step guide to take you from start to finish*, Bristol: Policy Press.
A helpful, practical resource for researchers from any discipline who are new to working with documents.

Quantitative methods

'Quantitative methods in social research: A topical bibliography.'
This document is free to download from the British Library. It lists lots of useful websites, journals and other helpful information and resources: www.bl.uk/socialsciences

Streiner, D. and Norman, R. (2014) *Health measurement scales: A practical guide to their development and use* (5th edn), Oxford: Oxford University Press.
This book begins by focusing on how to devise a new scale, but it has a useful appendix covering where to find existing measures, and lots of helpful information on how to use scales.

Treiman, D. (2009) *Quantitative data analysis: Doing social research to test ideas*, San Francisco, CA: Jossey–Bass (Wiley).
This is a very helpful how-to book that links theory with quantitative research techniques.

Terre Blanche, M., Durrheim, K. and Painter, D. (eds) (2006) *Research in practice* (2nd edn), Cape Town: University of Cape Town Press.
Section 2 is on quantitative research techniques and contains five readable and useful chapters.

Quantitative analysis

Dilnot, A. and Blastland, M. (2008) *The tiger that isn't: Seeing through a world of numbers*, New York: Profile Books.
A great introduction to the use and misuse of statistics.

Huff, D. (1991) *How to lie with statistics*, Harmondsworth: Penguin.
This book is old, but still very relevant, and easy to read.

Best, J. (2012) *Damned lies and statistics* (updated edn), Berkeley and Los Angeles, CA and London: University of California Press.

This is a more modern take on how statistics can be misused, and is useful for learning to think critically about reported statistics.

Etheridge, D. (2010) *Excel data analysis: Your visual blueprint for creating and analyzing data, charts and PivotTables* (3rd edn), Hoboken, NJ: John Wiley & Sons.

A really useful how-to book that will take you through the process step by step, with clear instructions.

Qualitative analysis

Silverman, D. (2015) *Interpreting qualitative data* (5th edn), London: SAGE.

This is a classic text, but it is very expensive, so borrow it from the library if you can.

Bazeley, P. (2013) *Qualitative data analysis: Practical strategies*, London: SAGE.

This is a very useful and much more affordable book; definitely a better bet if you want your own copy.

Mixed methods analysis

Creswell, J. and Plano Clark, V. (2011) 'Analyzing and interpreting data in mixed methods research', in J. Creswell and V. Plano Clark, *Designing and conducting mixed methods research* (2nd edn), Thousand Oaks, CA: SAGE, pp 203–51.

Teddlie, C. and Tashakkori, A. (2009) 'The analysis of mixed methods data', in C. Teddlie and A. Tashakkori, *Foundations of mixed methods research: Integrating quantitative and qualitative approaches in the social and behavioral sciences*, Thousand Oaks, CA: SAGE, pp 249–84.

These two chapters come from two seminal works on mixed methods research.

Quantitative reporting

Rowntree, D. (2018) *Statistics without tears: An introduction for non-mathematicians*, London: Penguin Random House UK.

This short and readable book is very useful for people who are new to statistics.

Knowles, S. (2018) *Narrative by numbers: How to tell powerful and purposeful stories with data*, Abingdon: Routledge.

This short, readable book explains what to do with your statistical findings.

Spiegelhalter, D. (2019) *The art of statistics: Learning from data*, London: Penguin Random House UK.

This book helps people to understand how statistics work, and how they are presented and misrepresented. It is particularly helpful for qualitative researchers who need to understand the statistics in others' research.

Abelson, R. (1995) *Statistics as principled argument*, Hillsdale, NJ: Lawrence Erlbaum Publishers, Inc.

Explains why and how researchers should use statistics 'to formulate good arguments explaining comparative differences ... in an interesting way' (p 17).

Rumsey, D. (2011) *Statistics for dummies* (2nd edn), Indianapolis, IN: Wiley Publishing, Inc.

This one is self-explanatory.

Field, A. (2016) *An adventure in statistics: The reality enigma*, London: SAGE.

This is a big book of almost 750 pages. The author has set his statistical textbook within a fictional story in the speculative fiction genre, illustrated with comic art. So it is definitely different, and some readers love it.

Bordens, K. and Abbott, B. (2022) *Research design and methods: A process approach* (11th edn), New York: McGraw Hill LLC.

This is an up-to-date statistical textbook that has more coverage of debates within statistics than most.

Writing for research

Pears, R. and Shields, G. (2016) *Cite them right: The essential referencing guide* (10th edn), Basingstoke: Palgrave Macmillan.

This is an excellent guide to citation.

Moran, J. (2018) *First you write a sentence*, London: Penguin Random House.

This is a very readable book on writing skills.

Murray, R. (2013) *Writing for academic journals* (3rd edn), Maidenhead: Open University Press.

A really useful text for anyone who wants to start writing for academic journals, this demystifies the process, step by step.

Thomson, P. and Kamler, B. (2012) *Writing for peer reviewed journals: Strategies for getting published*, Abingdon: Routledge.

This is an equally practical and helpful book.

Belcher, W. (2019) *Writing your journal article in twelve weeks* (2nd edn), Chicago, IL: Chicago University Press.

A classic guide that is very useful for first-time writers of academic journal articles.

Oliver, K. and Cairney, P. (2019) 'The dos and don't's of influencing policy: a systematic review of advice to academics', Palgrave Communications, 5(1), www.nature.com/articles/s41599-019-0232-y

If you're not an academic, don't be put off, because this article is open access, straightforward in style, and also relevant for practitioners.

Presenting and disseminating research

Daly, I. and Brophy Haney, A. (eds) (2014) *53 interesting ways to communicate your research*, Scarborough: The Professional and Higher Partnership Ltd.

This is an inspirational little book on presenting and disseminating research.

Evergreen, S. (2014) *Presenting data effectively: Communicating your findings for maximum impact*, London: SAGE.
Kirk, A. (2016) *Data visualization: A handbook for data driven design*, London: SAGE.

These two books are useful and readable for anyone who wants to delve further into the art of data visualisation.

Glossary

This Glossary contains definitions of words and phrases as they are used in this book. You need to bear in mind that not everyone uses research terms in the same way.

Words and phrases in italics are also defined within this Glossary.

Abstract   Summary of *academic research*, usually 250–500 words long.

Academic research   *Research* conducted for an academic qualification, such as a diploma, Master's degree or PhD, or in support of an academic career.

Action research   An iterative process of reflection and problem-solving in groups or communities.

Activist methodology   A *methodology* in which victims of oppression will research that oppression. Also known as *emancipatory methodology*.

Analysis   See *data analysis*.

Application programming interface (API)   A piece of source code that is being used to release some *open data* in such a way that external programs can communicate with it and access or exchange *data*.

Archival data   A subset of *secondary data* made up of historical records.

Arts-based research   *Research* that makes use of arts techniques such as drawing, photography or performance.

Average   See *mean*.

Background research   Part of a *research* project designed to give context to the *research question*, which may be in the form of a *document review* – for *workplace research*; or a *literature review* – for *academic research*.

Bibliography   A list at the end of a book or other written *document* containing *references*, some of which are cited in the text and some of which are not but may be useful to readers.

Bivariate statistics   *Descriptive statistics* that describe the relationship between two *variables*.

Case study   A *research method* in which a single 'case' (person, organisation, country, and so on) is studied in depth.

Citation   Giving the details of the source of an idea, fact or opinion that you draw on in your *research*.

Closed question   A question with predefined answers to choose from.

Code   A label for a piece of *quantitative data* or *qualitative data*.

Coding   Labelling quantitative data or qualitative data to facilitate data analysis.

Coding frame   A set of words or phrases to guide your *coding* of *qualitative data*.

Constructionist methodology   *Methodology* that views social phenomena as constructed by social actors, and recognises multiple realities rather than one independent reality.

Content analysis   A method of analysing *qualitative data* where you count the number of instances of each *code*.

Convenience sample   A *sample* where you choose the first *participants* you can find who are willing to help.

Copyright   The legal right of control over original written (or musical or artistic) work.

Correlation co-efficient   A statistical calculation that gives an estimate of the average distance of each point on a *scattergraph* from the regression line.

Covariant relationship   A relationship where two *variables* change in accordance with one another.

Critical realist methodology   A type of *realist methodology* that allows for an independent reality, but views that reality as only accessible through people's perceptions.

Cross–analysis of data   See *data synthesis*.

Data   Information collected for *research*.

Data analysis   Methods of analysing *data* to find out what it can tell you.

Data collection   Methods of collecting *data* for *research*.

Data mashup   A mixture of *data* from two or more *APIs*.

Data preparation   Methods of preparing data for *coding* and *analysis*.

Data repository   A place where *data* is kept, usually on the internet.

Data synthesis   Comparing and contrasting the *findings* of different segments of *data analysis* within the same piece of *research*. Sometimes called *cross-analysis* of data.

Data visualisation   Presenting data in the form of images such as *graphs*, charts and infographics.

Decolonising methodology   A *transformative methodology* in which colonised peoples research their own situations.

Deconstruction   An approach to separating meaning from content.

Dependent variable   A measurable characteristic that stays constant in the course of the *research*.

Descriptive statistics   *Statistics* that enable us to summarise and describe numerical *data*.

Digitally mediated research   *Research* using digital technology.

Dissemination   Sharing knowledge gained through *research*.

Dissertation   The write-up of a piece of *academic research* conducted for a qualification such as a Master's degree.

Document review   A review of relevant *documents* to provide context for *workplace research*.

Documents   Pieces of text that may be used for *background research* or as *data*.

DOI   Digital object identifier, used to uniquely identify electronic resources.

Draft   An unfinished piece of writing.

Edit   Work to improve a *draft*.

Emancipatory methodology   A *methodology* in which victims of oppression will research that oppression. Also known as *activist methodology*.

Emergent coding *Coding* based on whatever the researcher perceives to be of interest in *qualitative data*.

Ephemera Text and/or images that are not designed to be kept, but may be useful as *data*, such as advertising leaflets and social media updates.

Epistemology How knowledge of the world is learned.

Ethics The rules of conduct for a particular activity.

Ethnography A time-consuming *research method*, used in *qualitative research*, from the discipline of anthropology.

Evaluation A type of applied *research* used to assess the effectiveness of services or interventions, and make *recommendations* for improvement.

Excel Computer software by Microsoft designed for spreadsheets and with the ability to perform statistical calculations.

Executive summary Summary of *workplace research*, usually 1–4 pages long.

Feminist methodology A *transformative methodology* designed to redress the power imbalance between the sexes.

Findings The results of *research*.

Focus group A *data collection* technique in *qualitative research* that usually involves one or two *researchers* and several *participants*.

Formal theory A way of making sense of an aspect or aspects of the world around us, based primarily on thought.

Freewriting A technique to help writers overcome blocks or solve problems.

Frequency distribution A way of showing how many times a particular *variable* has occurred, both of itself and in relation to other variables.

Gatekeeper Someone who is able to help you reach potential *participants*.

Generalisability The extent to which the *findings* of *research* apply in situations beyond that in which the research was conducted.

Generated theory *Theory* that is built as part of the *research* process.

Geographic information system A way of working with *data* that contains location or place information, and plotting it on a map or doing calculations related to its position on the Earth.

Graph A diagram to show changes in one *variable* or the relationship between two variables.

Grey literature *Documents* that are not formally published, but that may be available in hard copy and/or electronic formats from individuals, organisations or governments.

Grid A table designed for keeping records, for example of *documents* or *literature*, or making notes, for example of *observations*, for the purposes of *research*.

Grounded theory A form of *generated theory* that is grounded in *data*.

Hermeneutic methodology An *interpretivist methodology* focusing on the principles of interpretation.

Hypothesis A hunch, guess or suspicion about something unknown.

Impact The effect research has in the world, which may be positive or negative.

Implementation Making use of research findings.

Independent relationship A relationship where two *variables* change independently of one another.

Independent researcher A researcher who is not part of an academic or other institution.

Independent variable A measurable characteristic that changes in the course of the *research*.

Inferential statistics *Statistics* that enable us to infer something about a *population* from a *sample*.

Informal theory A way of making sense of an aspect or aspects of the world around us, based primarily on experience.

Instrument See *measuring devices*.

Intellectual property Original ideas or words, which are held to belong to the person who created them.

Interpretivist methodology *Methodology* suggesting that reality is interpreted by people as they work to make sense of the world they experience and of their place in that world.

Interval data *Quantitative data* in ranks with a defined numerical distance between them, such as age in years.

Interview A *data collection* technique in *qualitative research* that usually involves one *researcher* and one or two *participants*.

Inventory See *measuring devices*.

Knowledge exchange A view of research as an arena where people are continually exchanging knowledge.

Literature Academic texts that may be used for *background research*.

Literature review A review of relevant *literature* to provide context for *academic research*.

Location A researcher's position, which may be geographical, political, theoretical, and so on.

Mashup tool A technological tool for combining *data* from different APIs (*application programming interfaces*).

Mean A statistical calculation for *quantitative data* in which the total of all values is divided by the number of values. Also known as the *average*.

Measuring devices Scales, tools, instruments or inventories designed to measure human characteristics and conditions.

Median The middle value in a set of *quantitative data* after it has been ranked in order.

Meta-analysis Similar to a *systematic review*, but also includes a statistical summary of *findings* from *quantitative research*.

Metadata records *Data* about *data*, such as grids designed for recording data during *observation* or for coding *visual data*.

Methodology A coherent and logical framework for research based on views, beliefs and values.

Mixed methods research *Research* drawing on both *quantitative data* and *qualitative data*.

Mode The value occurring most commonly in a set of *quantitative data*.

Nominal data   *Data* in categories with labels, such as categories of ethnicity.

Non-probability sample   A *sample* in which every member of the *population* does not have an equal chance of becoming a member of the *sample*.

NVivo   Computer software designed to support the *coding* and *analysis* of *qualitative data* including text, audio and images.

Objectivity   Considering or managing a situation on the basis of facts and logic without the involvement of emotions, values or other intangibles.

Observation   A *data collection* technique in *qualitative research* that usually involves one *researcher* and many *participants*.

Ontology   How the world is known.

Open access   Free access for everyone, for example to academic journal articles.

Open data   *Data* collected by governments and made freely available to everyone.

Open question   A question with no predefined answers.

OpenOffice   Freely available software that is compatible with Microsoft Office, including Microsoft *Excel*, and that performs the same functions.

Ordinal data   *Quantitative data* in ranks without a defined numerical distance between them, such as the first, second and third places in a competition.

Participants   People who participate in *research*, for example by completing a *questionnaire* or taking part in an *interview*.

Participant observation   A time-consuming method of collecting *data*, often used within *ethnography*.

Participatory appraisal   Sometimes called participatory rural appraisal, a set of participatory and mostly *arts-based* techniques for use in community-based *research*.

Participatory methodology   A *transformative methodology* in which *participants* are involved throughout the *research* process.

Participatory action research   Similar to *action research*, but with a slightly stronger emphasis on partnership.

Phenomenology   An *interpretivist methodology* focusing on how people experience the world they live in.

Pie chart   A circular chart with 'slices' that show the proportions of different *variables* in a dataset.

Pilot   A test run of a *data collection* method to assess its quality.

Plagiarism   Presenting someone else's ideas or words as your own original work.

Polish   The final stage in the writing process, to remove any remaining errors and finalise structure, grammar, word choices, and so on.

Population   All of the people you could, in theory, include as *participants* in a *research* project.

Positivist methodology   *Methodology* originating in the natural sciences that places a high value on *objectivity*.

Postmodernist methodology   A *methodology* that holds objective reality to be inaccessible and knowledge to be relative.

Post-positivist methodology   A form of *positivist methodology* that accepts that a researcher will influence what they observe.

Practitioner   Someone who works in *public services*, whether paid or unpaid.

Primary data   *Data* collected specifically for your *research* project.

Probability sample   A sample in which every member of the *population* has an equal chance of becoming a member of the *sample*.

Public services   Services run by society for society, such as health, social care, criminal justice and education services, from pre-school to university.

Purposive sample   A *sample* of people who, in the researcher's judgement, have most to contribute to the *research*.

Qualitative data   *Data* in the form of words, images, sound, or anything except numbers.

Qualitative research   *Research* based on *qualitative data*.

Quantitative data   *Data* in the form of numbers.

Quantitative research   *Research* based on *quantitative data*.

Questionnaire   A *data collection* instrument primarily used for *quantitative research*.

Quota sample   The *population* is divided into segments on the basis of characteristics (for example, gender, age, geographical location) and then a different type of *sample*, such as a *convenience sample* or *purposive sample*, is taken from each segment.

Random sample   A *sample* where random numbers are used to select *participants*.

Range   The difference between the smallest and largest values in a set of *quantitative data*.

Realist methodology   *Methodology* that uses theory, recognises complexity and acknowledges context.

Recommendations   Suggestions for how *workplace research* can be put into practice.

Reference   The full details of a *document* or piece of *literature*, signposted by a *citation*.

Reference list   A list at the end of a research report, dissertation or thesis, containing *references*, all of which are cited in the text.

Reliability   The extent to which a *research method* will produce the same results when used in different situations.

Research   Systematic investigation, using a predefined *research method*, to gather information with the aim of answering a predefined *research question*.

Research commissioner   Someone who holds a budget for a piece of *research*.

Research method   System for conducting *research*.

Research plan   Similar to a *research proposal*, most commonly used in *workplace research* to inform people such as research commissioners, managers and colleagues.

Research proposal   A written explanation of what you intend to *research* and why, and how you intend to carry out the research, to inform people such as potential funders or PhD supervisors, most commonly used in *academic research*.

Research question The stated question that a piece of *research* aims to answer.

Research report The write-up of a piece of *workplace research*.

Research topic The subject area of a piece of *research*.

Researcher A person who does *research*.

Sample The people you include as *participants* in a *research* project, drawn from a *population*.

Scale See measuring devices.

Scattergraph A *graph* that gives an overview of the relationship between two *variables*.

Secondary data *Data* that was not collected specifically for your *research* project, but that you can use in your research.

Service user A user of *public services*.

Snowball sample A *sample* where one or more *participants* help the researcher to find other participants.

SPSS Statistical Package for Social Scientists, computer software designed to perform statistical calculations.

Standpoint A person's own position from which they view or judge things.

Statistics A branch of mathematics that enables the *analysis* and interpretation of numerical *data*.

Stratified random sample A sample where the *population* is divided into segments on the basis of characteristics such as gender, age or geographical location, and then a *random sample* is taken from each segment of the population.

Stratified sample A *sample* where you use one number generated at random to select the first *participant*, then choose other participants at regular intervals, for example every third or every tenth person.

Subjectivity Taking emotions, values and other intangibles into account when considering or managing a situation.

Survey A piece of *research*, often large-scale, to investigate people's experiences, attitudes, behaviours, judgements, beliefs, and so on.

Systematic review A review of all the *research* previously conducted around a specific *research question*.

Thematic analysis A method for identifying themes within coded *data*.

Theory A way of making sense of an aspect or aspects of the world around us. See also *formal theory*, *informal theory* and *generated theory*.

Thesis The write-up of a piece of *academic research* conducted for a qualification such as a PhD.

Third sector Organisations and groups that provide *public services* and are neither state-funded nor run purely for profit, such as charities, social enterprises and community groups.

Tool See measuring devices.

Transcribe To convert *data* from audio to text.

Transformative methodology *Methodology* suggesting that research will not only investigate, but also create, change.

Univariate statistics *Descriptive statistics* that describe a single *variable*.

URL Uniform resource locator, that is, the address of a web page.

User-led methodology A *transformative methodology* where the *research* is led by *service users*, with or without help from a professional *researcher*.

Validity The extent to which a *research method* does what it claims to do.

Variable A measurable characteristic.

Variance In *quantitative data*, an estimate of the average distance of each value from the *mean*.

Visual data *Qualitative data* in the form of images, such as photographs, paintings, drawings, collage and video.

Viva An oral examination for *academic research* such as a PhD.

Workplace research *Research* conducted to support professional work, such as *evaluation* research, skills audit, training needs analysis.

Index

References to information in figures, tables and boxes are in *italics*
References to glossary entries are in **bold**